D0966319

CONNED

Also by Sasha Abramsky

Hard Time Blues: How Politics Built a Prison Nation

CONNED

How Millions Went to Prison, Lost the Vote, and Helped Send George W. Bush to the White House

SASHA ABRAMSKY

NEW YORK
LONDON

Published in the United States by The New Press, New York, 2006
Distributed by W. W. Norton & Company, Inc., New York

LIBRARY OF CONGRESS CATALOGING-IN-PUBLICATION DATA

Abramsky, Sasha.
Conned: how millions went to prison, lost the vote, and helped send George W. Bush to the White House / Sasha Abramsky.
p. cm.
Includes bibliographical references and index.
ISBN-13 978-1-56584-966-2
ISBN-10 1-56584-966-3
1. Ex-convicts—Suffrage—United States. 2. Political rights, Loss of—United States.
3. United States—Politics and government—2001. I. Title.

JK1846.A27 2006
324.6'20869270973—dc22
2005054352

The New Press was established in 1990 as a not-for-profit alternative to the large, commercial publishing houses currently dominating the book publishing industry. The New Press operates in the public interest rather than for private gain, and is committed to publishing, in innovative ways, works of educational, cultural, and community value that are often deemed insufficiently profitable.

www.thenewpress.com

Composition by Westchester Book Composition
This book was set in Palatino

Printed in the United States of America

10 9 8 7 6 5 4 3 2 1

This book is for my wonderful daughter Sofia.

May all her dreams come true.

Contents

Acknowledgments

I spent many months researching *Conned* and, during those months, I visited numerous places—big cities I'd been to before and little villages I had not previously heard of until research took me to them. Wherever I went, however, people I had never before met opened up their lives to my scrutiny; they gave me permission to ask intimate questions and to place the answers to these questions in my book. For the kindness and trust of these strangers, I will be forever grateful. Were I to acknowledge by name everyone who talked with me, these opening pages would swell to an unwieldy length. Instead, let me proffer a collective "Thank you."

There are, however, many whom I do want to thank by name. For their support of my work over the years, and for their understanding of the need to shed light on the underside of America's criminal justice system, I owe a tremendous debt of gratitude to the staff of the Open Society Institute, Demos, and the JEHT Foundation. Helena Huang, currently of the JEHT Foundation and previously of the Open Society Institute, has been especially supportive of my work.

For their generosity with time and information, I give warm thanks to Marc Mauer of the Sentencing Project and to professors Chris Uggen and Jeff Manza—all three of whom have answered my many questions with great patience and selflessness over the years. Their research on the topic of disenfranchisement has been groundbreaking, and their statistical analyses of the impact of disenfranchisement laws have shed new light on the topic. *Conned* could not have been written without the cooperation of each of these individuals. Likewise, the staff of the Brennan Center and the Right to Vote Campaign have all proven helpful beyond the call of duty. The contacts they provided me with around the country, many of whose stories found their way into the pages of *Conned*, taught me much about the ins and outs of disenfranchisement laws and their practical impact on millions of citizens.

My agent, Sam Stoloff, and my editor at The New Press, Andy Hsiao, grasped the importance of this topic from the get-go and worked tirelessly to bring the project to fruition.

Many friends helped me frame the issue and talked me through the complexities of writing about the American political system. They were there for me when I had questions, or when I simply needed to talk about what I was finding; they shared my moments of neurosis and they smoothed my feathers when events conspired to ruffle them. Some read drafts of my chapters and offered thoughtful, always helpful advice; others suggested ways to overcome obstacles and stay focused on the topic at hand. Particular thanks go to Nell Bernstein for her perceptive editing; to Robin Templeton for lending a sympathetic ear from day one until the closing bell; to Jason Ziedenberg for his comprehensive grasp of how criminal justice decisions impact the broader political system, as well as for his sardonic sense of humor; and to Eyal Press, Adam Shatz, and Andrew Lichtenstein for numerous wonderful freelance kvetches over the past decade. Raj Patel, Maura McDermott, Kim Gilmore, Carolyn Juris, Jessica Garrison, Michael Soller, Nicole Hala, and Ben Ehrenreich also all lent sympathetic ears and offered invaluable words of encouragement throughout the writing of this book.

Thanks to *Rolling Stone* for allowing me to include in my book extracts from interviews I conducted while writing an article for the magazine in 2001, and to the editors at *Mother Jones*, the *New York Times*, and the *Los Angeles Times* for publishing my writings on disenfranchisement in the years since the 2000 election.

To my mother and father, Lenore and Jack; to my brother, Kolya, and my sister, Tanya; and to my grandparents—quite simply, thank you for being wonderful.

My biggest pool of gratitude, however, is reserved for my daughter, Sofia—a continual ray of sunshine in my life who never fails to fill me with awe—and for my wife and companion, Julie Sze, who has had to tolerate my many absences during the genesis of *Conned*. Despite having just started teaching at the University of California, Davis, she took on the added burden of looking after Sofia by herself during the many weeks, and ultimately months, I was away from home on reporting expeditions. I very much doubt whether *Conned* would ever have seen the light of day without the understanding shown by Julie and the seeds of joy contained in Sofia's baby smiles and gurgles and enthusiasms.

CONNED

Introduction

De Tocqueville's House of Mirrors

Conned began as a small book with a narrow focus. Originally, I hoped only to report on how a handful of states permanently removed the vote from anyone convicted of a felony—crimes deemed by state and federal statute to be serious enough to send a person to prison for at least a year, should the presiding judge choose to do so—within their jurisdiction. Most of these states are in the old Confederacy, and I envisioned a book essentially limited in geographic scope to the southeastern quadrant of America. As my reporting developed, I realized I was actually studying a much broader phenomenon: in fighting the twinned "War on Drugs" and "War on Crime," modern America has created such a vast penal network that the very cultural and institutional underpinnings of the country's democracy are now under threat. And so my focus changed.

In 1831, a young French aristocrat by the name of Alexis de Tocqueville toured Jacksonian America at the request of the French government. Originally, he crossed the Atlantic to report on one of the young country's more novel experiments in social control: the widespread use of prisons to house and, it was hoped, to rehabilitate convicted criminals who, in most European countries at the time, would either have been branded, deported, flogged (or otherwise physically abused), or executed. As he journeyed around the states, however, de Tocqueville realized he was witnessing something far more profound than a mere social experiment in penal theory; the society out of which the prisons had emerged was, he believed, embarking on a radical new experiment in democracy. And so he wrote what became one of the great political classics: *Democracy in America.*

Soon after I started reporting for my book I picked up a copy of de Tocqueville's writings and began carrying it around with me as I traversed the country. Like de Tocqueville, I had grown up in Europe (in London). Unlike him, however, I am a U.S. citizen and had lived in America for over a decade when I began writing *Conned.* De Tocqueville's outsider-looking-in approach appealed to me, as did his fascination with a country that he came to love but never to adulate uncritically. I first opened the pages of *Democracy in America* while sitting at the bar of a rundown casino in Nevada one night in late June, and I closed it, dog-eared and tattered, its pages ornamented with my hastily scribbled notes, five months later on Miami Beach. In the intervening months, I had visited nearly one third of the states in the Union.

In the summer of 2004, as the presidential campaign hit high gear, I realized I was, in many ways, reporting on a perversely distorted mirror image of de Tocqueville's world—a place where the prison system had spiraled so out of control that it was ripping millions of people away helter-skelter from the body politic. Instead of being one of the boys on the bus, an election-year journalist attending staged political rallies and reporting on all the gory details of the quadrennial horse race, I was very much off the bus, traveling around the underside of an election from which millions of Americans had been legally excluded. Had time and resources permitted, I would have visited all fifty states. Since this proved impracticable, I chose instead to concentrate on states that either had particularly egregious disenfranchisement laws or had active political battles shaping up around this issue. Several states, chief among them Alabama and Florida, had statutes permanently disenfranchising anyone ever convicted of a felony; others imposed long waiting periods after a person came out of prison or off parole before he or she could apply to have their vote restored; other states, such as Utah, restored the vote when a person left prison but neglected to inform these same released prisoners; and still other states, including New York, which formally allowed ex-prisoners to cast ballots, were sending them letters demanding that they produce a nebulous "proof" of eligibility to vote.

When defenders of these rules and regulations responded with words to the effect of *"Well, these people don't care. They wouldn't vote even if they could, so what's the big deal?"* I began asking voteless people about whether they wanted to vote. And, time after time, they told me they did.

In Nashville, Tennessee, I met a young white woman named Jamaica S., an anxious lady with green-blue eyes and long brown hair, wearing a green checkered shirt, black cord pants, and sneakers. Less than a year before the 2000 election, she had been put on probation for fifteen months and had lost her right to vote.

Jamaica was twenty-five years old in 2000, had a seven-year-old son from a failed marriage, and had recently gotten her license to teach elementary school in Tennessee. She was the first person in her family to graduate from college and was by the far the most intellectual and politically aware of any of her relations. Her father lived in rural North Carolina, where she'd been born and spent her early childhood; she, her mother and stepdad, her sister, and her grandfather lived in Nashville. Hardly anyone in her family ever voted. None of them followed current affairs the way she did.

A year earlier, Jamaica, a fan of jazz music and National Public Radio, an avid reader, and an amateur artist, had been dating a man heavily addicted to painkillers. He'd gotten worse and worse, and, during the summer of 1999, while she worked as a substitute teacher, he lived in her house and began driving around town in her car robbing stores to get money to buy his drugs. She claims she did not know what he was doing—or, as she rephrases it, that she probably was subconsciously aware he was up to no good, but because she didn't want to know, she didn't let herself know. After the passage of so much time, there's no way to determine exactly how much she was, in fact, aware of.

Sometime during that summer, Jamaica picked up a speeding ticket and, as a result, had to attend an evening driver education class. Her boyfriend told her he would drop her off at the class. He stopped the car at a store, told her to wait, and then went inside. When he came out, he was being chased by a woman; he jumped in the car and screamed at Jamaica to drive. She did. Straight back to her house, where the police were waiting for them.

Jamaica's boyfriend was charged with aggravated robbery. So was Jamaica. To avoid a prison sentence, she pled guilty to a lesser charge—accessory after the fact—and, in January 2000, was put on probation. It was her first arrest, her first conviction. Over the years, it remained her only arrest and her only conviction. She did her fifteen months on probation, stayed out of trouble during those months, and stayed out of trouble afterward.

But that conviction, a low-level felony that came about because of someone else's crime, was enough to bar her from voting in Tennessee, to *permanently* deny her the right to vote until such time as she could either convince the governor to pardon her, or convince the district court that she was somehow worthy of having her rights restored—neither of which was an easy task for an ex-felon in a tough-on-crime Southern state. It was also enough to destroy forever her embryonic teaching career. During the more than four years that had elapsed since her conviction, Jamaica had obsessed over her loss of the vote; had compiled huge ring binders full of information on her case and on Tennessee's disenfranchisement laws; had phoned politicians, civil rights groups, community associations, the district attorney's office, the board of pardons, the officials responsible for administering elections, and anyone else she could think of who might be able to help her get her rights back; and had spent a vast amount of time thinking through all the implications associated with a felony conviction—from the loss of voting rights to all the limitations placed on employment for people with a record.

"I pled guilty to accessory after the fact," Jamaica told me over coffee at the Nashville public library, "in January 2000. And so I was really hopeless about there being any future." She went on: "I couldn't use my degree or my license to teach and I knew the law said I could not vote. I felt less than human, and felt very bad about myself. I gave up custody of my son. My ex-husband had just gotten married and had a house. I felt *I'm so unstable*. I was so depressed, so depressed. Then it became even more devastating that I didn't have my son. But I was trying to do what was best for my son.

"It seems when you're convicted of a felony, the scarlet letter is there. You take it everywhere with you. After my conviction, my job opportunities were very limited. I've done a little bit of everything since then. It's hard to get a good job and to keep it. I was a nanny for two years. I worked at a private school—they did not ask me about my background and I did not tell them. But they went out of business. I'm on unemployment right now. I do some side jobs, not a lot. A little babysitting. Housecleaning. Other than the one private school, everyone else I've worked for has known about my conviction.

"I have a lot of shame. I've told myself that I don't deserve it [the vote]. That I do make bad decisions. Why should I make decisions for anyone when I can't take care of myself? But it's been five years, and I realize my point of view is very important. I feel like not a whole person in many ways. It makes me feel like there's a caste system and I've become one of the untouchables. It's unbelievable it could happen in America. It's ironic they go overseas and seek to promote democracy in other countries—force it on other countries—but in America they deny the right to vote to so many people. It's the hypocrisy of our democracy. They assume anyone who's been in trouble is not intelligent and probably don't care about their right to vote.

"When I think of how it affects me, I want to bow my head. I feel like I'm not as good as other people, and I hate having to avoid questions like Who are you going to vote for? I'm shamed and humiliated every time I'm faced with the question. When I got convicted, a box was ticked on my judgment sheet: 'The defendant having been found guilty is rendered infamous.' Even just saying that—'I'm infamous'—it blows my mind. I'm interested in politics, issues and current events, and then I think, What does it matter how much I know; I can't do anything, I can't vote."[1]

In state after state, I heard stories of people who had been turned away from polling booths; people who were sent letters telling them they'd been struck from the electoral rolls; people who spent hours, then days and weeks, trying, and failing, to navigate bureaucratic mazes set up to make the process of getting one's vote back as onerous as possible; and finally, and perhaps most depressingly, entire families for whom the very culture of political participation had been shattered by the pervasive impact of the juiced-up criminal justice system of late twentieth- and early twenty-first-century America.

And, as the stories came in, I realized that, in many ways, mass incarceration was unraveling the very fabric of democracy, of mass participation in the process of political decision making that had so impressed de Tocqueville way back in the 1830s. In Alabama and Mississippi, over 7 percent of all adults had had their right to vote permanently removed. In both of those states, as well as in Florida, Virginia, Washington, New Mexico, Kentucky, Tennessee, and Iowa, more than one quarter of African American men were voteless. In many other states, including Texas, one in five black men had been removed from the electoral rolls.[2]

At the same time, as I interviewed dozens, and then hundreds, of people around the country who were working flat out in 2004 to educate voters about their rights in states where ex-felons *did*, in fact, have the vote, and to campaign for the restoration of the vote in states that still practiced permanent disenfranchisement, I realized I was watching a latter-day civil rights struggle unfold before my eyes. De Tocqueville's democracy was not dead; in fact, some of its fiercest proponents were those seeking to shine the light of publicity on America's hidden disenfranchisement epidemic—seeking to restore a universal suffrage so grievously damaged by the carelessly widespread use of the criminal justice system over the past three decades.

At its heart, *Conned* is a book about freedom. Most of us take our freedom for granted; in fact, it is a most precarious condition.

The thought of liberty lost produces, in me, a gut-wrenching, existential fear. The idea of living out my one life chained down, restricted in my movements, my choices, my associations, my chances of experiencing the world in all its wondrous variety, leads to an almost physical reaction. The shock of nausea. The weakness of legs gone wobbly with nerves.

In many ways, that instinctual fear has shaped my life. It has propelled me to travel, to explore, to seek new friends and new adventures. It has shaped my choice of work, my relationships. And, with sickened fascination, it has drawn me into a decade-long obsession with writing about prisons and prisoners—about the populous underbelly of an American democracy increasingly defined by a punitive societal attitude to its most impoverished and addicted lower strata. To me, prisons should be viewed as a necessary evil, never as a "good" in and of themselves. We need them because there *are* some people for whom we have found no better, more humane way of removing them from a society upon which they prey. Yet, in the years during which I have traveled the country exploring its prisons and its ever-growing prison population, I have become increasingly cynical about the cavalier way in which policies have, in recent years, been crafted, about many politicians' glorification of incarceration, about decisions that have resulted in America producing fully one-quarter of all the world's prisoners.

What does it feel like to know you will live out your days, however many they may be, serving a life sentence in a supermax prison? What does it feel like to live in a world bounded by walls and razor-wire fences, minutely controlled by uniformed guards and continuously filmed by security cameras? For those with sentences shy of life who serve their time and come out, what does it feel like to remain a second-class citizen, barred from a host of jobs, often permanently removed from participation in the political process, until the day you die? What does it mean to live in a society whose very laws say, in essence, *Once a criminal, always a criminal. We don't believe in second chances. We don't believe in rehabilitation.*

Nationally, there is a growing debate within criminal justice circles about whether a felony conviction should, in any way, be linked to the loss of voting rights. There are some who argue that access to the ballot in a democracy is a right rather than a privilege, and that a person convicted of a crime should pay a penalty—a fine, community service, or time spent behind bars—but should not be removed from the political process. There are others who believe that a person who breaks the social contract—in other words, someone who flouts laws agreed upon by the community as a whole—cannot be trusted to participate in the rule-making process; that, in order to preserve the smooth-functioning mechanism of the political system, the rights of at least certain lawbreakers must be forfeit. It's an argument that has a long pedigree, going back at least as far as seventeenth-century liberal theorists such as British philosopher John Locke. Personally, I think this is a moral gray zone, a place without perfect solutions, a space within which the arguments both in favor of and opposed to removing the vote from those currently serving a sentence have their good points and bad. Were we living in a world lacking all the biases and differences in opportunities that affect the life chances of different individuals and groups, and were all the laws that were used to convict people near universally acknowledged to be fair and just, I would say that temporarily removing the vote as a part of a felon's punishment makes philosophical sense. After all, those who violate fundamental social norms, particularly by wreaking violence on others, have, in a sense, expressed their contempt for the code that binds us together into a community. Thus it doesn't strike me as implausible to say that, for a while, they should not have a say in shaping that community.[3] Opinion polls in America tend to show pretty consistent popular support for such *temporary* disenfranchisement.

In the real world, however, where a young, poor, black, or Latino man is far more likely to be arrested, incarcerated, and disenfranchised than a more affluent white man, where the fairness of many of the contemporary laws—in particular those relating to drug sentencing—that put people in prison is hotly contested, I would contend that disenfranchisement, even temporarily, overall does more societal harm than good. It is too heavily laden with the baggage of a culture divided along racial and class lines ever to be viewed as simply a criminal justice matter; its impact is too predictably absorbed by the economically marginal and the racially discriminated against to be viewed in isolation from broader social tensions.

Be that as it may, in 2004 the more pressing issue was to explore how disenfranchisement *after* people's sentences were served reverberated through the political system and down the generations. That doesn't mean there shouldn't be, or isn't, a debate about whether those in prison should be able to vote *while* serving their sentences. After all they can, and do, in many other countries, including Sweden, Israel, and South Africa, as well as in the states of Maine and Vermont. And, as far as I can tell, in none of those countries or states has the political process been hijacked by a group of felons with a collective "felonist" agenda of tearing apart the societal fabric. But, because the policy of disenfranchising people after they have rejoined the "free" community beyond the prison gates poses such a unique, and extraordinary, challenge to so many fundamental democratic beliefs, and so destructively reinforces so many other deep-rooted social divisions, I chose to focus my book largely on the issues raised by post-prison disenfranchisement. After all, America is a nation that prides itself on treating all people fairly, that attaches great import to the notion of equality under the law. And permanent disenfranchisement serves as a slap in the face to such values.

Conned tells a story of mass disenfranchisement within America at a moment in time when America has both positioned itself as the world's democratic bulwark against forces of reaction and, increasingly, reshaped its foreign policy—its relationship to the rest of the world—using the rhetoric of a messianic democracy. This saga began a generation ago. Each passing year has dumped more people, especially more poor, black, and Latino people, into prison, creating an ever-accumulating mass of subcitizens at the back end of the system. These people are released from prison with a few dollars and a bus ticket but without the basic political rights most of us take for granted and assume to be universal.

In June 2004, I met Jazz Hayden, a sixty-something activist from New York who had spent much of his adult life behind bars on charges ranging from drug possession all the way up to attempted murder. He earned four college degrees in prison before his release, after which he established a reputation as a no-nonsense policy advocate. Hayden told me that voting was "the coin of the realm." Politics, he said, was a game, and to stake your place in the game you had to vote. "The voting issue," he argued, "is the only issue that addresses questions of power and power relationships between prisoners and prison administrators, and communities prisoners come from and the state. It's *the* key issue. It's the one right you have to have to protect all your other rights—to choose who's going to lead, [who are] going to be policy makers and who's going to run things, and *how* they're going to run things."

Disenfranchised by felony convictions, however, millions of Americans simply *can't* vote. They are now removed from the game before the starting pistol is even fired. And thus they drift through life on the outside as citizen-ghosts, as taxpayers and neighbors and service users, but not as voters, not as people to whom those seeking office have to pay attention. I think of the melancholy song sung by the cuckolded husband in the musical *Chicago*: "Mr. Cellophane should have been my name, 'cause you can see right through me, walk right by me, and never know I'm there." Lacking the vote, come election time those barred from the process simply do not count.

Felons are individuals, and their political preferences defy easy stereotyping. In the two highest-profile lawsuits on the issue in recent years, *Farrakhan v. State of Washington*, in Washington, and *Johnson v. Bush*, in Florida, the lead plaintiffs are extremely conservative African American men who have publicly stated their sympathies for the Republican Party. Mohamed Farrakhan couldn't vote in 2004, but he told me he would have voted for George Bush had he been able to. Thomas Johnson could vote—the state had suddenly restored his suffrage soon after he filed the lawsuit—and he told me that not only was he voting for Bush, but he was also telling all and sundry in the town of Gainesville, where he lived, that they should also support the Republican candidate. Yet experts such as sociologists Chris Uggen and Jeff Manza, of, respectively, the University of Minnesota and Northwestern University, who have studied the effects of felon disenfranchisement, believe that, on the whole, it serves to reduce the pool of Democratic Party voters—to disastrous effect for the Democrats in an era in which the American electorate is almost evenly divided between the two main parties. In many ways, though, the Democrats are themselves to blame for this: in the 1990s, in particular, they made a Faustian bargain, trying to shore up support among crime-weary suburbanites by throwing their voice behind so-called "tough on crime" initiatives that, inevitably, would ultimately lead to the disenfranchisement of another pool of their supporters—the urban and rural poor.

Whatever the political antecedents of the problem, this infection of America's body politic came to a head with the 2000 election—when, for the first time, a strong argument could be made that modern disenfranchisement had actually helped determine the outcome of a presidential contest. After all, upward of half a million Floridians were unable to vote because of felony convictions. Given the closeness of the election result in that state, if those men and women had been entitled to cast ballots, even if only one in fifty of them had bothered to go to the polls, had those few split 60–40 in Al Gore's favor the Democrat would have been the president come inauguration day 2001.

In the years since 2000, a powerful new civil rights movement, backed by an increasing number of state and federal politicians, has emerged to push for the restoration of voting rights for those caught within the country's ballooning criminal justice web. Going into the 2000 election, thirteen states permanently disenfranchised felons. Going into the 2004 election, only seven states continued to have blanket disenfranchisement laws. In the intervening four years, political pressure resulted in reform in Delaware, Maryland, New Mexico, Nevada, Washington, and Wyoming. Even Florida and Alabama, the two states most affected by felon disenfranchisement going into the 2000 election, eventually passed provisions making it somewhat easier for ex-felons to apply for a pardon from the governor and, by extension, to have their names put back on the electoral rolls. In the months following the 2004 election, Nebraska and Iowa also eased restrictions on ex-cons' ability to vote.

In many ways, this is a saga of successful grassroots pressure rectifying an obvious political injustice. Yet, for various reasons, the reform has been only a partial success. The states where permanent disenfranchisement remains, or where the vastly complex restoration and pardon processes that have been in effect for a century have survived largely unchanged, are the states where the majority of the disenfranchised lived going into the 2000 elections—in particular, Florida, Alabama, Mississippi, Virginia, Tennessee, and Kentucky. Florida *did* enact some changes after the 2000 election, but they were modest in the extreme, and still left many hundreds of thousands of Floridians voteless and voiceless. The same holds true for Alabama. In Washington and Wyoming, permanent disenfranchisement has been replaced by waiting periods and complex restoration procedures, which have the effect of still serving to disenfranchise tens of thousands; and, equally important, most ex-felons appear to be unaware of the process by which they can get their voting rights restored.

Thus, in practice, those with felony convictions continue to be driven out of the political process in a significant number of states around the country. Precisely because reenfranchisement methods in many of these states are so cumbersome, very few people complete the complex task of regaining their right to vote, and far more continue to be disenfranchised each year by new felony convictions than are reenfranchised. Despite some tinkering at the margins, therefore, the cumulative effect of disenfranchisement grows worse with each passing year. Finally, even in states such as Utah, where ex-prisoners can, theoretically, vote as soon as they are released, most ex-cons believe they can't vote, and many parole officers and other government officials are also ill informed, unaware that their clients *do* actually have the right to vote—or, if they are aware, they are unwilling to share that knowledge.

Because so many people have been driven out of the political system by disenfranchisement laws, the broader culture of voting has been damaged to an extraordinary degree. At least in part, America's low voter turnout of recent decades can be attributed to felon disenfranchisement contributing to a culture of political disengagement. For a generation now, only slightly more than half of adult citizens in America have voted in most presidential elections and far fewer have cast ballots in less high-profile contests. In 2004, when a higher percentage of Americans came out to vote than had been the case in decades—approximately 60 percent of those eligible—pundits initially predicted this would aid the Democrats. When the votes were tallied, it turned out it had actually helped the Republicans. Quite possibly, in contrast to the Republicans, who were able to mobilize the Christian Right and other core voter blocs in record numbers, Democrats had hit their natural limits. At least in part, those limits may have been reached because many millions of economically impoverished Americans—traditionally crucial Democratic voters—had literally lost their right to vote.

So much attention has been paid to the issue of voting rights since the 2000 election that it seems quite likely that over the next several years many, if not all, states will modify their disenfranchisement laws. After all, an earlier wave of reform in the post–World War II decades removed the notion of the permanent political banishment of felons from most states' law codes. In the states that retained such provisions—most of them states of the Old South where post–Civil War constitutions specifically used felon disenfranchisement to minimize black political participation—the spirit of the age at least forced lawmakers to camouflage the more overtly racist intent of such laws. It wouldn't be too surprising, therefore, if a second wave of reformist zeal swept away the remaining permanent-disenfranchisement statutes.

Yet, as I journeyed around the country reporting for *Conned*, I began to realize that none of this would be anywhere near enough. The injustice entailed by the enforcement of current disenfranchisement statutes cannot be redressed merely by states passing expedient new laws and then washing their hands of the issue. Nor can the problem be resolved simply by banning obviously egregious practices such as Florida's hiring of partisan private companies to "scrub" the electoral rolls of possible felons. There is far too much historical baggage behind these laws for them to be overcome that easily.

Felon disenfranchisement in the United States has historical roots that lie deep in the Medieval European notion of "civil death," which is the placing outside of all of the state's protective structures of those convicted—or sometimes only accused—of treason or outlawry. Today, disenfranchised Americans are burdened with a crazy-quilt patchwork of state laws (some of which, taking their cue from European civil death laws, date back to the Colonial era, others to the Jim Crow period), numerous state and federal court decisions amending these laws, and various provisions of state constitutions and their revisions. Overlying all of these is the miasma of American race and class relations. After all, until the recent past, the chattering classes still debated whether access to suffrage should be restricted solely to the educated and property-owning classes. Felon disenfranchisement, in other words, is not a mere side effect of misguided social policies or strategies of law enforcement. Rather, pruning the voter rolls has been, in the view of a significant portion of the American power elite since the end of the Civil War, a good in and of itself.

To overcome this legacy, state and federal governments will have to fund massive public education campaigns and outreach drives informing communities of the restoration-of-voting-rights process. They will have to educate not just the already politically aware but also the marginalized and the alienated—the people who have been through the criminal justice system, or who have friends and family members with felony records—the classes and categories of people who, throughout American history, have been most frequently denied their political rights. Only in this way will the country be able to regenerate the nerve endings that create a culture of universal political participation.

At the same time, state and federal lawmakers will have to devote time and attention to figuring out why America's incarcerated population has boomed to such historically exceptional numbers in recent decades, to looking at the reasons that explain why America has utilized its criminal justice system as a first-resort social intervention mechanism in a way no other democracy in the world has chosen to do. For as long as so many tens of thousands of people are being sent to prison each year for nonviolent crimes that would not have landed them in prison in the United States in the past and would not land them in prison in most other countries on earth today, the collateral impacts on the electoral system will continue to accumulate, and de facto disenfranchisement will continue to increase. Finally, to really tackle the problem of millions of Americans either being prevented from voting by statute or being so discouraged that they think they no longer have the right to vote, both major political parties will have to commit themselves to shoring up participation rather than tamping down the numbers who bother to go to the polls on election day in order to reap short-term partisan advantage.

The story of disenfranchisement will, therefore, continue to be one of the great political sagas of our time. The 2000 election marked the moment the issue hit the mainstream. By 2004, voting rights for ex-felons had been firmly defined as a story with national political ramifications and one with powerful implications for how America defines civil rights and voting rights, as well as the notions of rehabilitation and second chances, in the years and decades ahead.

As I flew and drove around this huge and wonderful country reporting for this book, I was continually floored by the degree to which loss of liberty and loss of political rights has come to be something taken for granted by large swaths of the population, has come to be a regrettable but largely inevitable part of life for millions of Americans. As the new century speeds along, reenfranchising the millions removed, both legally and emotionally, from the voter rolls during the heavy-handed and poorly strategized "wars" on crime and drugs will be one of the great political challenges of our times.

1
Permeating the Entire Confederation

> The doctrine of the sovereignty of the people came from the townships and took over the government. All classes of society committed themselves to its cause.
>
> —Alexis de Tocqueville

> At some point, you have to ask yourself whether . . . expanding the franchise to just everyone who has two arms and two legs is the best way to govern a democracy. . . .
>
> —Tom Feeney, ex-Speaker of the Florida House of Representatives

In some ways, November 2000 is a world away—as remote from the realities of today as, say, the fall of the Berlin Wall. So much has happened in the years since the Supreme Court stopped the post-election recounts and declared George Bush the winner of Florida's Electoral College votes. Our world and our certainties have been jarred in so many ways that it's sometimes hard to remember just how momentous those weeks in Florida really were. Then again, Florida 2000 will in other ways continue to cast its long shadow over American politics—and, by extension, over developments around the world—for years, perhaps decades, to come. Whether the Electoral College votes in the Sunshine State were, in the literal sense, stolen, or whether a series of dirty tricks, combined with happenstance, simply proved enough to give

George W. Bush the slimmest of slim electoral margins, the result is the same: America's domestic and foreign policies were taken in dramatically new directions by a president who, in 2000, assumed power lacking any clear mandate—and who then used that power to shore up his party's dominance over the political system in a way few presidents in American history have managed to do.

There were many flaws in Florida's electoral process at the start of the twenty-first century. And central among these was its exclusion of hundreds of thousands of ex-felons—or, at least, possible ex-felons—from the voter rolls.

A few months before Election 2000, disturbing stories began surfacing in the Florida media about the electoral rolls being "scrubbed," or "purged."

Hundreds of thousands of Floridians were technically not allowed to vote because they had been convicted of a felony at some time in the past; yet the state was worried that several thousand of these men and women (though still less than 10 percent of the state's total number of felons) might have registered to vote anyway and that county officials might have failed to notice that these people were ineligible to vote. And so state officials decided to clean up the rolls.

A private company named Database Technologies, or DBT, was hired by the secretary of state's office to create lists of people thought to have felony records. The secretary of state then sent the lists to county election supervisors and ordered them to remove voters from the rolls if their names showed up on the purge lists. The criteria for potential "matches" of felons' names with the names of people on the electoral rolls were so vague that if only 70 percent of the information overlapped—if a person's name was the same as a felon's nickname or alias, for example—a person would be sent a letter telling them they were being taken off the list of eligible voters because of a prior felony conviction.[1]

As the reports flowed in, it became clear that something had gone very wrong: the vast majority of those being removed from the political process were African American, and a grossly disproportionate number of those removed were likely Democratic voters from Democratic precincts.

None of this should have come as a surprise.

At the very least there was a credibility gap. It turned out that DBT—hired by Republican apparatchiks in a state that everyone knew was going to be closely fought over between the two main political parties that November—had close ties to the Republican party. And the Republican party clearly had an interest in minimizing the numbers of poor and black people who would be voting in the upcoming presidential election.

Later on, after the proverbial shit hit the fan, DBT would argue that it had simply been hired to create usable databases out of raw information handed them by a variety of state agencies. If that was the case, they were paid an extraordinary amount of money simply to make telephone calls, key data into computers, and do some statistical sampling: the contract with the state of Florida, signed in November 1998, was reported to be worth $4 million over three years, with over $2 million the first year—up from a $5,700 annual contract Florida had previously signed with a small local company to generate an updated initial felon purge list.

Whatever the motivation behind the construction of the list, the result was, to put it charitably, a mess. Florida was forced to admit that 8,000 names provided by the state of Texas had been wrongly included in the list. Voting rights activists alleged that people were being disenfranchised for crimes committed in the future. The criteria allowed those compiling the list to reverse a felon's first and last name, thus flagging people whose first name matched a felon's last name, so long as their last name matched a felon's first name. The matching criteria didn't even require that a voter's race match a supposed felon's race.

After the election, DBT was bought by a company named ChoicePoint. ChoicePoint argued that it bore no responsibility for DBT's decisions. But the company wasn't in a hurry to open up its inner workings either: ChoicePoint refused to allow its executives to be interviewed on this, instead responding to my repeated requests for information and for interviews with a long, pass-the-buck e-mail sent by the director of its external affairs department. "ChoicePoint has never been involved in the review of voter registration rolls in Florida or any other state, and has no plans to do so in the future," Director Chuck Jones wrote. "ChoicePoint did not perform the legally required review of Florida voter rolls used in the 2000 elections. Rather, ChoicePoint acquired the company that did—Database Technologies—after DBT had delivered the initial 2000 voter exception list to Florida officials for verification." Jones went on to say that while DBT was contracted to create lists of potentially ineligible voters, it "did not remove anyone from a voter registration roll. . . . DBT did not independently 'generate' any names for or from any lists. DBT's job was to review names that appeared on lists it had been provided by the state of Florida for potential matches with names of registered voters who were possibly deceased, may have been registered in more than one county, or may have been convicted felons. In 1999, DBT employees assigned to the project had advised the state that the review criteria developed and required by the state could produce a list that would be overinclusive. As a result, such a list could misidentify some individuals as deceased, registered in more than one county and as convicted felons, who, in fact, were not. State officials replied that was acceptable because county election supervisors were legally required to verify the information before any voter was removed from the registration rolls by local officials."[2]

In other words, a series of potentials, possibles, maybes, could-bes, and might-be-the-cases were being used to insulate a multi-billion dollar corporation from any responsibility in errors that had resulted in thousands of voters being wrongly told they couldn't vote in the 2000 presidential election. When the National Association for the Advancement of Colored People (NAACP) sued Database Technologies, the secretary of state's office, and the seven large urban counties that had sent out you-can't-vote letters to large numbers of people—in a case known as *NAACP v. Katherine Harris*—memos uncovered during discovery showed that the company had indeed warned the state that it was generating inaccurate lists because of the overly broad matching criteria used by the state. Yet, when the state had turned around and said something to the effect that We're aware of these problems but we want you to go ahead and generate the lists anyway, the company had simply agreed, and, its legal rear protected by the memos, had plowed right ahead into the lucrative territory of voter purges.

Meanwhile, Florida's state agencies were denying that the mess was their fault because, they claimed, they believed the company was providing accurate lists, and anyway, it was up to individual counties to double-check the accuracy of the information as it related to residents of each county. Finally, the county officials themselves were arguing that they didn't have the resources to investigate every single name handed them by the secretary of state's office and that they therefore shouldn't be held to account if wrongful purges had taken place at the local level.

Apparently a national presidential election's outcome could hinge on the mistakes and cavalier behavior of unaccountable private companies and unresponsive state bureaucrats . . . and yet nobody was to blame.

Two issues were being played out in Florida 2000. The first was a straightforward, almost technocratic question: were the "right" people ending up on the purge lists, and being removed from electoral rolls, or were these lists being populated by "wrong" names, by people who had never been convicted of felonies? Given the ineptitude of those who had compiled the "purge lists," this problem alone—even though it only dealt with a tiny percentage of the total number of disenfranchised in the state—was of a magnitude large enough to have prevented the Democrats from cleanly winning Florida.

The second issue was more complicated, more philosophical: should "purging" of electoral rolls occur in the first place? Was there a credible intellectual defense of the practice of removing, permanently, the vote from anyone ever convicted of a felony, even if they were living crime-free in the community and paying taxes like everyone else? Most states had, at one time or another, permanently removed at least some categories of felons from their voter rolls; yet, by 2000, the vast majority of states had abandoned these laws, replacing them with temporary bans on voting that generally mirrored the length of a person's prison, parole, or probation sentence. Two states, Maine and Vermont, actually let people vote while in prison—a practice that didn't appear to have much public support in America but which was the law of the land in many other countries, including allies of America such as Israel and postapartheid South Africa.

In Florida, by contrast, most politicians seemed pretty content with keeping the reenfranchisement bar as high as possible. The state's constitution mandated that all felons be automatically struck from the voter rolls, and it also declared that these individuals could only regain their right to vote through receiving something called "executive clemency"—essentially a second-chance pass issued via a state clemency office headed by the governor, with input from all of the state's cabinet members. Over the years, governors had varied enormously in how they had interpreted the clemency rules. Traditionally, they had pushed for rules that forced most felons to journey to the state capital, Tallahassee, to argue their case in person. Then, in 1975, Democrat Reubin Askew created an assumption of eligibility—removing from the rules a list, known as Rule 9A, of the categories of crimes that mandated a person to appear in person before the Office of

Executive Clemency to plead their case for vote restoration. Thenceforth, the language of the reform implied, anyone who applied for their rights to be restored would get them back without any kind of hearing.[3] It was a deft legal maneuver designed to sidestep the constitutional provision that created permanent disenfranchisement in the first place. In essence, Askew was saying, "You've lost the right to vote forever unless you ask for this to not be the case."

Two years later, however, Askew's successor, Democrat Bob Graham, revived Rule 9A. Under Graham, many felons would again have to appear in person to argue their cases—but the presumption remained that, if they did so, they would ultimately get their rights restored. By the 1980s, however, things were getting tougher in Florida again. Under Governor Martinez, fewer and fewer felons got their right to vote restored. In 1991 lists of crimes were put into the statutes, the perpetrators of which had no way to get their rights back other than to beg their case before the governor at the quarterly meetings of the Office of Executive Clemency, in Tallahassee.[4]

By the time Jeb Bush came to power as governor in 1999, touting a tough-on-crime agenda titled "tough love," the vast majority of Florida's felons could get their vote back only by applying for a hearing. Bush's office added two hundred crimes to the lists of those requiring such a hearing. As a result, only 30 percent of ex-cons were eligible to apply for restoration without a hearing. Yet of these, if a single member of the governor's cabinet objected, they'd be bounced into the "need a hearing" category. Since the cabinet objected to approximately half of these 30 percent, in reality only about 15 percent of ex-cons were eligible for the speeded-up restoration process—and of those, very few actually knew they could apply in this way, and far fewer ultimately got their vote back.[5]

The remaining 85 percent had to fill in the application form (the Department of Corrections was statutorily obligated to give it to them upon release, though in most instances failed to) as well as gather personal references, produce proof of employment, find copies of all of their court records and sentencing documents, produce bank statements, submit to fingerprinting, and then wait while the Department of Parole filtered the list of applicants and clemency office "investigators" further filtered it.

It would routinely take years after a person filled in the application form before they even got their chance at a hearing. After all, the Office of Executive Clemency met in Tallahassee only four times a year, and at each of these sessions—presided over by the governor, who asked probing personal questions of the supplicants before him, many of whom had had to cobble together what little savings they had to make the journey north to the panhandle from Miami, Palm Beach, Orlando, and other cities to the south—it heard about fifty applications. In a year, therefore, only two hundred people appeared to argue for their voting rights. Of these, about half were granted their rights back.

In other words, while tens of thousands of Floridians were losing the vote each year, only about one hundred were getting it back via clemency hearings, and at most, 15 percent of the remainder were getting their vote back without a hearing.

I had been researching felon disenfranchisement since the late 1990s, fascinated by what it meant to surreptitiously remove millions of citizens from the political process. It seemed a topic tailor-made to raise eyebrows; yet, in the months leading up to the 2000 election debacle, and in the months following, it was hard to get editors fired up about the issue. There were simply so many other things to write about. Beforehand, there was the aftermath of the Monica Lewinsky scandal and all the juicy gossip of the primary season campaign: Would John McCain bolt from the Republican Party? Would Clinton jump into the fray to save Al Gore's bacon?

Afterward, of course, there were the hanging chads and dimpled ballots, and there was Pat Buchanan's improbable surge among elderly Jewish voters in south Florida thanks to the creation of an ingeniously incomprehensible "butterfly ballot."

With the result still up in the air in Florida, I wrote a couple of quick-turnaround articles for the online edition of *Mother Jones* magazine. Then, having failed to convince any other publications to let me devote my time to the story, I went off and wrote about other things—about the three strikes law in California, about mental health services in prison, about redistricting battles in Texas.

But the voting scandal continued to nag at my consciousness. I knew that two sociologists, University of Minnesota professor Chris Uggen, and Jeff Manza of Northwestern University, along with the D.C.-based Sentencing Project and Human Rights Watch, had done some in-depth analyses suggesting that the quadrupling of America's prison population and the continued existence of nineteenth-century felon-disenfranchisement codes were coming together with brutal effect throughout huge swaths of the country.[6] And I knew that the cumulative nature of permanent disenfranchisement provisions—if convicted felons could never vote again, then the more convicted felons there were over the years and decades, the bigger the pool of nonvoting citizens would become—meant this was a problem that, like a tumor, would keep on growing, would keep on eating away at the core of the country's democratic institutions, until stopped by some form of dramatic intervention.

In the second chapter of *Democracy in America*, Alexis de Tocqueville wrote of how the original principles of confederation developed by the New England pilgrims for self-government "spread first of all to neighboring states; subsequently, they reached successively the more distant, ending up, if I may put it this way, by permeating the entire confederation. Now they exert their influence beyond its limits to the whole American world."[7] Reporting on political and cultural shifts in this country, I've thought for a while now that the New England political roots of contemporary America have gradually been taken over by the spreading tendrils of Southern political culture—albeit one carefully tailored to a postsegregationist civil-rights era—in particular the corrupt political culture of Florida and the self-aggrandizing, strutting politics of Texas. I'm not the only one to have come to this conclusion. In his book *Made in Texas*, the scholar Michael Lind writes that "the failure of the nation to Americanize the South has made it possible for the South, under leaders like George W. Bush, to attempt to Southernize the United States. . . . Southern conservatism has always hurt the South. Now, thanks to the South's influence in Washington, Southern conservatism is hurting the United States and the world."[8]

It's not simply that Southern Republicans have temporarily staked their claim to positions of leadership in Congress, or even in the Oval Office. Rather, Southern political values, shaped in isolation from the rest of America and, more generally, from the wider world and adapted to function in a polity from which overt racism has ostensibly been banished, have come to hold sway over the political institutions that make the societal machinery run. Southern fundamentalist religious values. Southern anti–trade union, anti–workers' rights values. Southern hostility to anything resembling a welfare state. Southern glorification of all things martial. And, of course, Southern attitudes to crime and punishment.

If such is the case, perhaps it is no surprise that disenfranchisement laws—developed in their purest form in America in the post–Civil War South—are once again impacting national politics and governance such that, in de Tocqueville's turn of phrase, their influence is now "permeating the entire confederation." What began as a rather devious way of legally removing thousands of newly freed blacks from the political process in such states as Florida, Mississippi, and Alabama over one hundred years ago has now—in a period during which "tough-on-crime" legislation has radically increased the number of Americans, particularly those with black and brown skins, with some direct experience of the criminal justice system—come to affect the politics of an entire country. And, ironically, it has done so during a time in which virtually all politicians claim to abhor racism, and in an era in which America has trumpeted its mission to sow the seeds of democracy in the far corners of the earth.

A few months after the raucous endgame of the 2000 election, with the dust having settled somewhat and Bush ensconced in the White House, and with more people starting to talk about the significance of disenfranchisement, *Rolling Stone* asked me to write a story about how legal restrictions on access to the ballot box had affected the election result. And so, I flew to Florida.

After November 2000, African American politicians in the Florida assembly and senate had pushed the issue to the forefront, and several of them were now working on reform bills that would make it easier for felons who had done their time to apply to get their voting rights restored.

I drove from Miami north to Tallahassee to interview some of these men and women, stopping along the way to interview ex-prisoners who had tried to get their vote back as well as lawyers and political figures who were attempting to help them in their quest.

"A lot of these folks are first-time offenders and they end up getting their rights nullified," thirty-five-year-old Florida state senator Kendrick Meek, who represented a largely Haitian district in Miami, told me in a tone of disgust that could have sliced through metal. Many, said the cigar-smoking, khaki-wearing senator, were young people arrested on petty drug charges. "They get their rights taken even before they're old enough to vote. They're paying a bill that they'll never pay off."

After I'd heard the reformers' side of the story, I arranged to interview Florida House Speaker Tom Feeney, a Republican and staunch opponent of restoring the vote to felons who'd completed their sentences.

Sitting in his spacious, wood-paneled office, I mentioned to Feeney that a young colleague of his was hoping to secure a floor debate on the issue, and Feeney made it pretty clear, pretty quickly, that as long as he controlled the House machinery, a full-blown airing of the topic was highly unlikely. "I've told him it's not a big issue to me in terms of rectifying the situation," the Speaker candidly stated. "I wouldn't go out of my way to bump an education reform bill or a growth management or a cut-the-costs-of-prescription-drugs bill so we could hear automatic restoration of felons' voting rights. People in my district don't think that the problem we had was insufficient numbers of ex-felons qualified to vote." To my amazement, Feeney then went on to express his reservations about the whole concept of universal suffrage, talking in a manner reminiscent of the old Southern gentry from generations past. "At some point you have to ask yourself whether or not an electorate that is increasingly less likely to be literate, whether expansion of the franchise to just everyone who has two arms and two legs, is the best way to govern a democracy for the future. It's less important to me that I have the right to vote than the people that do are upholding the integrity and legitimacy of the society and culture. The fact that an individual, because they've permanently lost the right to vote, for example, is not going to be able to go vote every two years, as long as the voters who do vote vote responsibly, it shouldn't [affect] his ability to enjoy the blessings of the First Amendment and the Twentieth Amendment and all his constitutional rights."[9]

* * *

The past, they say, is prologue.

Four years after an election in which the presidency had arguably been determined by the inability of hundreds of thousands of Floridians to cast ballots, and in a world radically transformed, I found myself on the road again, this time charting the impact of disenfranchisement around the country as Bush geared up for reelection.

2
The Legal Literacy Test

Unlike many cross-continental trips, this one doesn't start in New York or California. There is no dramatic scene on the Venice boardwalk, with sun-soaked palm trees reaching up toward the deep blue sky and gorgeous, suntanned beach bums promenading along the sand at the edge of the waves.

Instead, it begins on a rainy day in Seattle, with the seagulls squawking overhead and the salty smells of Puget Sound and the Port of Seattle wafting in over the bars and cafes and musty old restaurants of Pioneer Square. It starts there, because Washington made it all but impossible for large numbers of felons to ever get their right to vote restored. By contrast, California's suffrage was no longer so restrictive.

There were many other things wrong with California's criminal justice system—I've spent much of the past decade documenting ills in the state ranging from a terribly expensive and catchall three-strikes-and-you're-out law to widespread brutality within its prisons—but permanent disenfranchisement was no longer one of its flaws. That wasn't always the case. In 1974, when the state did still disenfranchise ex-felons, it was challenged by prisoners in a lawsuit known as *Richardson v. Ramirez*.[1] The case went all the way to the U.S. Supreme Court, which, in a decision penned by William Rehnquist, upheld the right of states to deny ex-felons the vote. Meanwhile, as the case developed, California's voters decided it would be easier to abandon permanent bars on voting and to replace them with temporary bans running concurrently with felons' prison and parole terms. In the November election, they voted in favor of amending the state's constitution to this effect. And so, in 1974, the state moved away from permanent disenfranchisement, despite the Supreme Court's having validated the state's old law by declaring that the Fourteenth Amendment to the U.S. Constitution allowed states to deny the vote to felons (a decision used by proponents of ongoing disenfranchisement in several states to swat away legal challenges over the past several decades). Once a Californian's sentence was up, the state posted no bureaucratic hoops to jump through before a person could rejoin the electoral system. Those on probation and those who had finished their sentences could vote.

The vast scale of California's prison and parole system meant that, even with the less restrictive franchise laws, some quarter of a million citizens in the state still were temporarily voteless at any one time. And, in neighborhoods heavily affected by incarceration, that in turn meant that several congressional and local elections had been significantly affected by people having been taken off the electoral rolls in this way in recent years. Close races in Southern Californian cities such as Long Beach—an industrial port community just south of Los Angeles airport with a large population of African Americans, Hispanics, and working-class whites—could well have turned out differently were so many residents not currently serving time in one or other of the state's more than thirty prisons.

But, powerful though this impact was, suffrage issues in California were not nearly as devastating, or as controversial, in their impact as they were in Washington. In raw numbers, more Californians were voteless at any one time than were Washingtonians.[2] But as a percentage of the adult population, a far larger number of Washingtonians had been removed from the state's policy-making process, and, in most instances, they remained removed long after they had rejoined the community.

And so I headed north, flying up the Pacific Coast to Seattle.

* * *

Seattle, with its hills and sparkling skyscrapers, its jazzy rhythm and stunning waterfront, is one of the most beautiful of American cities, a place custom-made for dreams. Yet it has an underside—an impoverished class of drug addicts and petty criminals, of poor people struggling to make ends meet, and of homeless men and women who scavenge for food and money and the thrown-away remains of other people's days along the avenues and alleyways of the late-night city. And, with a large number of ex-prisoners living within its boundaries, it has become the epicenter of Washington State's recent experience of mass disenfranchisement.

Although, technically, Washington State does not permanently disenfranchise convicted felons, it creates so many hurdles to their regaining the right to vote that, in practice, huge numbers of felons never vote again. Such is the way in almost all the states that have a practical form of permanent disenfranchisement.

Thirty miles south of Seattle, past the great industrial cranes of the port and the nondescript suburbs climbing up the hilly landscape of coastal Washington, I met a man in a county jail (we talked via telephone, sitting on either side of a bulletproof glass divide in a tiny visiting booth) who had spent the better part of a decade trying to prove that these hurdles were illegal.

In 1995, Mohamed Farrakhan—an African American man originally named Ernest Walker, who had converted to Islam and changed his name—filed a lawsuit against Washington State, arguing that because minorities were so overrepresented in the criminal justice system, the felon disenfranchisement laws were a violation of the Voting Rights Act.[3] Thirteen years earlier, Congress had amended the landmark 1965 law to bar policies that had the effect of placing hurdles in the way of minority access to the ballot box even if those policies were not deliberately crafted to subdue the minority vote. Farrakhan—in prison for writing several thousand dollars' worth of bad checks—and five other plaintiffs from various minority backgrounds, all of them incarcerated at the time, argued that, because of this, Washington's disenfranchisement codes should be ruled illegal. It was a long-shot lawsuit, and many Voting Rights Act experts thought that it would have no legs. In fact, privately, many wished the case would disappear, fearing that, if Farrakhan lost, it would do widespread damage to a range of other voting-rights cases.

But nearly a decade later, after ping-ponging back and forth between a district court in the middling city of Spokane nearly three hundred miles east of Seattle on the other side of the grandiose Cascade Mountains and the San Francisco-based Ninth Circuit Court of Appeals, the case was still alive. By now, Farrakhan had come out of prison; had run for office as an assemblyman in the state legislature (he called himself an independent Republican) and been sued by the state attorney general's office for illegally running while still being disenfranchised; had embraced a somewhat eccentric black nationalist ideology known as Muir, which contended that black Muslims from northern Africa had colonized America centuries before Columbus; had adopted the name Mohamed Shabazz Farrakhan-Bey (all followers of this movement added the name Bey to their surname), and had bounced back into the county jail for neglecting to pay his restitution fees—the monies he owed as compensation for his original crimes.

While Farrakhan-Bey was busy doing all of this, his lawsuit had been shepherded along by an attorney named Dennis Cronin; by Professor Larry Weiser, of Gonzaga University's legal clinic in downtown Spokane; and by a series of law students interning at the clinic, who worked out of a poky second-floor office overlooking the university's soccer field.

I drove over the thickly forested Cascades to visit the legal clinic. Weiser was a short man, somewhat shy of five and a half feet tall, a feisty activist-lawyer originally from Boston who played saxophone in local klezmer and funk bands, and who had worked with the legal clinic since its inception in the early 1980s. One of his music combos was called Funk Pro Tunc, a play on the legal term *nunc pro tunc* ("now for then"—the retroactive application of something that should have been done earlier) that, in all likelihood, only fellow legal eagles would understand. Luckily, all of the band members were public interest lawyers. When he wasn't making music, Weiser put in long hours at the clinic and had the bloodshot, watery-red eyes to show for it. Over the years since he'd gotten the phone call from Cronin asking him to come aboard the Farrakhan case, a huge amount of his time and energy had been spent mustering information on disenfranchisement laws and finding historians and other experts who could talk him through the linkages between criminal convictions and loss of voting rights in America.

In 2004, as the election neared, the state of Washington challenged rulings by a panel of judges from the Ninth Circuit Court of Appeals first overturning a lower court's summary judgment dismissing the case and then refusing a state request for an *en banc* hearing in front of all of its judges to review this ruling. The state asked the U.S. Supreme Court to hear their challenge.

Weiser was torn. On the one hand, the attorneys working the Farrakhan case believed the state's appeal to the U.S. Supreme Court had no merit, and they wanted the Supreme Court to send it back to the state so that they could finally begin preparing for trial; on the other hand, if the Supreme Court took the appeal, there would be an opportunity to appear before the highest court in the land to argue a case that Weiser had come to see as presenting fundamental questions about the nature of American democracy. Weiser could hardly contain his excitement at this possibility. It would, he said, be the experience of a lifetime.

For better or worse, that experience was not to be. In November 2004, a few days after the election, the U.S. Supreme Court declined to hear the case, dealing a hefty blow to Washington State's legal strategy and paving the way for a high-profile trial that could have dramatic implications regarding voting rights across America in the years ahead.

"The Ninth Circuit's opinion provided that evidence of bias in Washington State's criminal justice system could be considered under the totality of circumstances test to determine a violation of the VRA [Voting Rights Act]," Weiser explained. "We will now be preparing for trial on that basis. We will be looking for additional expert evidence to support the notion that the criminal justice system discriminates against minorities. We will also be working to provide additional evidence on other relevant social and historical factors that the court may consider in determining whether disenfranchisement laws discriminate on account of race."

There was a lot of history behind Farrakhan's lawsuit. Over the years, citizens in Washington looking to regain their vote could either seek a pardon from the governor—which involved filling in several pages of questions on a form issued by the governor's office, as well as providing a list of personal references, a copy of the judgment from the original sentence, a description of how they had rehabilitated themselves, and the addresses of all places of employment over the previous five years, with no guarantee the governor would act on the request—or they could get a document known as a "Certificate of Discharge" from the Department of Corrections indicating that they had fulfilled all the terms of their sentence. However, of the thousands who had finished their sentences and paid off their fines, many had still been unable to successfully navigate the bureaucratic maze constructed for those seeking to have their voting rights restored.

Nearly 4 percent of adult Washingtonians, or more than 150,000 people, were, according to the D.C.-based Sentencing Project, barred from voting either because they were in prison or because they hadn't been able to fully complete the terms of their sentence. In many instances, that simply meant they could not pay the fines and court fees—known as Legal Financial Obligations (LFOs), which accumulated interest at the rate of 12 percent per year from the moment they were imposed, including throughout a person's stay in prison—levied on them in increasing quantities and amounts in recent decades as a part of their conviction.

Since the 1990s, the LFOs, as they are known, had been made so onerous that few people managed to get them off their backs. All prisoners now had to pay something called a Victim Penalty Assessment, only the first of many court-ordered fees. In 2000, legislators in Washington passed what was called the Offender Accountability Act, raising this assessment from $100 to $500. An array of other fees were also now levied against felons. Since most people coming out of prison found, at best, minimum-wage jobs, this had, in practice, proven an extremely powerful block to people being able to get their vote back. Indeed, Washington's Department of Corrections estimated that, a few years after the Victim Penalty Assessment Act's passage, only one quarter of the felons under its supervision in the community were making their payments regularly.

Yet, the Department of Corrections did have the authority to terminate a person's supervision even if they hadn't finished paying their debts, meaning that they were no longer bound by the restrictions of probation or parole even though they hadn't technically fulfilled all of the requirements of their sentence. At that point, it became extremely difficult for a felon ever to get the paperwork from the department that would subsequently allow them to vote, even if they did succeed in paying off their debts. They were cast into a sort of Kafkaesque legal limbo, unsupervised by the correctional system and, because of this, unable to regain their civil rights.

Not surprisingly, few managed to get their rights restored. Data provided to the American Civil Liberties Union by the state's Department of Corrections in late 2001 indicated that in 2000, fully 10,000 people had their cases "terminated" by the department while only 3,000 had their cases "discharged," meaning that far more people than not came off of parole with no paperwork from the department that could be used to speed up their reenfranchisement applications. The same was true every year previously going back to 1995. From 1995 back to 1988 (the earliest year for which the department crunched the numbers), more people were receiving discharge papers than were being simply terminated, but out of a far smaller total pool.[4] And of the two to three thousand being officially "discharged" each year, by no means all successfully managed to complete the application and review process required before they could once again cast their votes in elections.

"I don't think there's any real understanding in Olympia [the state capital] of the practical impact of the $500 fine," said attorney D'Adre Cunningham of Seattle's Defender's Association Racial Disparity Project. "I don't think it even occurred to people it would interfere with people's ability to get discharged, to restore their rights. It's kind of messy."

In 2002, 2003, and 2004, bills were put before the legislature that would have separated the issue of voting rights from that of unpaid Legal Financial Obligations. Each time, prosecutors in the state opposed the measure, as did victims' rights groups. Unwilling to contradict these powerful lobbies and reluctant to present as a hostage to fortune a yes vote that could be portrayed as somehow being "soft on crime," legislators killed the bills in committee.

Shortly before I decided to visit Washington, the Department of Corrections made a bad problem worse. Seeking to clean house, they went through old files and terminated tens of thousands of people from their caseloads, thus unintentionally making it even harder for these men and women to reclaim their right to vote. "A large number of offenders who had not paid in full the Legal Financial Obligations associated with their sentence, in essence, ran out of time," Department of Corrections secretary Joseph Lehman wrote to the American Civil Liberties Union in response to a query on this. In other words, the department washed its hands of these people and sent them off with all of the handicaps that accompany an incompletely finished sentence.

Finally, in June 2004, a milder reform was passed. It allowed ex-felons to apply for a Certificate of Discharge if they paid off their LFOs after the Department of Corrections had terminated their supervision. Yet to get this process started, applicants still had to get the department to sign off on their petition. Not surprisingly, this wasn't exactly a priority for the state's corrections officials, and reports soon started coming in that few people were successfully completing the new, supposedly streamlined, process.

Victoria S., for example, was convicted of welfare fraud in the early 1990s for claiming $4,000 in welfare while her then-husband was earning money on a fishing boat. At the time, she was raising her son and stepdaughter while attending college and claimed not to have been aware that her husband was earning money. In the fishing business, often the fishermen do not earn cash while preparing a boat for an expedition, so her claim was not as outlandish as it might otherwise have seemed.

While the courts didn't buy her plea of ignorance, neither did they deem Victoria to be a hardened criminal. She was convicted of a low-level felony, spent a total of three days in jail, and was ordered to pay back the money plus about $1,500 in miscellaneous court costs. In April 2004, Victoria, now living on a small island a couple of hours' drive north of Seattle and dividing her time between making canvas tops for sailboats and working on an orca whale–watching boat, finished paying her debts. She applied to get her vote back and was wrongly told by the county clerk's office that she had to buy something called "Criminal History/Records: A Guide on When and How to Seal, Vacate Non-Violent Class C or D Felony Convictions." As if the stolid title weren't enough to scare anyone off, the office told Victoria she had to fork over $20 for the privilege. "I bought it and there's a petition for a certificate of rehabilitation. Another for the right to bear and own a firearm. The paperwork was so overwhelming, all these different petitions that needed to go to court, go to the police department. I had to get my fingerprints taken." At that point, she called the Washington office of the ACLU, who told her that she was not legally required to go through any of this to get her vote back in the state. All she had to do, they said, was to apply for a Certificate of Discharge, which required a signature from an official in the Department of Corrections.

So Victoria approached the department and asked them to sign off on her paperwork. In July 2004, she received the necessary signatures. But then she found yet another obstacle placed in her path: after the paperwork was received back from the Department of Corrections, the prosecutor's office that had tried her case had to look up her records and determine whether she had paid off all of her obligations. When she phoned the prosecutor's office, they told her the county clerk's office still had her paperwork. Of course, when she phoned the county clerk, they told her the prosecutors had it. And, so, as Election 2004 approached, forty-eight-year-old Victoria S. was still denied the right to vote, caught in a maze of paperwork and bureaucratic inertia.

"I've been going through this for six months," she blurted out angrily when I phoned her. "I voted in every election before this. I was an avid voter, very alert, aware of what's going on in the world. I've got two college degrees—in fisheries biology and English. Whenever my boyfriend goes to vote, and my mom and family, it hurts me. I'm a citizen of the United States. I want my voice to be heard. I've paid taxes since I was a teenager and I want the right to vote."

Meanwhile, in the mixed-income, mixed-race neighborhood of Beacon Hill south of downtown Seattle, forty-three-year-old

Michael Carter, a tall man with a trim gray goatee, was still trying to regain the vote after a bloody brawl with an Asian shopkeeper nearly twenty years earlier, a fight he had always claimed followed on from the shopkeeper refusing to sell Carter and his friend beer and calling him a nigger. In the ensuing melee, as a crowd of local onlookers egged the twenty-four-year-old on—the shopkeeper had, apparently, angered many of his black customers—Carter, who at the time used drugs and hung out with local toughs, drew a pocket knife. He didn't use it, but, when added to the fact that he badly beat the storekeeper, it was enough to get him convicted of second-degree assault with a deadly weapon.

Carter spent six months in the county jail and also had to pay restitution and fines. He spent his time in jail on a work release program, working as a certified nurse's assistant at a nearby nursing home. In the two decades since then, Carter picked up two misdemeanors: he was ordered to attend anger management classes after knocking down the door to his house and sitting on his second wife (he had been married three times by the time I met him) during a domestic quarrel, and in 1998 he was arrested for driving under the influence. Other than that, he got his life back together, stopped using drugs, and got himself regular employment. His third marriage stuck, and, after he and his wife had children, the family's little house in Beacon Hill filled up with the normal clutter of childhood: plastic toys, a fish tank in the cramped living room, and sports trophies won by his son on the mantel above the fireplace.

Carter's was hardly a perfect record, but also hardly cause for lifetime disenfranchisement either. When Carter tried to regain his vote in 2004, however, after a voter registration worker knocked on his door and said the law had recently been changed to make the process of restoration easier, the Department of Corrections told him that because his case happened so long ago, his papers were all buried deep in the archives, and, because they couldn't find them, they couldn't know for sure whether he had paid all his fines. Thus they couldn't approve his application to have his voting rights restored. Attorneys from the ACLU reviewed Carter's case and determined that he was, in fact, eligible to get his vote back. They advised him to write to the Department of Corrections. Yet, when Carter did write to the DOC to ask how he could get approval for his petition for the Certificate of Discharge, he received a dismissive handwritten reply scrawled on the bottom of his own letter: "Mr. Carter, you can petition the court with an attorney to review your case at any time, in front of your sentencing judge. The prosecutor's office will inform your sentencing judge as to if you meet all court ordered requirements." Of course, there was no guarantee his sentencing judge was still on the bench, or even still alive, twenty years after the events in question, and even if he was, the prosecutor's office would not have been able to tell the judge whether all the requirements were met because the Department of Corrections had already acknowledged they couldn't find the original documents in their archives.

It was either a Catch-22 or another series of self-contained impossibilities worthy of a Kafka novel. Whatever it was, as the election approached, Carter, too, was still unable to vote.

As if all of the rigmarole surrounding Legal Financial Obligations weren't complicated enough, a few days into my trip I found out that in Washington there were also requirements for those convicted prior to mid-1984 under old indeterminate sentencing guidelines that were different from those that applied to people convicted after that date. These old guidelines allowed for a sentence to range between a minimum number of years and a maximum, with correctional authorities having discretion over when a person would actually be released based on their behavior inside prison and evaluations as to whether they had been rehabilitated;

the newer guidelines set up a more rigid sentencing code. And to further complicate matters, different counties requested different degrees of proof before putting a person back on the electoral rolls.

In fact, the system in Washington was so complicated and cumbersome that when the ACLU surveyed the state's thirty-nine county auditors—the men and women in charge of each county's election process—a few months before the 2004 elections, they found that about half of them had no idea how felons could go about getting their right to vote restored.[5] An activist group from Seattle that requested a meeting with the secretary of state in 2004 to ask him about the process received from him a series of grossly inaccurate answers.[6] The literacy test may have been abolished as a gateway to the franchise, said ACLU attorney Aaron Caplan, but in states like Washington a "legal literacy test" remained in place for the growing number of felons living out in the community after the completion of their sentences.

Staggeringly, nearly one in four black men living in Washington, a state that prides itself on its laid-back, live-and-let-live ethos, were legally disenfranchised by 2004 because of involvement with the criminal justice system—a number ratcheted up in recent decades largely as a result of the dragnet strategies utilized by the warriors fighting the "War on Drugs" and the vastly disproportionate number of African Americans caught up in these sweeps. By the early twenty-first century, the U.S. Bureau of Justice Statistics was reporting that over 2 percent of blacks in Washington were incarcerated. In other words, one in fifty African Americans (of all ages and of both genders) was living behind bars in the state.

The problem wasn't limited to African Americans. Across the board, more and more people were winding up in prison—or at least with felony convictions—and, by extension, were losing their right to vote. According to Washington State's Sentencing

Guidelines Commission, 10,100 felony convictions were imposed in 1986 (the total number of people convicted is less than this, since many offenders are convicted of more than one felony). By 2002, that number had shot up to 27,835—at a time when only about 3,000 felons per year were qualifying to get their vote restored. But the incarceration epidemic had certainly hit the black population particularly hard. In the Seattle area, African Americans were sentenced for drug crimes at a rate twenty-five times higher than that for whites (as a percentage of their respective populations) in the area.[7]

These figures are truly extraordinary, yet we have become so blasé about sensational crime data that few people today even bat an eyelid at such numbers, much less sit down and actually think through the implications of such vast disparities. As I drove around Washington listening to talk radio and eavesdropping on election conversations in diners, I didn't hear anyone mention the huge numbers of residents who couldn't vote—although, in recent years, the issue had cropped up enough times in the media that, going into a closely fought national election, it should have been an issue. There was talk about Iraq, talk about the war records of John Kerry and George Bush, talk about jobs and health care and, away from the political arena, major sporting events, but nothing on Washington's epidemic levels of disenfranchisement and its possible impact on the upcoming elections.

And yet, disenfranchisement of the proportions experienced in Washington speaks volumes about America's contemporary political culture. We are at risk of becoming something absurd: a culture that prides itself on, even defines itself by, its democratic institutions and then systematically removes entire subgroups of people from political participation. We are becoming a country that boasts of its universal suffrage yet disenfranchises millions. In short, we are evolving into an oxymoron.

Over the years that I have reported on the criminal justice system in America, I've come to loathe these three words: War on

Drugs. Not because I have any sympathy for drug kingpins, nor because I think using drugs is smart—I don't—but because the "war" has always targeted the marginal and the sick rather than the wealthy and the powerful and has, from the get-go, been tragically intertwined with the politics of race in the United States. I've come to detest the futility and smashed dreams those words encompass, come to hate the wasted lives they enclose—lives fractured by the drugs themselves, then further violated by a criminal justice strategy that locks up low-level offenders while allowing those higher up the drug-smuggling food chain to trade information for light sentences, that encourages addicts to rat out fellow addicts, that creates a numbers game that rewards police officers and prosecutors for arresting and sending to prison evermore young men and women regardless of whether society is best served by their imprisonment. I've come to abhor the policy choices, both about drugs and, more generally, about how the country deals with nonviolent crime, that have made America the number-one incarceration nation in the world today.

Wars that cannot be won generally should not be fought, especially not when there are other, realistic alternatives available. Strategies that are fundamentally flawed should not be stubbornly adhered to in the face of overwhelming evidence that they are not working. Yet the "War on Drugs" is still being fought, and hundreds of thousands of addicts and two-bit dealers dealing to make a few dollars here and another few there are going to prison and jail rather than into community treatment or community service programs, even though the evidence—continued drug availability and use, the replacement of arrested dealers and drug mules with new dealers and mules as fast as they are taken off the streets, the continued power of drug cartels—all points to a massive policy failure.

One of the consequences of this war is a startling increase in the number of felons in America, and, because of this, a contraction of the franchise on a scale not seen since the consolidation of the South's Jim Crow laws in the latter decades of the nineteenth century and the first years of the twentieth. Every week, Seattle, and Washington State as a whole, convicts hundreds of people on felony charges. They are by no means all drug felons, but, as in every other state, if you dig below the surface you find that a hefty majority of felons have some kind of substance-abuse issue. They may not have been convicted of a crime relating to drugs, but a large number of them will have committed their crime while under the influence, or in order to fund an untreated addiction. There's probably no way of knowing for sure, but it's at least possible that if America spent even a fraction as much money on treating addiction as it does on waging the "War on Drugs," many of these individuals could have been helped before their addiction catapulted them into the prison system. Every week, the courts in each of the state's thirty-nine counties send lists of these newly convicted felons to their county auditors—the people who oversee each county's electoral machinery. Those individuals' names are then removed from the list of eligible voters. But no streamlined process exists at the tail end of their sentences for reinserting their names back onto the rolls. "The process for canceling voting rights is very prompt and very automatic," asserted Nancy Talner, of the ACLU of Washington. "And that's in contrast with how difficult it is to restore voting rights."

As the Farrakhan case wended its way through the courts, the numbers of Washingtonians denied the vote steadily increased. In fact, they had been increasing since the early 1970s, when the nation's prison population began booming. Not coincidentally, according to statistics generated by the secretary of state's office, a sharp, and continuing, falloff in voter participation began in Washington in the early 1970s, as it also did nationally.

For years, commentators have bemoaned the rising political apathy of America's population, but the secretary of state's numbers hint that perhaps disenfranchisement rather than apathy is to blame for some, though certainly not all, of the decline in political participation. Between 1952 and 2000, the percentage of registered voters who voted in Washington stayed fairly constant, bouncing between a high of 82.35 percent in 1960 to a low of 74.52 in 1996. In 1972, 76.96 percent of registered voters went to the polls in the presidential election that resulted in Richard Nixon's reelection. In 2000, 75.46 percent of registered voters in Washington voted in the election that resulted in George Bush's assuming the presidency. However, during the second half of the twentieth century the percentage of the *total* voting-age population who voted fell from 72.8 percent in 1952 to 57.62 percent in 2000—a huge decline, most of which occurred after 1972, which is the year the prison boom began.[8]

In other words, those who registered to vote were almost as likely to actually vote in 2000 as in 1972, but a smaller percentage of the population was registering to vote in the first place—at exactly the same time as more people were getting entangled in the criminal justice system and being legally barred from registering to vote. In 1970, according to Bureau of Justice Statistics numbers, Washington had 4,128 prisoners. By the end of 2003, that number had shot up to 16,148. Since the disenfranchisement problem in the state was cumulative, this meant that exponentially higher numbers of people had been removed from the voting rolls. In 1972, 85 percent of Washington's adults were registered to vote. Then the numbers began slipping. In 2000, barely three-quarters were registered.

There are, of course, also other reasons for the falloff in voter registration. In 1972 the voting age was lowered from twenty-one to eighteen, thus bringing into the pool of eligible voters millions of young men and women who, simply because they were young and often immature, were less connected to the political system than older adults and therefore less likely to vote. Yet youth alone cannot explain the decline in the numbers of eligible adults registering to vote. To understand much of the rest of this downturn, one must appreciate the scale of the growth in incarceration in America. Since the early 1970s, the number of Americans behind bars has more than quadrupled. The number of Americans on parole and probation has also skyrocketed. Year in and year out for thirty years, regardless of whether crime rates were rising or falling, the prison population—and, by extension, the number of ex-prisoners with felony records walking around communities, many of them prevented from registering to vote by state laws—increased. By 2004, there were more than 1.4 million people living in prison in the United States and well over half a million living in jails. All told, over two million Americans were living behind bars on any given day. Another several million were on parole or probation. Many millions more had been through the criminal justice system and had served time behind bars at some point in the past.

Looked at in this light—amid a disenfranchisement epidemic seen only once before in America, at the onset of the dark days of Jim Crow—it's hardly surprising that a smaller percentage of the total adult population votes today than a generation ago. It would be practically miraculous if it were any other way.

After driving around Washington for the better part of a week, I returned to Seattle. But before I flew back to Sacramento, I met up with one more felon, a forty-four-year-old musician named Dan who had spent decades as a fairly hard-core environmental, animal rights, and antinuclear activist roving the country from protest to protest before being slapped with a felony for something as far from political protest as you could imagine.

In 1996, Dan and his wife were living in Seattle with their young son. His wife, he said, had been diagnosed with schizophrenia several years earlier, and her condition had deteriorated. Dan himself was suffering from undiagnosed bipolar disorder. The couple had abandoned their wandering political ways and moved back to Seattle so that Dan could go to a community college to study photography and his wife's parents could move in and help take care of her. Dan and the in-laws didn't get along, and, as they fought, he became more and more depressed. By June 1996, he was suicidal. After yet another fight with his wife and her parents, Dan went into the bedroom and grabbed a hunting rifle that was stashed in his wife's backpack. His mother-in-law yelled to her husband to call the police. As Dan tried to explain, "At that point I said, 'You guys don't understand what's going on,' and sat down with the rifle and put it in my mouth. My mother-in-law grabbed it by the barrel and pulled it away. And I pulled it back and cut her finger [on the barrel of the gun]. I got up and left, and the next thing I know I'm getting arrested for assault with a deadly weapon."

By the time Dan's case came to court, he'd been sitting in jail for six weeks. The prosecutors told his attorney that if he went to trial, they'd ask for a fifteen-year sentence, but if he took a plea bargain, they'd accept two years' probation and a $100 fine. There really wasn't much choice involved. Dan pled guilty to a third-degree felony (the lowest level felony Washington has on the books), was put on probation, and was fined $100 and also ordered to pay his mother-in-law's medical bills and the mandatory Victim Penalty Assessment. He went straight to the hospital, where he was put on medications for bipolar disorder and extreme depression.

Since that dalliance with death, Dan had been on Supplemental Security Income (SSI). He received about $500 per month, and out of that he paid off about $15 of his court debts. It was barely enough to cover the 12 percent annual interest, and it certainly wasn't enough to help him get his vote back. The Department of Corrections had terminated its supervision of Dan in 1999 after he had stayed out of trouble for several years, and, without a Certificate of Discharge, Dan had become yet another member of Washington's numerous voteless underclass. This seemed particularly ironic, given the number of years he had spent in a variety of political undergrounds.

We sat in an art café, surrounded by political posters and advertisements for upcoming music events. Grunge kids, or their next-generation heirs, wandered in and out, and Dan swapped chitchat with them. He seemed to know everyone—from bands he had played with, from other bands he hung around, from protests and community meetings, and just from the cafés he spent an awful lot of time in. "I feel like they're treating it like voting is a gun almost," Dan suddenly said, laughing bitterly, as our meeting neared its end. "They're saying I'm dangerous with a gun. But how would I be dangerous as a voter? Wait a minute. Voting should be an indication of someone's willingness to be a citizen. I still have feelings about political things. I have very strong feelings about how the system is."

3
S-Man and the One-Armed Bandits

By the time I settled into the Casbar Theater Lounge in Las Vegas's Sahara Hotel, with de Tocqueville, a cold beer, and an earful of 1970s cover tunes blasting from the stage, I imagined my aristocratic French traveling companion to be thoroughly mystified. The hotel—at which I had finally arrived, following a delay occasioned by both of my car's front tires shredding on the scorching asphalt on the way into town—mimicked a giant mock-Moroccan palace, complete with ornate turrets. The yellow neon sign advertised its presence on the northern end of the fabled Strip with two huge camels; the entrance to the parking lot tower was guarded by a couple of giant Lawrence-of-Arabia-style statues; a roaring roller coaster thundered past the main entrance to the hotel and up a vertical incline; and, just to the south, a multistory blue water slide was depositing hundreds of screaming kids, teenagers, and adults into the cool waters of a giant pool sitting in the middle of one of the hottest deserts on earth in a city of more than one million people.

Then again, perhaps de Tocqueville—who believed that anything west of the Mississippi was part of the Great American Desert—would have understood the innate democratic brilliance of this strange fantasy-sandscape. After all, he'd written that "In America, the people constitute a master whose pleasure has to be satisfied to the utmost level."[1] I had my doubts; the more I was coming to know de Tocqueville, the more I concluded he was a bit of snob—that intellectually he had grasped that the future belonged to the masses, but, in his heart, he felt a great nostalgia for a more discerning, aristocratic culture. I was pretty sure that my companion would have been more comfortable with a mellow place like Seattle than one with all the razzmatazz of Vegas. He seemed to me to be more of a martini-and-jazz type than a diet-Pepsi-and-Muzak man.

Las Vegas is an amazing place: the few miles of the Strip are among the most famous, most loved and hated, most visited, and weirdest few miles on earth. The casinos are air-conditioned palaces oozing decadence from every corner; they are places where the world goes to forget its woes, to sunbathe, drink, gamble, frolic, and do all the other things that people do when they're looking for high-intensity fun. Their buffets seat thousands and the waste from these mega-kitchens could, I dare say, feed a small, and hungry, African nation. Their theaters and cabarets and circuses combine the glamour of New York with the kitsch and decadence of a Roman orgy.

And then there's the other Vegas, the underside of the city that, like the tin shacks and piles of garbage off the tourist route in some paradisiacal Third World island, you're not supposed to see. (Or, if you do see it, politeness dictates that you certainly do not talk about it.)

The northern end of the Strip is heralded by the soaring Stratosphere Tower, a knockoff of Seattle's Space Needle, topped by a vast outdoor red roller coaster—the highest scare-ride in the world—hundreds of feet above the ground. North of there, Las Vegas Boulevard, the official name for the Strip, becomes very seedy very fast. Once upon a time, the area, called Meadows Village, was a ritzy locale, in the dwellings of which the city's upscale casino showgirls lived. Rumor has it they used to lie nude out by their pools. True or not, Meadows Village acquired a nickname: the Naked City. And it stuck. Nowadays, there's still a lot of nakedness, but it's the sort you find in lap-dance spots, twenty-four-hour adult video arcades, one-hour motels, and shabby little dives with names that lustily hint at hours of masturbatory pleasures behind the tinted windows of their paint-peeling facades—light years away from the manicured world of the large casino topless revues.

Around the Naked City live Las Vegas's poor communities: blacks, Latinos, a smattering of impoverished whites. There are a lot of drug users and dealers in these parts, high unemployment levels, rinky-dink mom-and-pop stores, taco stands, fast-food venues, liquor outlets, bail bondsmen, and extremely large numbers of ex-prisoners—many of them having served time in the Southern Desert Correctional Center, forty miles north of town and surrounded by red-rock mountains so devoid of vegetation under a sky so lacking in moisture that it might as well be on Mars. Ironically, the prisoners at Southern Desert produce the decks of cards that are used in Vegas's casinos—which is about as close as these men will get to the dollars generated by all the gambling, since most casino jobs are actually off-limits to anyone with a felony conviction.

Under the fierce desert sun, and away from the multibillion-dollar casinos of the Strip, the Naked City could be the poorer seedier heart of any major Southwestern city. Except for the fact that, because of a long history of severe restrictions on felons' voting rights in Nevada, it is now an epicenter both of disenfranchisement and also of a grassroots campaign to restore the vote to these people. Approximately forty thousand ex-prisoners live in Nevada.[2] Because Las Vegas is home to most of the state's residents, most of the ex-prisoners live there; today, somewhere in the region of four to five thousand prisoners return to Clark County, of which Las Vegas is the major center, each year. And because the Naked City is among the poorer neighborhoods of town, a great many of them concentrate inside its boundaries. If the prison boom continues for another few years, many tens of thousands of ex-cons will be living in the poorer parts of Vegas.

* * *

The Naked City was part of Democratic assemblywoman Chris Giunchigliani's district. The other part of her district was made up of affluent inner 'burb communities, including the Scotch Eighties, a toney neighborhood that the city's mayor called home. Giunchigliani had been an assemblywoman since 1990. It was a part-time position, and, until 2002, when she wasn't legislating she was a special-education teacher at a local middle school. (That year she decided to focus on politics full-time.) In the 1980s Giunchigliani, who was born in Lucca, Italy, and grew up in Chicago before moving west in her mid-twenties, was also president of the state's teachers' union.

When I visited her at her home, she was in full-on campaign mode. A "Reelect Chris Giunchigliani" poster stood in her desert garden—a sparse, cactus-studded lot in front of a down-to-earth house decorated with eclectic artwork: a reproduction of an Egyptian hieroglyph graced the living room; a poster of the turn-of-the-twentieth-century radical activist Mary Harris "Mother" Jones, "the most dangerous woman in America," hung in the assemblywoman's home office. Her home phone, her fax, and her cell phone were ringing nonstop, and her husband was getting ready to take her to a stump event. For several years, Giunchigliani had led an often lonely fight to if not repeal then at least modify Nevada's disenfranchisement laws. It was, in fact, largely thanks to her efforts that Nevada's law was changed in 2003.

Until 2001, once a person lost his or her voting rights in Nevada, the only way to get them back was to spend thousands of dollars going through an extremely convoluted legal process that would culminate in applying to the governor for a pardon. That year, a coalition of civil rights groups and community activist organizations teamed up with some politicians in the legislature and made a concentrated push for reform. They succeeded in passing a very mild legislative change that provided some felons with access to the ballot after an approval process supervised by the parole or probation department. The new law, however, was complicated and very unpopular with the agencies mandated to enforce it. And, in the state's large cities, the electoral registrars' offices simply chose to pretend the new law didn't exist. As a result, hardly anyone who had lost his or her vote got it back.

In 2003, the reformers tried again. This time around, they introduced a bill that would automatically restore the right to vote to first-time nonviolent felons who had completed their sentences. It was, by most standards, a very modest bill, and it would still leave many thousands of Nevadans—who would have had the right to vote had they lived in, say, California or Vermont or Ohio—outside the political process. Nevertheless, everyone involved agreed that it was as broad a reform as was politically feasible. The Democrat-controlled assembly passed the bill by a large majority, but the Republican senate, urged on by the district attorneys' association, then blocked it. Opponents of reenfranchisement tried to undermine the bill by attaching an amendment that would also give felons the right to bear and own firearms; since no one was arguing that this was a good idea, this gimmick came close to sinking the entire proposal.

At its first reading, the bill was defeated. It was then reintroduced as an amendment to another law. After Democrats in the assembly threatened to hold up all legislation originating in the senate unless the upper house passed a restoration-of-voting-rights bill, it finally passed and was signed into law by Republican governor Kenny Guinn in June 2003.

"I have a lot of poor, a lot of motels downtown," Giunchigliani explained. "I'd say 10 percent [of her constituents in the poorer parts of her district] are ex-felons. I have approximately fourteen thousand [registered] voters, out of forty-eight thousand residents." In a presidential election, she estimated, perhaps only 5,000 of these people actually came out to vote. "If you want people to come back into society, let them earn their rights back so they can participate in society. As a teacher, [I know that] you teach something, you reenforce it. If you have a family member who's disenfranchised, the spouse says 'You can't vote. I'm pissed off. I'm not going to vote either.' The kids see this. We're losing another generation."

Over the years, Giunchigliani had become convinced that laws restricting felons' right to vote were playing a large, and generally underexplored, role in local elections. "Most assembly races are generally won by fifty to two hundred and fifty votes. We had one won by eleven votes last year. [U.S. Senator] Harry Reid [a Democrat] was elected by six hundred and forty three votes statewide." Meanwhile, in state senate races, a margin of victory of "one thousand votes is huge. Two hundred votes is not bad. Ex-felons can make a difference in a race." And the issue didn't stop at the state, or even the congressional, level. Nevada was one of those states with a population almost equally divided between registered Democrats and Republicans. In 2000, it was one of the most closely contested states in the presidential election. In the end, its five Electoral College votes went to Bush by a margin of only 21,597. Before the 2000 election, five Electoral College votes might easily have been dismissed as a footnote. After the election, each and every vote became a nugget of gold.

Four years later, in 2004, both parties threw all they could into Nevada, with the candidates repeatedly stopping in to whip up their crowds. The 2003 reforms had put several thousand more potential voters into play, and voting rights groups were doing their utmost to convert "potential" into "actual" as the countdown to Election Day began.

On an old industrial strip near a large Las Vegas Police Department building in northwest Las Vegas, an organization named EVOLVE was running a program to help ex-prisoners rejoin the community. One of its missions was to inform clients of the change in the law that allowed them to register to vote. In the year since they'd started, over 1,200 people had walked through their doors, the majority of them African American or Latino, most of them from four particularly impoverished zip codes in the city. Most hadn't heard a word about the new law. They told EVOLVE staffers they had assumed they could never vote again.

In this bizarre political netherworld of rights lost and information flows blocked, strange champions emerge. It fell to an ex–drug dealer, prisoner, and enforcer named Shawn Smith to inform EVOLVE's hundreds of clients of their newfound rights. Sitting in his light pink, carefully uncluttered office, behind a desk dominated by a blue globe on a gold mount, the staffer counseled clients and urged them to do whatever they had to do to get their vote restored.

Smith was large in every sense of the word. In his mid-forties, he weighed in at 373 pounds and change, had been a locally well-known footballer and wrestler in his younger days, and, under the street moniker of S-Man, had acquired a fairly fearsome reputation while working as a muscleman in the 1980s for a drug dealer who operated out of one of Sin City's many nightclubs. He got arrested in December 1988, was sentenced for possession of a controlled substance (an additional charge of using a firearm during drug trafficking was dropped as a part of his plea bargain), and spent most of the 1990s behind bars. It was in prison that S-Man grew up. He realized that he was wasting his life and he began reading and thinking about politics. He had never voted before he got arrested. Now, he wanted to vote the way a man with an itch wants to scratch.

Originally sentenced to over seventeen years, Smith was deemed rehabilitated and was released after serving eight years. He immediately founded an organization named Guiding Individuals From Trouble (GIFT), and began working with other prisoners coming back into the community after years on the inside. The street reputation he'd acquired a decade earlier now gave him the credibility to talk to the ex-cons. "Oh, you're S-Man," they'd say, and then they'd relax a little and let Shawn give them his spiel. When EVOLVE began, Smith was one of its key figures.

I met S-Man a few months before the November 2004 election. He had just begun the paperwork process that would, he hoped, result in getting his vote back. The presidential election, he told me excitedly, would be the first time in his life that he had ever voted. "You know what," he averred, gesticulating with his soft, pudgy hands, his eyes lit up, "it's almost like being released out of prison again. Being free. Being one of the ones who can provide an opportunity for someone else. Here I am, voicing my opinion to enhance what I believe in. That's a freedom in itself. Prior to incarceration I didn't know the significance of it. I'm fired up about it. When you know better, you'll do better."

S-Man was optimistic, but his optimism didn't tell the whole truth. All around the city, tens of thousands of residents still weren't aware that they could vote. When I joined up with a group of young college students registering voters inside a poorly air-conditioned, and thus incredibly hot, music superstore in a poor part of town, about a dozen people told them over the course of one afternoon that they couldn't vote because they were felons. Many others, most of them young and black, simply stared away and walked past silently with an expression, or rather a lack of expression, I have come to recognize over the years of my reporting as a classic blank-slate prison face. "I don't know anything about a law change," one young man said when I mentioned I thought the rules had recently been modified. "I'd like to vote. It's an important thing. I guess some people say it's important. Sometimes I think it doesn't matter."

A similar situation held in New Mexico as well, another sparsely populated Southwestern desert state, won by Al Gore in 2000 by a mere 366 votes. Like Nevada, the state had, in the wake of that election, replaced its permanent disenfranchisement provisions with a law allowing felons to vote after they had fully completed their prison, parole, or probation terms. Yet New Mexico, too, was having problems educating voters about the new provisions. And in neighboring Arizona, about 150,000 people had lost their right to vote, thanks to a state law that not only disenfranchised prisoners, parolees, and those on probation, but also permanently removed the right to vote from anyone convicted of two or more felonies.

Back in Las Vegas, the New Voters Project, a group that works to bring young adults into the political system, told me they kept meeting up with young men and women fresh out of prison who assumed they could never vote again. A Catholic padre working in Latino neighborhoods of town explained that his twelve canvassers were also meeting people every day who told them they were not allowed to vote because they had been to prison.

Perhaps in a city where residents are used to having a replica of Venice's St. Mark's Square next to one of the Eiffel Tower, where across the street from the Empire State Building are the Statue of Liberty and various other glorious New York City landmarks, and where down the road from Caesar's Palace in all its imperial Roman splendor stands a sheer glass "ancient" Egyptian pyramid, there's nothing weird about going to prison on a marijuana charge as a teenager and being told as an old man that you still can't vote for mayor, senator, president, or, for that matter, the school board that runs your grandkids' schools because of your felony record. But in the same way that I find it weird to see a marvel of ancient Egyptian architecture next door to a reproduction of a giant green statue placed in New York harbor four thousand years later, so I find it strange to think about lifelong removal from the political process.

"I had a man crying over the phone, saying he hadn't been able to vote in forty years," said a community organizer with wonder as she registered people to vote in the run-up to the election. "A drug conviction in 1964 or 1965. This man hadn't been able to vote since then. He was at least sixty years old."

I left Las Vegas and continued on my travels.

In Reno, the state's second city located several hundred miles to the north of Las Vegas, Washo County district attorney Dick Gammick decided not to talk with me about his opposition to reenfranchisement. State senators Maurice Washington (from the small east-of-Reno suburb of Sparks) and Dennis Nolan, who had led the charge against Giunchigliani's bill in the senate, also ignored numerous phone messages left at their homes and Carson City offices. But there were plenty of others who did want to talk.

By the old, dusty railway tracks, a world away though hardly more than a stone's throw from the massive (albeit not Las Vegas–quality palatial) concrete-and-neon casinos of downtown Reno, Denny owned an auto repair shop. The shop was made of wood, with dirty blue horizontal slats at the base and vertical once-white slats making up the walls. It looked like something out of Depression-era small-town America. The early-summer desert wind whistled harshly and hotly down the tracks from the dry mountains that surround the Reno bowl, sucking the moisture from out of my skin; scrubby twigs and grasses and miscellaneous detritus blew loosely out of the Nevada wilderness.

Denny was fifty-seven years old, tall and lean—almost Jimmy Stewart–lanky. He had big bones and graying hair brushed up and back away from his temples and an intelligent, earnest expression on his face—like a neighborhood shopkeeper in a 1930s black-and-white feature film. He had hearing aids in both ears and his skin was weathered—the hardy skin of a man who had spent much of his life working on cars under one of the hottest suns on earth. He looked in good shape, though somewhat older than fifty-seven.

I'd been told the mechanic would be a good person to navigate me through the maze of proceedings that Nevadan felons seeking to get their vote back used to have to go through and that many, not eligible under the 2003 law change, still had to face.

Denny was born in northern California, the first of what eventually turned out to be a family of twelve children. He went to Catholic school, got interested in the activism of the 1960s, married young, and had a daughter. In 1969, he said, bothered by the images of police brutalizing civil rights and anti–Vietnam War protestors, he decided that he could do better, that he could wear the uniform without succumbing to violence. And so he became a policeman, working in the small community of Menlo Park, California. For eight years he rose through the ranks, accumulating a reputation as a no-nonsense cop when it came to violent criminals and sometimes, he admitted, turning a blind eye to those committing what he saw as less serious crimes—dope possession, in particular. Like many small-town officers, he saw himself as part hand of the law, part social worker, part good neighbor.

But then the policeman's marriage hit the rocks, he grew increasingly frustrated with his life, and, running out of emotional strength, he turned in his badge, moved to the Truckee Mountains just over the state line in Nevada, and began working for one of the big casinos.

By the end of the 1970s, Denny was "broke and discouraged." And he was hobnobbing with some decidedly shady characters. Denny had a pilot's license, and some of these shady characters were looking for someone who could fly in shipments of marijuana from Mexico. And so, he admits, he became "pretty much an escort." In 1979, the ex-cop was arrested at Minden airport, on the outskirts of town; the charge was possession of marijuana for sale, and, in February 1981, the thirty-four-year-old divorcé, who'd spent the time between his conviction and his sentencing working in auto-repair shops, was given two years in prison. In many ways, it wasn't a bad deal. Given the quantities of marijuana involved, he could easily have received a far longer sentence if ex-colleagues and a host of friends in the criminal justice system hadn't testified to his good character. Had he been arrested a few years later, after the "War on Drugs" really took off, he almost certainly would have been dealt with far more harshly.

All told, Denny spent seven months in a minimum-security prison and another five months in a halfway house. He went home in early 1982, and by September of that year he was off parole, in the process of separating from his second wife, and trying to get his life back together again. Because he had a felony conviction, he couldn't get the sorts of jobs that his education and his employment history normally would have qualified him for. He was barred automatically from any job that required a state license, and so he returned to cars. By the mid-1980s, Denny was married for the third time. This time, the relationship gelled. He and his wife bought a house together, and they opened an auto-repair shop. Because Denny, as a felon, couldn't get a license to carry out smog checks, the business had to be in his wife's name.

The car shop was a success, and Denny and his wife prospered. They gave money to charities and progressive social organizations; if they had a customer they knew was having hard times, without any great fuss they quietly knocked a chunk of change off his bill. Many of their customers became firm and fast friends. Denny got into no more trouble with the law—he was, you could argue, a perfect example of a rehabilitated ex-prisoner. "Since getting out and being deeply in debt and thinking the best I could do for myself was being a gas pump jockey someplace, I believe that with my wife and myself together and having this business we've become members of the community and an asset to the community. And that's very gratifying to me. Because I had it at one time," he stated with just a trace of bitterness, "and through sheer stupidity threw it away."

Although Denny had left the crazy days of the late 1970s long behind him, the one-time cop, who had always followed politics avidly, still could not vote. Nevada was, at the time, one of over a dozen states that, in effect, permanently barred felons from the ballot box. And, like everywhere else in the country in the 1980s, it was putting more and more of its citizens behind bars—thus, in effect, removing more and more of its voters from the electoral rolls. The love of excess that had fueled the casino boom was now resulting in excessive faith that the criminal justice system could solve ingrained social problems, excessive numbers of people being locked up on felony charges that, in decades past, would have resulted in a slap on the wrist and a warning, and excessive numbers of Americans being declared, in effect, subcitizens.

In about 1986, Denny recalled, "I went to my attorney and asked him to start on a process for restoration of civil rights. My attorney started working on it. He was told by somebody close to the then-governor that I'd have to wait. That it wasn't time." But, stubborn to a point, Denny didn't give up. As he pursued his pardon, he had to submit to being fingerprinted numerous times; he had parole officers make surprise visits to his house (despite his no longer being on parole); and he had to provide stacks of paperwork, ranging from details of his original conviction and sentencing to character references from friends and colleagues in the community proving that he was morally worthy of having his right to vote restored.

Thirteen or fourteen years later, and $17,000 in legal fees down the line, Denny finally got his pardon and won back the right to vote. Afterward, when he voted for the first time, he was "very proud. It felt like," he paused, a long pause, punctuated by his rocking back and forth on his chair, "like I was stepping back into respectability."

Denny's perseverance was the exception rather than the norm, however. In Nevada, until the laws were changed in 2001 and again in 2003, hardly any ex-prisoners ever managed to vote again. Nor is it terribly surprising that most people who emerged from prison during a period when they knew they'd have to spend thousands of dollars in legal fees to get their vote back weren't exactly rushing to vote after the laws were changed. By now, many of them had simply resigned themselves to lives of political silence. "I doubt whether a high percentage of the people coming out of prison are going to take advantage of the new law," Denny said, sitting in his stuffy office, the walls of which were plastered with magazine photos of lush tropical beaches, and with sepia images of steamships docking at San Francisco's Fisherman's Wharf. "When they come out, they generally have no want or desire to become involved with anything official at all."

4
The Great-Grandmother Brigade

To test the notion that ex-prisoners in states where they actually were eligible to vote were walking out of the prison gates under the misapprehension that they couldn't vote, I drove east to Utah.

Until 1998, Utah was one of only four states in the country—the other three being those Yankee redoubts of Massachusetts (which also later abandoned voting rights for prisoners), Vermont, and Maine—where prisoners had the right to vote from behind prison bars. The conservative state had embraced such a liberal notion in reaction to late nineteenth-century U.S. congressional statutes aiming to break the Mormon religion's embrace of bigamy.

In 1870, the territory of Utah had decided to allow women to vote as a way to boost the political power of their polygamist husbands. In 1882, the U.S. Congress passed the Edmunds-Tucker Act, overturning Utah's law and once again removing the territory's women from the political process. The law also barred "bigamists, polygamists and any person cohabiting with more than one woman," from voting or serving on juries. Until then, Mormon juries had routinely refused to convict men charged with the crime of bigamy in Utah. When the disenfranchisement law was challenged, the U.S. Supreme Court upheld it. Afterward, the territorial legislature (Utah was prevented from becoming a state until 1896, largely because of the emotions aroused by the "Mormon question") went even further, requiring all prospective voters to swear that they were "not a member of any order, organization or association which teaches, advises, counsels or encourages its members, devotees or any other person to commit the crime of bigamy or polygamy."[1]

The anti-Mormon voting oath was overturned with the coming of statehood in 1896. And the new state then did away with felon-disenfranchisement codes in their entirety, again presumably to preserve the voting power of men with multiple wives, since bigamy remained a felony under federal law.

Surprisingly enough, Utah's social order hadn't collapsed under this dispensation; prisoners hadn't organized into satanic political parties whose platforms endorsed rape, legalized murder, mandatory drug use, and other hellish pastimes—the cartoonish scenario painted by many opponents of restoration of voting rights today—and Utah had remained a Republican-controlled state. But even though many thought, as one state senator reportedly put it in 1998, "if the system ain't broke, why fix it?" a conservative legislator decided to push a bill that would permanently remove the right to vote not just from prisoners but from anyone ever convicted of a felony in the state.

That proposal went nowhere; but, as proponents of various sides of the issue hashed out their positions during committee hearings, it became clear that the easiest compromise solution would be to take away the vote from those currently serving time behind bars. And so in 1998 Utah disenfranchised citizens serving a prison sentence for a felony.

That law still left Utah's access to the ballot far less restrictive than in the dozen or so states that continued to permanently disenfranchise felons, and less restrictive than the majority of the remaining states, where parolees, and in some cases those on probation, also couldn't vote. But, in a sense, the small print was lost on many ex-prisoners. Having been told they now couldn't vote while in prison, they generally came out convinced that they couldn't vote on the outside either. According to many of them, prison officials, parole officers, and other state employees did nothing to disabuse them of this notion.

* * *

Somewhere along Route 80, heading east through Nevada toward Utah, it struck me that felon disenfranchisement is somewhat like chaos theory, or the law of unintended consequences. A butterfly flaps its wings in the Amazon and somehow sets in motion a chain of events that ultimately leads to a thunderstorm in Antarctica, and so on. Change enough laws, turn enough minor crimes into serious felonies, put enough people in prison who previously would have been fined, or perhaps even ignored, and eventually, because a felony conviction at least temporarily removes a person's right to vote, a state skews the electoral rolls enough to change the outcome of a presidential election. Bubba makes enough traffic stops on the I-95 and searches enough cars for drugs, and an idiot takes up residency on Pennsylvania Avenue.

It had been an interesting drive. An eerie, high-pitched wailing wind seared across the desert, and ominous black storm clouds pounded the bleak mountaintops as I passed one poor hamlet after another—tiny places with names like Winnemucca and Battle Mountain, made up of trailer parks, rusted antique mobile homes that looked like a tornado had deposited them on the desert sometime back during the Eisenhower years, sordid casinos, crumbling motels, and the occasional legalized brothel.

After spending the night in Elko, a small town populated by a surprising number of Basque immigrants and in which Bing Crosby lived and served as honorary mayor from 1948 until his death in 1977, I headed down into the blinding glare of the Great Salt Lake Desert. No wonder the Mormons had visions of whatever it was they had visions of once their wagons reached Utah. Within a few minutes, I also felt that I was hallucinating. The salty flats literally shimmered so much that the great rocks rising out of the ground in the distance looked like they were floating on water. Then the road began to rise; the Pequod Mountains, lashed by storm clouds, stood in front of me, striding north-south across the desert landscape. The road picked up what felt to be several inches of water, and the traffic slowed to little more than a crawl. The salty flats were replaced with real water—the edge of the Salt Lake itself—with white frothy waves rippling healthily in the wind. Then sunshine. And then the Cedar Mountains soared upward and a second helping of a truly Biblical thunderstorm descended on me.

By the time I arrived in Salt Lake City, a miserable, frightened wreck, the rain was once more easing off, and, out of the clouds, mountains rose on all sides—not undulating hills but real, snow-covered aeries from which winter had never retreated, hauntingly beautiful crests and peaks and dagger-like inclines.

Salt Lake City is built entirely on a grid structure, and all roads, built wide enough for a twenty-horse wagon team to be able to turn around, are named by how many blocks south, west, north, or east of the massive gray Mormon Temple they are. I took the 1300 South exit—thirteen blocks south of the temple—and headed west. I turned north on the 700 West block and left into the driveway of 980 South. By now I was so confused by the directions that, despite the grid, I didn't know what was up, down, east, west, Mormon, or anything else.

Marianne Johnstone, the founder and organizer of the Prisoner Information Network (PIN), was at the door of the orange-brick industrial warehouse–cum–office space, waiting to let me in. She was a short, slightly dumpy woman, with a thick head of gray hair, blue eyes, and a frenetic energy, an almost messianic organizing zest that would leave many younger activists gasping for breath. Ten years earlier, her husband had died in a car wreck during a getaway weekend in Idaho, a crash that also seriously injured Marianne, kept her out of commission for months afterward, and ultimately convinced her that she wanted to get out of the housing management business and do something more fulfilling with her life. Her forty-eight-year-old son was in prison—he kept getting let out and returning to prison on parole violations—and her three daughters lived in other states.

The PIN chief loved cherry-butterscotch milk shakes and onion rings from the Iceberg Diner, she loved feeding the classic jukebox there and listening to fifties hits, she was a great fan of Saturn cars, she did exactly eight minutes of stair exercises every day, and she had made a hobby of going into the Mormon genealogy archives—where starry-eyed young Latter-Day Saints direct you to air-conditioned rooms crammed with state-of-the-art computers, each loaded up with state-of-the-art databases—and studying her family history. She claimed to have traced her family back to the seventeenth century; her husband, she informed me almost conspiratorially, was confident of having found details of his family lineage going back to the tenth century. Her favorite restaurant was the little-bit-of-everything One World Café, half a mile southeast of the Temple—and it was there that, a few weeks earlier, she had met a heavy-set dishwasher nicknamed Scoop (he had $coop tattooed across his back), who was adorned with heavy-metal-type barbed wire necklaces and green prison tattoos and who'd been convicted of possession of an illegal substance as well as having (consensual) sex with a sixteen-year-old girl when he was twenty-one. It was there, in the alley off to the side of the restaurant where the workers sat and relaxed during their breaks, that she made his day by telling him that he was, in fact, eligible to vote in the upcoming elections, to cast a ballot for many of the environmental initiatives that he had been following closely in the news.

I know all of this because Marianne Johnstone didn't hide her likes and dislikes, the things that interested her and the things that pained her. As we walked and drove around Salt Lake City over two days, she took me to her favorite spots, told me stories about her life, talked incessantly. I got the feeling that, despite all her work, despite her nonstop activities, she was somewhat lonely. Perhaps she buried herself in her work precisely to avoid her demons.

When we met, Marianne Johnstone was sixty-eight years old and had three great-grandchildren. Most of her PIN friends were at least as old and had at least as many descendants. Almost all of them were retired women like herself—church friends, scrabble partners, fellow members of the local community board, activists in Salt Lake neighborhood watches. Jimmy (named after her grandfather) Hartley was a retired nurse, who, in her youth, hiked most of the mountains surrounding Salt Lake City, and who, when I met her four months before the presidential election, was dividing her time between working with PIN and her Bible studies. She had one great-grandchild. Seventy-year-old Virginia Stringham, a bubbly, still-pretty retired teacher, had grandchildren but hadn't yet hit the great-grandkids landmark. Annie, aged sixty-two, was an ex–house cleaner with a daughter addicted to meth; the daughter was in and out of prison on drug charges. Annie had two great-grandchildren. Sylvia Wadlow was an eighty-one-year-old onetime truck driver—she and her husband drove farm produce around the West during the World War II years before they moved to Utah; she abandoned the truck business in order to raise her children. Perhaps the feistiest of the lot, Sylvia had a baby great-grandson.

Every Tuesday, when state prisoners were released from Draper Correctional Facility, a prison twenty miles south of downtown Salt Lake City surrounded by supremely magnificent mountains, Marianne got up early. She collected boxes of "hygiene kits"—Ziploc bags containing toothbrushes, toothpaste, soap, shampoo, little towels—secondhand books (mainly, as far as I could tell, Harlequin romances), pamphlets on voting rights, thrift-store clothes donated by the Church of the Latter-Day Saints, and miscellaneous folders containing voter registration forms, food stamp applications, and other vital paperwork for newly released inmates. Her car filled with all of these items, she drove from her office out through the poorer parts of south Salt Lake City, past miles of suburban tract housing, past the world's largest copper mine, and, after presenting her driver's license to the guards, through the prison security gates.

There, she met up with other PIN volunteers, all wearing the blue PIN T-shirts. The women set up their table in the Glass House, a waiting room made of shatterproof glass just the other side of a security door from the main prison buildings. A double row of chain-link fencing topped by three layers of rolled razor wire headed off toward the eastern mountains. The view straight down the gravelly open-air corridor between the two fences was of unforgiving mountainsides truly worthy of the Winter Olympics held in Salt Lake City back in 2002.

De Tocqueville came to believe that private civic associations were one of American democracy's greatest assets. And, sitting with these great-grandmothers as they waited for tough, often gang-tattooed male cons to emerge through the prison gates to ask them if they needed clothes, soap, and other basics, to inquire of them if they were registered to vote—all this just moments after they had reacquired their freedom and when, in all likelihood, all they were thinking about was how and when they could get laid—I had to agree with my young French traveling companion.

Many years ago, when Marianne's husband was in the military, she lived in Japan, Washington, D.C., San Diego, and a slew of other places. When they moved to Salt Lake City, she started up a building management company, then later worked for the Salt Lake City Housing Authority. One day, she told me, she planned to retire in the small Nevada desert town of Mesquite, where she could plant a cactus garden and avoid the harsh winters of Salt Lake City. "I like going to winter rather than it coming to me," she explained matter-of-factly. But that would be later. When I met her, she was pretty much a full-time activist. Having failed to keep her son out of trouble, she perhaps felt she could make amends by helping hundreds of other young men and women as they struggled to make a success of their newfound liberty out in the communities on the freedom side of the prison gates.

For close to three hours that Tuesday morning in early summer, I sat in the Glass House with the women. Annie brought over several filled-in voter registration forms from the women's prison unit down the road. Virginia approached an extended family waiting for their twenty-two-year-old relative to come out of Draper and somewhat halfheartedly tried to change their minds about the importance of voting. None of them, it seemed, cared terribly much about the political process. When, at 9:25 A.M., the young man—his arms tattooed, his hair slicked back, a pencil-thin mustache decorating his upper lip—and two other prisoners, all dressed in white Utah Department of Corrections jumpsuits, finally walked through the door of the Glass House to freedom, the PIN women watched while the family surrounded him, the women sobbing, the young children jumping up and down with excitement. They waited while he ran off to the waiting room toilet to change into his new Fila sweatsuit and brand-new out-of-the-box sneakers handed him by a friend of the family who had come to see him get released. And then Virginia approached him to ask him if he wanted to register to vote. "Nah," he said, brushing the old woman off with scarcely a glance. "I'm all right. Thank you."

They had more luck with Keith, a thirty-seven-year-old house burglar, who said the prison guards told him he could never vote again. As his girlfriend watched, he sat down at the PIN table and enthusiastically filled in their forms. "This year, I might vote," he said slowly. "I like Bush." His woman stood behind him, gently stroking his back. He got up, gave over his voter registration form, and, arms interlocked, the two lovebirds practically danced out to the parking lot, a passionate kiss, and freedom.

That's when Marianne realized the burglar hadn't signed his form. That's when the sixty-eight-year-old great-grandmother burst out of the Glass House and, improbably, ran full-speed toward the couple, shouting after them to wait for her. She caught them halfway down the row of cars, and, as the released prisoner leaned against an old black Nissan Maxima, she got that all-important final signature.

By 10:30, everyone who was going to be released had come through the security exit, into the Glass House, and out to begin their new lives on the outside. It had been a slow, somewhat confrontational morning. The week before, the PIN people had registered seventeen people as they came out of prison. That morning, they registered only five.

A middle-aged white woman who herself had served twelve years, and who was now at the Glass House to greet a friend as he reemerged into freedom, had shouted combatively, challengingly, at the volunteers, "I thought convicts couldn't vote. I thought it was all across the board. I thought I'd heard they were given paperwork saying they couldn't vote." Afterward, as Marianne tried to argue with her, the woman said in exasperation, "I never vote and I don't really care. I just never have. I'm too busy doing my own thing. I'd assume most inmates don't care about that. Yeah, there are some who are into that, but the majority don't care. You learn to worry about your own business and not others'. You just mind your own business. That's what you're supposed to do, in a sense." Her friend, dolled up to the nines and waiting for her twenty-two-year-old son to emerge from three years behind bars, jumped in: "I don't care who the president is," she boasted, with I'm-so-tough-I'm-not-going-to-cry bravado. "It don't matter to me. We're still in a mess. The rich are getting richer and the poor are getting poorer."

The old women packed up their donated clothes and their voter registration forms and wheeled their boxes back to Marianne's Saturn on a small plastic dolly. We headed back to the city. There, I met Sylvia Wadlow, who hadn't been at the prison that particular morning. She had set up a table outside an Albertsons supermarket in a poor part of town with a high concentration of ex-prisoners. The retired trucker couldn't see too well anymore, and so, as the presidential election approached, her husband had been driving her to the supermarket most mornings and leaving her there with her table of pamphlets and voter registration forms for a few hours. When I approached with Marianne at 11:30, she was positively beaming with joy, having registered several people in the previous hour—including a couple of ex-felons who had assumed that, because of their felony convictions, they could never vote again.

Sylvia's ex-felons were hardly unique in their assumption that they had lost their voting rights, which, in Utah, wasn't even remotely true. So pervasive was the word on the prisoners' grapevine that a felony conviction resulted in disenfranchisement that, until the PIN women began their work, few ex-cons were bothering to register. Even now, the misconception remained pervasive. The night before, Scoop had explained to me that his halfway house administrator had told him, "Voting, along with handguns, was banned to me for life because I had a violent crime. I tried to see if there was a way around it, but the staff there really didn't help. By word of mouth, you hear from other parolees the same thing. After hearing other guys saying it, I assumed it was gospel. You take a guy's right to vote away, you take away his right to say anything. You feel like cattle. If you don't have a right to say what's going to happen to your life, you're cattle. You're a cow. I hope, in my life, I have more ranking than a Guernsey."

That day, at the Adult Probation and Parole Office, Marianne approached several waiting parolees. Almost all of them told her they'd also heard on the prisoner grapevine that they could never again vote. Like Scoop, but unlike the family at the prison, many of them were desperately keen to take part in politics again.

Thirty-five-year-old choreographer Danielle had picked up a

felony conviction for methamphetamine possession in 2001. Prior to her conviction, she said, she had made a point of always voting. Afterward, she stopped taking part in politics. After all, if you can't vote, you can't vote, and why cry over spilled milk? "I'm a felon. I've been a felon since '01," she explained slowly. "Possession of methamphetamine. I didn't go to prison. I went to diversion, then a daily reporting center and a women's reporting center." Then, after she missed a drug diversion class, she ended up spending a few months in jail. "A lot of people in those facilities don't think we can vote and no one told us otherwise. I'm pretty liberal. It bothers me. We're all human. We all should have the same rights. [Now] I absolutely will vote."

As Marianne was registering Danielle, her ride drove up in a white four-by-four Ford pickup truck. Danielle tripped over to the driver's side window, her long brown hair glowing in the afternoon sunshine. "Just a sec," she shouted to the driver, her voice bubbling over with excitement. "I'm just registering to vote. I can vote!"

"It's very interesting and it teaches you something about life," Sylvia explained of all the varying responses to PIN's voter-awareness drive. She was standing under the Albertsons awning just outside the store's entrance, a little old woman in wrap-around eye shades, a straw hat that only partially obscured a thick head of extraordinarily curly white hair, dark denim jeans, and the ubiquitous blue PIN T-shirt out of which emerged liver-spotted, suntanned forearms. She laughed heartily. "Of course, there's not much I need to learn at my age." But, she went on pensively, "I'm glad I can do it at my age. I do it because my grandson was in there [in prison on drug charges] and because I care. It's because you care that you do anything like this. Because you care about people. Most people think prisoners deserve everything they get. We do it to show they do need help, they are people."

I liked Sylvia. She reminded me of my grandmother. I liked her even more when, as I was getting ready to leave, she turned to me with a broad, impish grin, opened her arms wide, and said, "Hey! How about a hug? I haven't had a California hug in a while," and, before I could answer, she entangled me in a great big warm grandmotherly embrace.

When I left Salt Lake City, the lure of Highway 50, known to fans as "the loneliest road in America" proved too strong to resist. Instead of heading back to Sacramento due west on the 80, I headed south on the 15, connected to State Highway 6, drove southwest through splendidly remote mountain villages and down toward the Nevada desert, hitting Route 50 just outside the Santaquin Delta. I was glad I did: halfway across the Casino State, about one hundred miles west of one hamlet and forty miles east of the next, as the temperature soared to near triple digits, I passed a black man on a unicycle, peddling furiously in the opposite direction. For a moment I thought I was hallucinating. Then I thought I'd whip my car around and chase after him to get his story. And then I realized that a black man on a unicycle in the middle of a desert might not be too pleased to be chased after by a white stranger trying to run him off the road to ask him questions about his mode of transportation. So, I continued west, and chalked the moment up to one of those "only in America" experiences that you can't help but come across when driving the back roads of this enormous land.

5
Sent to Prison for Cooking Sausages

In mid-July, I took a break and flew to France for a two-week vacation with my family. On the way home, as the Democrats' convention in Boston got underway, we stayed a night in Brussels, in a hotel just off of the Grand Place—an ornate, late-seventeenth-century masterpiece of a square, perhaps second only to St. Mark's in Venice for sheer, overwhelming spectacle; each stone building, built as headquarters for the guilds and as houses for the merchant elites of the period, competed in its extravagant, statue-bedecked exteriors with its neighbors. The whole thing was towered over by a magnificent cathedral. From there, we returned to California, a long, tortuous route that took us through New York, then Los Angeles, and finally on to San Francisco.

Somehow, while we were away, the issue of the disenfranchisement of ex-prisoners had become a major news story. The *New York Times* had run an editorial calling for reenfranchisement, and a host of other papers and media outlets had jumped into the fray. One pundit had even gone so far as to write that it should be made a crime to disenfranchise people who had completed their sentences. In Florida, the beleaguered secretary of state's office had essentially been forced to throw out its much-criticized purge list after it became clear that the company hired to create the list had constructed it in such a way that blacks were far more likely to be struck off the rolls than were Floridians of Hispanic background. In New Orleans, Washington, D.C., and a handful of other cities, voters' rights groups were successfully entering jails and registering inmates awaiting trial as well as those serving misdemeanor sentences.[1] And in Ohio—a state that was shaping up to play a huge role in the presidential election—attorneys for the Prison Reform Advocacy Center were heading toward a legal victory that would, in mid-September, force the state to send out one hundred thousand letters notifying parolees, and everyone else released from prison within the previous five years, that they *could* vote while still on parole in the state of Ohio.[2]

Yet in the states with permanent disenfranchisement, there didn't exactly seem to be a legislative stampede to reform in the face of these criticisms, and (despite the Ohio lawsuit being all about people not being made aware of their rights) none of the newspapers were discussing the deeper problem of *perception,* of the millions of Americans with felony convictions who lived in states in which they actually did have their right to vote restored, but who hadn't been made aware of this. In a sense, all the publicity about permanent disenfranchisement might actually have been having a perverse effect on the process—reinforcing the notion that felons as a class were barred from voting and not adequately explaining that in most states at a certain point ex-prisoners *do* regain their political rights.

Three days after returning from France, I headed back to the airport again, on the way to Montana. The state's prison population had increased from 1,500 to 6,000 over the previous couple of decades—and although it only had about 10,000 ex-prisoners dotted across its 147,046 square miles of territory and among its approximately 700,000 adult citizens, it had to look forward to the prospect of far more ex-prisoners down the road as the current crop of inmates rotated out of the system and back into the community.

The newspaper headlines were full of Senator John Kerry's acceptance speech at the Boston convention, as well as news of a $445 billion federal deficit. On the mounted TVs in the airport, Bill Clinton was talking to Larry King about his newly published memoirs. In the book I carried in my briefcase, de Tocqueville was busy explaining the divvying up of power between state and federal institutions in America.

I flew via Salt Lake City, over the same Wasatch mountains that I'd driven through a month earlier, circled down over the salt flats, and came in low over the massive network of marshy, slightly fetid-looking patches of water that, as a whole, make up the Great Salt Lake. And, from there, I took another flight north to Bozeman.

I've been to Big Sky Country before, in the near-arctic freeze of winter in the year 2000, reporting on a commune of radical environmentalists who were going head to head with state livestock officials who were shooting diseased buffalo from the country's last truly wild herd that had strayed out of Yellowstone and onto neighboring ranchland. That time around, I had skied, snowmobiled, and snowshoed my way through the brutal landscape; now, in the calm of summer, there wasn't a snowflake to be seen.

I got into town late on a Saturday night at the very end of July. The mountains were vague silhouettes against a dark sky, and the hugest full moon I have ever seen lurked like a gigantic orange Halloween pumpkin low in the sky behind a veneer of misty cloud wisps. Of course, I'd forgotten to book a hotel room, and, Bozeman being one of the gateway cities to the Yellowstone area, every place in town was full. Finally, I managed to find one hotel that had one room available—a very smoky room that smelled as if someone had holed up inside it chain-smoking cigars for about a month. It was absurdly overpriced. I took it.

The next morning, I saw the vast mountains in their true colors. They were mottled green, with exquisite cloud formations heading off into infinity in the gaps between the peaks.

I was in town to meet Casey Rudd, a fifty-four-year-old woman I had heard had been surveying election officials and thousands of ex-prisoners about voting rights and an array of other issues for the past several years. I was pretty sure it was the biggest survey of ex-cons on the topic of voting ever conducted. And, from what I'd been told, the results provided strong backup to the idea that people were grievously ill-informed about voting rights. Unlike Washington to the west, and Wyoming and Nevada to the south, Montana had actually had a rather permissive attitude to ex-prisoners' voting rights since the early 1970s. But, apparently, the relevant authorities had neglected to inform their staff of this fact. Rudd had found that well over half of the ex-prisoners she made contact with thought their conviction disqualified them from voting; as disturbingly, she'd discovered through her surveys that the majority of state election officials also believed that a felony conviction barred a person from voting. "Oh gosh, I don't know," one official answered in a semi-panic when asked about this over the phone. "They can't run for office, I know." Another responded, "Oh man, I think if they've been convicted as a felon they've lost their voting rights, but I'm not certain of that." Another answered, "Call back Monday." On Monday, when Rudd's researchers called back, he asserted, "If they are a felon, they cannot vote."[3] They were all wrong: like Utah, Montana allowed people to vote as soon as they came out of prison—it was just that until Rudd's team started putting the spotlight on this, prison and parole officials generally either failed to tell prisoners anything about their voting rights, or, in many instances, actually told them that they could *never* vote again.

Casey Rudd turned out to be a true character. She was a large lady, red-faced, blue-eyed, with powerful, no-nonsense arms sticking out from a gray Montana Grizzlies T-shirt. Her curly gray hair was bunched up on top of her head, with combed-straight bangs hanging down over her forehead. And her voice had the confidence of a political spokesperson and the warm tinkle of a grandmother. For most of her adult life, she'd been a drug addict and dealer. She freely admitted that she had roped her own children into the trade, and that, when the law finally caught up to her in the early 1990s and sentenced her to twenty-eight years behind bars for selling $120 worth of marijuana, in truth she was being sentenced for a host of more serious offenses which the police had been unable to pin on her definitively.

Because she was making a genuine effort to go clean, Casey managed to get her sentence reduced. First off, a panel of judges conducted a sentence review and lowered her term to fifteen years under the custody of the Department of Corrections—giving the department discretion as to whether to keep her in prison or monitor her in another way. After two years, Corrections felt that she was rehabilitated enough to be released from prison and placed under supervision on the outside. She spent another nine months under house arrest and four more years on probation. During those years, Casey finally managed to kick the drugs, set up an organization named Connections,[4] began traversing the state giving talks to inmates and ex-prisoners on health care, safe sex, how to apply for jobs, and how to register to vote, and eventually managed to attract considerable amounts of grant money—including $5,000 in Help America Vote Act (HAVA) federal funds—to support her work.[5]

Casey's current husband, Eddie, was fifteen years her junior, wore his mouse-brown hair long, and sported a Charles I–style pointed goatee. The day I met the Rudds in their office space on the northern edge of Bozeman, Eddie was modeling a white T-shirt with the biker logo "Choppers Till You Die." He had grown up in San Diego and had gotten into progressively worse trouble from the age of about ten on. In fact, Eddie had spent most of his life behind bars, first in California, then in Texas, and finally in Montana. His arms were heavily tattooed. Disconcertingly, down his right forearm were permanently inked the words "White Pride," the initials "SWP" and "FTW" (for Supreme White Power and Fuck the World), two lightning bolts, and a swastika—earned, he admitted, for "taking care of business" behind the bars of California's Folsom prison back in the 1980s, presumably for doing something vicious to a person of another color in one of California's endless race-based prison wars. Eddie claimed to have left all of that behind him; he was now, he asserted, a political liberal looking for a way to permanently tattoo something more politically appropriate over his arm. I wished he'd done that long before.

Surprisingly, however, behind the horrific tattoos, Eddie seemed a reformed man. He and his wife, in a program supported by the state parole office, brought recently released inmates into their Bozeman home while they tried to readjust to life on the outside. And they spent the better part of each week driving up and down the length and breadth of Montana in Casey's Plymouth Voyager, talking in prisons, halfway houses, drug treatment facilities, and anywhere else that felons might benefit from salty, down-to-earth words on medical issues, on sex education, on looking for jobs, or on voting rights. Eddie claimed to have gone right through three old minivans over the past few years. They had to have been driving close to a thousand miles per week. "It keeps us busy and keeps us out of prison," Eddie said, and laughed. "That's why I do this work. It keeps me out of trouble."

Everywhere the Rudds drove, they distributed their survey forms, which included questions on whether those being surveyed could or could not vote, and, if not, why not. The results were filed in dozens of cardboard folders in file cabinets and boxes in their small Bozeman office. "Everywhere we go we give those, and last year we made five thousand contacts. At least three thousand of those were ex-felons," Casey proudly explained, with perhaps just a hint of exaggeration. In one month alone, the Rudds reaped 385 survey forms, over half of which included answers suggesting the respondents believed they'd forever lost their voting rights because of their felony convictions.

It was a very personal issue for Casey. In 1996, her parole

officer had told her that she'd forfeited her right to vote upon picking up a felony conviction. He was wrong and she knew it, but the thought that many others who might not have known the law were being told the same thing bugged her. The Rudds lectured on voting rights, they gave out the surveys, and they also registered ex-felons to vote. In the run-up to the 2004 election, they managed to register several hundred people in Montana. Yet many thousands more remained outside the political process.

In their cluttered office, I began to open folders, each one containing a batch of forms filled in during meetings the Rudds had addressed (one folder per meeting), and spread out the contents. In the first batch, ten wrote that they could vote and six said that they couldn't—but those forms were filled in *after* the Rudds had given a presentation on voting rights. Another batch: three yes, three no; another, one yes and ten no; seven no and four yes; fourteen no and not one yes; five no out of five answers, and so on. After a couple of hours of this, I had a pretty good picture. At most of the meetings with ex-felons, the Rudds were finding that before they spoke, most in the audience were unaware they could vote—and even after the lectures, considerable numbers had still failed to absorb the message and still believed they'd forfeited their suffrage.

As a result, in a state that actually had liberal enough suffrage laws to allow ex-felons to flex their political muscle should they be so inclined, few ex-prisoners even knew that they were allowed to participate in the political process until the Rudds started spreading the word on voting rights. Had they known, they might have been able to press for certain criminal justice system reforms. They might, for example, have been able to push the state to modify its particularly harsh parole system, a system that was notorious for sending parolees back to prison for minor infractions.

Eddie Rudd himself claimed to have been returned to prison for a year while on parole in Montana, after getting into a dispute with administrators at the prerelease center he was living in. He was the chef in the program, and the staff had asked him, he told me, to cook bacon. Instead, he cooked sausages, for which he was written up for "disobeying a direct order," which led to his receiving a technical violation and ultimately being locked up again.

Stories like this usually can be played in different ways. Most likely there was some shouting and arguing involved, and the sausage incident proved a trigger for larger discontents. Rudd felt he had been returned to prison for cooking the wrong breakfast item. Quite possibly his parole officer felt there were bigger issues in play. But the point was, Montana had one of the harshest parole regimens in the country; of the parolees who returned to prison, about three-quarters of them were sent back on technical violations of the terms of their parole rather than because they had committed new crimes.

In 2004, with the state now collaborating with the Rudds' efforts to educate felons on issues ranging from how to safeguard against the spread of hepatitis C to how to register to vote, prisoners did indeed begin flexing their political muscle. Members of the committee in charge of allocating money from the state's inmate welfare fund contacted Chris Christiaens, a balding, gentle-voiced, sixty-four-year-old lobbyist, who previously had served over a dozen years as a state senator, asking if he would be willing to lobby on behalf of some of their pet proposals in the state capital of Helena. The lobbyist agreed to consider their proposal.

Christiaens, an insurance manager for a Great Falls car dealership, was elected to the senate as a Democrat in 1983. In 1985, he was defeated by fifteen votes in his reelection bid by a conservative Republican who shortly afterward achieved notoriety by being arrested for drunk driving. He returned to the senate in 1991 and remained there until 2001, when he ran up against Montana's term limits.

As a state senator, Christiaens gained renown by fighting for rehabilitation services, substance-abuse programs, education for prisoners, alternatives to incarceration for less serious offenders, and help for those returning to the community, at a time when few other politicians would have touched such issues with a ten-foot barge pole. Perhaps if a handful more ex-prisoners had been aware that Montana's constitution had been amended in the early 1970s to allow them to vote, he would never have lost that 1985 election by a mere fifteen votes. After all, Christiaens was pushing for policies that would have made Montana safer by providing prisoners and ex-prisoners with real opportunities to turn around their lives. Perhaps, too, if more ex-prisoners had voted, Governor Judy Martz—who won election by only about 4 percent as a staunch law-and-order conservative—would have felt more pressure to take their concerns seriously, to appoint parole board members who would do more than simply look for excuses to turn down parole applications, to invest more money in medical and mental health services inside Montana's prisons.

Perhaps. In the meantime, Christiaens was about to start work as a lobbyist for the prisoners. And the Rudds were still traversing the state in their latest vehicle—a blue Plymouth Voyager, a beat-up old thing with more than 200,000 miles on it and a baby seat for Casey's granddaughter resting upside down atop the boxes of pamphlets and brochures in the back—holding presentations in prisons, juvenile centers, drug treatment facilities, and halfway houses, trying to hammer home the point that ex-prisoners in Montana *were* in fact entitled to vote.

I followed the Rudds north to the rather charmless little town of Great Falls. It was a smudge on the glorious landscape—its main street torn up by roadwork, dust everywhere, the sky interrupted by endless plastic signs announcing one fast-food restaurant, one motel, one gas station after another. The side streets, however, were pleasant enough. They were lined with old wooden houses and neat little yards. And amid the houses were larger brick buildings: churches, schools—and residential drug treatment facilities.

Casey was dressed for the occasion in a black Connections T-shirt, black shorts, and sandals. Her gray hair was down, falling onto her hefty shoulders in ringlets, and her bangs were brushed especially straight, down over her forehead. The Rudds bounced from meeting to meeting. They had their routine perfected: Eddie would give a ten-minute introductory presentation, complete with break-the-ice small talk about how he and Casey had met, about his criminal past, about the fast life he'd led and the realization that it was time to change. And then Casey would take over. She spoke with ease and confidence about how she'd been abused as a child; about the fact that her mother didn't believe her when she told her; about her desire to pay her mother back by taking drugs and drinking and generally behaving in a disreputable manner; about her spiraling into addiction and her son being born dependent on meth; about her promise to herself to never inject again; about her drug dealing over the years; and about her arrest, her conviction, her getting clean, her setting up Connections.

Casey and Eddie would talk about the hepatitis C epidemic inside prisons—as a prop, they brought along plastic models of healthy and diseased livers—and about how to minimize the risk of contracting the disease: don't share improvised prison tattoo guns and ink, don't share drug needles or snort from a piece of paper that has just been up someone else's nose, and so on. They'd talk about safe sex. And they'd talk about voting rights.

At the end of the show, after the questions had been asked and answered, they'd hand out bags of gimmick-condoms: condoms on sticks made to look like lollipops; condoms with packages painted to look like a man in a hat, or a cop (particularly popular with the women the Rudds talked with), or a smiling lady. While the audience was snickering over these treats, they'd hand out voter registration forms and get as many as possible to fill them in. Their goal, they told their audiences, was to register one thousand people in the run-up to the November election.

It was a smooth operation, and, as far as I could tell, it held their audiences' attention.

At the presentation in Grace Home (a drug treatment center), twenty-one-year-old Chereesa, a member of the Cheyenne-Navajo Native American tribe, told of how her probation officer explained to her that she'd struck out when it came to voting. Chereesa had picked up a federal marijuana-dealing conviction for crossing state lines with some pot when she was eighteen years old. She had been arrested on her reservation in August 2001, pled guilty in January 2002, and was sentenced to a year's supervised release in January 2003. Fourteen months later, she was sent to Grace Home after missing some court-mandated Alcoholics Anonymous meetings. "I asked her [the probation officer] if it would restrict me from housing, voting, TANF [Temporary Assistance to Needy Families], welfare and schooling, and she said 'Yeah.' I wanted to vote. I'm a public kind of person. I like to be around the public, and I'm a question kind of person too. It made me feel—I don't know the word—like I was *bad,* like I was not a citizen anymore."

The next morning, the Rudds talked to fifteen residents at another institution, the Rocky Mountain Treatment Center, in a day room with a ping-pong table and, on the walls, framed posters delineating the twelve steps of AA. One of the clients was a twenty-five-year-old named Eric, who wore a white T-shirt that left uncovered the heavy green prison tattoos running up and down both arms, baggy black pants, and a trimmed beard with just a sliver of hair down the cheeks and then a full beard under the chin. Eric had been convicted of robbery when he was seventeen—and a methamphetamine addict—and then was convicted again when he was twenty-one for failing to register as a violent offender. He served a total of five years behind bars. Like Chereesa, he reported that his probation officer "said I wouldn't be able to vote, wouldn't be able to own a gun. He said I lost my voting rights." Eric also wanted to vote. "I'd vote against people who want more prison beds. I'd vote for people who want reform, want to rehabilitate inmates; and for minorities; bias laws; stuff like that."

Had he heard from anyone other than his probation officer that felons couldn't vote? It was, he said immediately, "common knowledge" in prison that ex-cons had lost their right to participate politically.

While the Rudds were busy spreading the word that ex-prisoners in Montana *could* vote, far to the north at least one man was hoping that one day that would not be the case.

Five hours' drive northwest of Bozeman, past a series of spectacular mountains and the high-altitude waters of Flathead Lake, was the little town of Kalispell. It was a drab little place seventy miles from the Canadian border, ugly enough to almost undermine the beauty of the surrounding scenery. But, since it was the gateway to the intimidating and spectacular rocky citadel of Glacier National Park, there were plenty of motels and decent places to eat.

I'd driven the nearly 400 miles to see a man named Norman DeForrest, a retired UPS employee from California who had moved to Montana and, in 2001, decided to try to get a petition off the ground for a ballot initiative to impose on ex-cons in the state a series of waiting periods for the restoration of voting rights: twelve years to life for the most serious offenses, eight years for the next group, and two years for those convicted of minor crimes. He'd been egged on in this enterprise by a friend of his from Staten Island, New York, an ex-policeman who had begun distributing what he called "VIRTUE" literature. VIRTUE apparently stood for the somewhat forced title "Voting Is a Right That U Earn," and the memo that had set DeForrest along this path stated that "the unfortunate truth is that in most of the states in our union Felons who finish their sentence and a, [sic] usually brief period of probation or parole, are able to vote immediately. An uncounted number of Felons are now free to roam our streets and organize as a new protected victim class for the Left and its allies in the Democratic party pander to [sic]. At this very moment, the Felon/Leftist axis has its dream scenario in place."

Despite VIRTUE's stirring warnings, however, the petition had failed to achieve liftoff, and DeForrest, a local Republican Party activist, had gone on to focus his signature-gathering energies on a drive for an initiative that would create a state constitutional amendment banning same-sex marriages.

DeForrest was a striking man: a sixty-six-year-old with a limp, in a flowery-blue Hawaiian shirt, with a shock of white hair brushed neatly back on a supersuntanned face. Over his upper lip quivered a thick dyed black mustache (dyed, he informed me, to offset the yellow of his teeth). Above his eyes, bushy black eyebrows bristled. In addition to his somewhat extraordinary appearance, DeForrest also came fully equipped with a host of rather extraordinary views on life.

"How do you decide who should vote or who shouldn't?" he mused. "If I were king for a day, I'd have some kind of requirement to test people. People should speak English. They should not have ballots in a foreign language. And they should have a knowledge of how the Constitution works. The only thing to do is to have a scale of limitations on felons. People take citizenship for granted. Putting some restrictions sends a message that our system of government is not something to be taken for granted—that it's very important; that the right to vote is very important." It sounded, to me, something akin to the old Vietnam War logic that you sometimes have to destroy a village in order to save it. But then it got better, as DeForrest came to the heart of his objection to felons having the right to vote: "The majority of felons, I'd say about 75 percent of them, are liberals or Democrats. Only about 25 percent are conservative or Republicans. It's one reason I feel there should be some limitation—because the Democrats will go out of their way to get anybody to vote for them. Including illegal immigrants. So why not felons? Whatever they can use." He laughed derisively and sipped his Budweiser. And then it got better still. DeForrest moved away from discussing crime and punishment and began denouncing the "eco-Nazis" he believed had "infiltrated the Forest Service" and, through their network of lobbyists, taken over the country. He talked about how radical environmentalists had "bought all the Democrats," and he bemoaned the ignorance of an electorate too befuddled to see what the environmentalists were up to. "I don't want people voting who don't know anything about what's happening," he explained. "If you don't know who you're voting for, you could very easily vote for someone who could affect your life very negatively." He lambasted an immigration process that let in too many illiterate, corrupt, crime-committing migrants from Latin America. And he fulminated against a political correctness in schools that went so far as to dare to lump European civilization in the same category as African civilization. "The word *Africa* and *civilization* is an oxymoron to me. Because there's nothing civilized about their civilization—any more than there is about Islamic civilization. Blacks should have the right to vote. But I think, if this had been a perfect society, we would have either sent all the blacks back to Africa, or started educating them and teaching them to be responsible citizens. But we didn't do that."

It would be easy to dismiss DeForrest as nothing more than a nasty misfit; and, after sitting through an hour and a half of his tirades while eating dinner on my dime at an overpriced and eminently mediocre restaurant, I was more than ready to do just that.

I felt dirty and wanted to rush back to my motel room and take a long shower. But then I realized that, while DeForrest was an anachronism—his stated views anathema to the modern mind-set, his explicit justifications for limiting the franchise deeply offensive to most modern theorists of democracy—his views *were* fairly much in tune with those of the Southern leaders and their Western sympathizers who had carefully crafted the disenfranchisement codes back in the post–Civil War years. De Tocqueville wrote that free societies always have, at their heart, a great divide between those who want to maximize popular power and those who seek to restrict it. "As one investigates more deeply the innermost thoughts of these parties," he scribbled, "some are seen to be pursuing the restriction of public power, others to widen it."[6] DeForrest was clearly on the side of the restrictors, his views closely aligned with such illuminaries as the authors of Alabama's 1901 state constitution. According to the historian Andrew Shapiro, and others, the felon codes from this period were specifically designed by postbellum Southern politicians to bar blacks from the ballot box. Indeed, in 1901, John Knox, the politician presiding over Alabama's constitutional convention, publicly stated that the aim of such provisions was to help preserve white supremacy without directly challenging the constitution of the United States.

In a sense, dining with Norman DeForrest as he discussed voting rights was like getting a behind-the-scenes view of an elderly dowager as she prepared her wrinkled, sagging face for public display. DeForrest was inadvertently giving me a glimpse of the views that shaped the policies and priorities of a previous era, and his defense of disenfranchisement laws was, in fact, arguably the most honest, bare-bones rationale for the continued existence of such laws that could be made. For, in the end, once all the intellectual wriggling was over, how else could such laws be defended other than through a broad-based philosophical attack on the very principle of universal adult suffrage, on the very notion that all adults have, as a basic right, the right to participate in the political process that governs their lives? And while DeForrest was cruder than any modern politician could afford to be, when it came right down to it, how different were his views from those Tom Feeney had shared with me in Florida three years previously?

Meeting DeForrest seemed as good a jumping-off point as any for leaving the West to begin my journey southeast, toward the heart of the old segregationist South, into a region that served as the crucible of America's first wave of mass disenfranchisement, and which today is at the forefront of its second wave of disenfranchisement.

I drove southeast from Kalispell along the southern side of Glacier National Park and out into the dry, rolling hills of Montana cattle country. North Dakota wasn't too far to the east, the prairies and pastures of the Midwest just over the horizon. I went to another one of the Rudds' presentations, and then returned to Bozeman for the evening. The little town was having a summer festival on Main Street and the entire community seemed to be promenading and eating from the outdoor stalls set up by local restaurants. I drank a couple beers, read some more de Tocqueville in a bar blaring disco classics, warded off questions from a few inquisitive women in cowboy hats as to why I was reading in a watering hole during a town party, and returned to my hotel room in time to catch five hours' sleep before heading to the airport in the small hours of the morning.

Next stop on the disenfranchisement tour would be Texas, a long, long, way south, then north again to Iowa, and, then, submersion in the heart of Dixie.

6
Snakes and Ladders

In the early 1960s, a young man at the University of Texas made a name for himself by orchestrating a petition drive against the university's integration of its sports teams and its school dormitories. More than three decades later, in 1998, the man, now middle-aged, told the *Houston Chronicle* that he "was one of those who wasn't for the integration issue. I was eighteen years old. I was raised in a segregated society, and I didn't like the fact they were picking on athletics."[1]

That man was Johnny Holmes. He was a large person, with a handlebar mustache and a bullying, gruff manner. He was also, by 1998, the district attorney for Harris County, Texas, which was dominated by the sprawling city of Houston. Holmes had reputedly once turned his own uncle in to law enforcement officers for evading income tax. More significantly, he was known as the most virulently pro–death penalty district attorney in the country, calling those he prosecuted "slugs" and arguing that even if one could guarantee a person would never step out of prison for as long as he lived, he still felt some people simply deserved to die. Since the death penalty was reinstated in 1976, Harris County had sent 246 people to death row. And, while Holmes claimed never to take race into account when deciding whether to ask for death, the county's statistics were, at best, far from reassuring. Almost 70 percent of those sent to death row were nonwhite, and more than half of them were black—figures far higher than both the national averages and the averages for the state of Texas as a whole, and, disturbingly, higher than Harris County itself generated back in the 1930s, 1940s, and 1950s, before the civil rights era supposedly brought a greater degree of accountability to the criminal justice system.[2] Many of the capital cases involved instances in which nonwhites had robbed and murdered white victims, a combination that, nationally, seems particularly likely to land a murderer on death row. In the months following my visit to Texas, eight capital defendants convicted in Harris County were slated to be executed.

Holmes's position was an elected office. Holmes himself had had to win the votes of Harris County residents, and, when he retired, the man he handpicked as his chosen successor also had to win the approval of the electorate. Given the extraordinary tough-on-crime posturing of the Harris County district attorney's office, it was particularly ironic that many tens of thousands of the county's residents had been barred from casting votes, precisely because they had previously been prosecuted by the office.

They didn't have a say because Texas removes the vote from anyone in prison, on parole, or on probation for a felony conviction. And, since the Lone Star State is notorious for handing out extremely long parole and probation terms (in addition to long prison sentences and the sickeningly high number of death sentences) many thousands of residents who have been living crime-free lives for years, and even decades, still cannot vote. I have heard stories of a man in Lubbock given lifetime parole on a drug charge, of a woman in Houston sentenced to eight years to life on parole. By 2004, nearly half a million Texans were on probation, and another 100,000-plus were on parole.

A similar situation existed in Georgia, a state that also removed the vote from those on parole and probation, as well as from prisoners. Approximately 200,000 Georgians could not vote because of these laws, and one in eight of the state's African American males had been removed from the political process. In one zip code in Atlanta, more than one in ten residents of both sexes and all ages were disenfranchised. In the summer of 2004, the Sentencing Project released a report on the impact of this; it found that a quarter of the black men in Georgia who weren't registered to vote were not registered for the simple reason that they weren't allowed to put their names down on the electoral rolls.[3]

"The judge sentenced me to ten years: 1986 to 1996," recalled one San Antonio man, who received the long sentence for a shoplifting offense because of a prior conviction for a violent crime. "But every time they send you back to prison, they take the good time away and you start off with your original sentence. When they sent me back [for missing a visit with his parole officer], I did thirty-three months. Then they violated me again." The man finally "got off of paper" in 2002—at which point he was *wrongly* told by his ex–parole officer that he couldn't even apply to have his vote restored until he'd been clean another five years. "I want to vote," he said, sitting in a nondescript Mexican restaurant on a quiet back street north of downtown. "Vote the right way, we can change the laws about the high gas prices, the cost of living. Right now I live in an RV. It's very important for one who's been incarcerated and is off of parole to be able to vote."

Until 1983, Texas, like most other Southern states, permanently disenfranchised felons. It had been that way for more than a century, since Southern Redeemers—white supremacist Dixie Democrats looking to end the North's post–Civil War influence in the region—rewrote the Texas constitution with a specific eye on finding ways to deprive freed blacks of the vote. Article 6, section 1 of the 1876 constitution stated "all persons convicted of any felony are not qualified to vote," and was written with the clear assumption that sheriffs would target nonwhites for arrest and that courts would also be more likely to convict nonwhites.

Article 6 flourished through the Jim Crow decades and remained intact through the first decades of the modern civil rights era. Then, under Democratic governor Mark White, a lawyer whose rise up Texas's political ladder began in the late 1960s, the state embarked on a fourteen-year process of gradual liberalization. In 1983, the lifetime disenfranchisement was replaced by a five-year waiting period, after a six-year campaign that had run aground against opposition in the state senate and from the previous governor. In 1985, the waiting period was shortened to two years. Finally, in 1997, it was abolished altogether. The reform was presented by its sponsor, House representative Harold Dutton, a Democrat from Dallas, as a cleanup bill, tying up the messy ends left by the reduction in the waiting period more than a decade earlier, and it didn't get on anyone's radar screen as being potentially "soft on criminals."

The governor who signed this into law wasn't known to closely monitor what the legislature was doing; nor was he particularly quick to use his veto. His name was George W. Bush.

The irony became clear three years later, when the governor's own brother, Jeb Bush, ruthlessly manipulated Florida's disenfranchisement provisions as a tool designed to help smooth the Texan's way to the White House.

But, while Texas's move away from permanent disenfranchisement was obviously better than nothing, in reality it didn't amount to a huge hill of beans. Neither the move to a waiting period in the 1980s nor the final abolition of that waiting period in 1997 was accompanied by any county or state spending to inform correctional officials and ex-prisoners or probationers about the law change. There were no mandates written into the law that required any sort of voter education campaign inside prisons nor, until a policy change in mid-2004, at parole or probation offices. There was no mechanism to notify people who had been out of the system for years and assumed there was still permanent disenfranchisement that the laws had been modified. A bill that would have required probation officers to provide a voter registration form to all clients being discharged from their supervision was killed in committee in 2003. A 2004 proposal by a Dallas Democrat that would have required the secretary of state's office to include in the Voter's Bill of Rights (produced as a part of Texas's Help America Vote Act legislation) a section on the right to vote of ex-felons was also defeated. Thus, unless you were an unusually well-educated, well-informed felon, the chances were pretty high that you'd continue in the erroneous belief that you weren't allowed to vote—and that, if you did cast a ballot, you risked being charged with a new felony and could, perhaps, be returned to prison.

At a summer 2004 job fair for ex-convicts in inner-city Houston, where voter registration teams had set up tables, an assistant for a state representative asked participants how many were familiar with the law restoring their right to vote after they came off of parole or probation. Not a single person in the overwhelmingly African American crowd raised his or her hand. Most ex-prisoners, said Robin May, a life-skills coordinator with Bread of Life, a local organization working with homeless and addicted Houstonians, "think that once they have a criminal background, voting for them is out the window. Forever. It's the miseducation of our population. I don't know if *malicious* would be the right word. Or if *racist* would be the right word. It's just been the predominant thing to *not* educate people about their voting rights. If they don't know, don't tell them. It's a handed down kind of miseducation. Almost generational miseducation."

"I thought I was permanently barred from voting," reported thirty-five-year-old Lyle Dorsey, in Dallas. Dorsey had spent ten months in prison after being convicted of forgery in 2001. "I'd hear it from incarcerated people that once you had a felony you couldn't vote." In fact, until the privately funded Unlock Your Vote campaign began sending people out into poor neighborhoods of Houston, Dallas–Fort Worth, and San Antonio in early 2004, no organization, public or private, had done any work educating ex-prisoners about their rights. When the Unlock Your Vote workers began contacting these people, they found that most ex-prisoners still believed Texas had permanent disenfranchisement, as did a good number of people who had never been to prison but had spent time in jail. "They were nineteen, twenty when they first got incarcerated," said one Hispanic activist working to register ex-felons in Houston. "They came out and thought their rights were taken away forever. Nobody tells them they can vote in Texas. By and large, probation officers do *not* let their people know they can vote again when they get released from probation."

Unlock Your Vote began running radio ads and doing other low-level publicity; volunteers started visiting churches and shopping malls and nightclubs and anywhere else they thought they might be able to establish contact with people who'd gotten into trouble with the law; and some of its member organizations even began sending out letters and voter registration forms to people whom the probation department told them had come off of probation within the previous five years. One organization, MASS Inc., ultimately sent out eighteen thousand of these letters to people who'd graduated from probation since 2000 in the Dallas–Fort Worth metropolitan area.[4] But, with limited resources and manpower, they couldn't reach many parts of the vast state—including the western metropolis of El Paso and the small towns of the desert and panhandle.

This clearly had huge implications for the state's politics, given the fact that because of Texas's extraordinary reliance on incarceration in recent decades, approximately one million Texans have spent some time in prison or jail in the past and another three quarters of a million are *currently* in prison, on parole, or on probation. In the 1990s alone, Texas added more prisoners than were held in the entire prison system of New York State, a state whose population is about the same as that of Texas. The only other state with numbers anywhere near this high is California, which has a prison population that is sometimes slightly higher and sometimes slightly lower than that of Texas. But California's total population is about thirty-six million, while Texas's is only twenty-two million. And California hasn't had permanent disenfranchisement provisions since 1974 and thus no longer has to battle quite as widespread a perception—in poor communities seeded with large numbers of people who have served time—that a felony conviction forever removes a person from the political process.

In fact, Texas now incarcerates approximately 1 percent of its adult population at any one time, a shockingly high figure bested only by Louisiana.[5] Add the huge parole and probation system, and one in twenty adults in the state is now under criminal justice supervision. This is partly due to a more generally zealous lock-'em-up approach pioneered by DAs like Johnny Holmes, and partly due to a particularly robust application of discretion to the state's rulebook. Thus you routinely hear stories of inner-city black and Latino residents arrested for very low-level marijuana possession and sentenced to months, and even years, in prison, whereas middle-class kids get a ticket and are sent on their way. In 2000, the Center on Juvenile and Criminal Justice reported that blacks in the Lone Star State were seven times more likely than whites to be living behind bars, with close to 4 percent of all African Americans in the state incarcerated.

When a person is convicted of a felony in Texas and has used up all of his or her appeals, the Department of Criminal Justice sends the information to the Department of Public Safety. Every week, that department forwards the data to the secretary of state's office, in the state capital of Austin. And the secretary of state's office, after cross-checking these lists with databases of registered voters, forwards it to the county election officials in charge of overseeing the electoral rolls. When the county officials are notified that one of their residents has recently picked up a felony conviction, they strike his or her name from the rolls, or flag the name in case the person subsequently tries to register. It's an efficient process and probably serves to ensure that almost all of the people deemed ineligible to vote are, indeed, taken off the list of voters.[6]

At the same time, the list also serves to warn election officials if ineligible voters have somehow slipped onto their electoral rolls. While Texas has tighter matching criteria used to take people off voter rolls than did the companies contracted by Florida to purge its rolls in the runup to the 2000 and 2004 elections, those criteria are still by no means perfect. Until March 2004, the Department of Public Safety would recycle the driver's license numbers of felons in prison for more than two years. Then they started getting complaints from irate citizens who'd been assigned these numbers and had then been sent letters telling them that because they were convicted felons they were being taken off the electoral rolls unless they could prove they weren't in fact felons within thirty days. Because the counties weren't required to check the accuracy of the names they'd been furnished by the secretary of state's office, the onus rested squarely with these individuals to prove their eligibility to vote rather than with the counties to prove their ineligibility.

There is, however, an even bigger problem. While the transfer of information between different government agencies works smoothly when it comes to taking people off the electoral rolls, Texas has no reverse mechanism in place to transfer information between agencies when a person becomes re-eligible to vote. It's like the children's game of snakes and ladders—all too easy to slide down the snake, very hard to clamber back up the ladder. Nobody bothers to tell the secretary of state's office or the county election registrars when a person comes out of prison, or comes off parole or probation. As a result, some of the 254 counties of Texas have been keeping old lists of felons and have been using those lists to deny people the vote, even if, in the years since the information was sent to the counties, the individuals have finished their sentences. "We were finding that some counties were holding onto the data," explained Ann McGeehan, the mild-mannered, freckled director of elections at the secretary of state's office in Austin, sitting in her third-floor office, its expansive windows looking directly out at the stunning, grandiose architecture of the capitol building. "Instead of just using it to flag people *currently* on the list, they were storing it and then using it when people were trying to register. And, of course, that's unreliable. It's not a good process and it's not authorized by state law."

Texas is vast—over a quarter of a million square miles in area. And that vastness serves as a geographic locus for the heart of the country, linking the South, the Midwest, and the Southwest. It has the prairie culture of the Midwest, farmed by the Anglo heirs of the westward-migrating pioneers as well as the descendants of German émigrés from the failed revolutions of central Europe in the mid-nineteenth century. It has the Southern land culture inherited from the old, slave-owning, plantation aristocrats. Its big, oil-rich cities, in particular Houston and Dallas, are, along with Atlanta and New Orleans, arguably the cultural and commercial capitals of the South. Its smaller eastern cities like Waco, and, in a geographic irony, its northern panhandle communities like Tulia, are centers of Southern Protestant fundamentalism rich with seams of the South's ugliest racist history. Waco was notorious as a center of lynching well into the twentieth century—and the region was only partially transformed by the civil rights revolution.[7] Its southern boundary with Mexico, snaking along from Brownsville, hundreds of miles southwest of Houston, all the way west to El Paso, has generated a potent border culture unique to Texas, with residents caught in a two-centuries-old tug of war between the countries of Mexico and the United States, and the Latino and Anglo cultures within these. Finally, as it bleeds into the southwestern deserts, Texas provides a gateway to the wide-open West and the Southwest—to the space where the Southern lynch mob metamorphosed into the Western posse, where the plantation owner was replaced by the do-it-yourself rancher, where the cotton fields and vegetable farms were traded in for grazing land for cattle and the mythology of the cowboy out on the range.

On a road trip, conquering Texas is one of the great psychological challenges. You feel like you're in the state forever. No matter how beautiful the scenery—the wildflowers dotting Hill Country, the monumental landscape of the mountainous southwestern deserts, the armadillos suicidally trying to navigate multilane highways—at some point it becomes an endurance test. You keep driving and you're still there. You drive, you sleep, you drive some more, and the road signs still say *Texas.* It's like one of those nightmares in which however hard you try to run you find that you're standing still. When you finally get to the other side, it's like being allowed to breathe again after having had to hold your breath for an obscenely long time.

Since my first trip to Texas—midway through a cross-country road trip with two friends made while I was still an undergraduate at Oxford University in England—I've been back to the state numerous times. This is partly because during my mid-twenties I made a point of driving across the country once a year, always from the East Coast to the West, in order to see places I would never otherwise encounter, to hike canyons and climb mountains (and unless you take the northern route, it's pretty hard to avoid Texas on the way west), and partly it's because I've been writing about crime and punishment for the better part of a decade and there's really no way to understand trends in criminal justice policy in America without understanding Texas.

In 2001, a photographer friend and I journeyed to Tulia, a scrubby little panhandle town controlled by a viciously conservative white elite. The town, which had a total population of about 5,000 and a black population of perhaps 500—who, until only a few years previously, had been concentrated in a honky-tonk slum, literally on the wrong side of the railway tracks, that was colloquially known as "Nigger Town"—had achieved national notoriety after employing a corrupt, pathologically untruthful freelance narcotics agent to entrap dozens of African Americans on drug dealing charges. The men and women were then arraigned before juries (although not, perhaps, juries of their peers, since they were almost all white, as the blacks in town were either on trial or the family members of people on trial), and those who didn't take plea bargains in exchange for lesser sentences were then shunted off to prison for terms that, in some cases, ranged up to one hundred or more years. It didn't take a genius to work out that something was wrong with the charges: a town that small couldn't have supported the dozens of drug dealers the DA claimed had set up shop there. And many of those labeled as "kingpins" were in fact impoverished farmers or unemployed high-school dropouts, people who could hardly read and write, couldn't afford to keep a car, and lived in shacks that a real "kingpin" wouldn't have even housed his manicured pet poodle in. More to the point, there was no physical evidence—no bags of drugs, no photographs of deals going down. Only the word of one undercover narcotics officer.[8]

The blacks in town swore that it was a racial purge, that the city's elite had decided to "take out the trash," and had brought in an undercover agent, a man who roamed from town to town entrapping people into selling him drugs and then moving on, with the specific mandate of fabricating cases against petty users and local down-and-outs. The whites in town swore that that was conspiratorial nonsense. And, since a goodly chunk of the black population was now barred from voting on account of having picked up felonies, and given that a hefty percentage of the white population was directly implicated in the events—either through being a part of the local administration, or through sitting on the numerous juries that railroaded Tulia's blacks—there wasn't really a whole lot of local political pressure that could be brought to bear on the local DA, the judges, or the city council and mayor to get to the truth of the matter.

But then, a year or two after we visited Tulia, with a glare of international publicity on the little town, Texas's appeals courts decided that the blacks had just about gotten it right. The testimony that had landed so many people in prison was either perjured or otherwise untrustworthy, and, since there was absolutely no other evidence against these people, their convictions were all overturned, and they were freed from prison.

All over Texas one hears outlandish stories from utterly impoverished underclass blacks and Latinos: stories of friends and relatives being sent to prison for years for possession of one marijuana joint; a story of a man caught with a fingernail-size rock of crack cocaine, sent away for forty-five years. Stories of people given decades of probation for two-bit drug possession offenses; of repeat offenders who face twenty-five to ninety-nine years in prison if they commit another high-level misdemeanor (a crime such as shoplifting that the district attorney can choose to charge as a felony). The stories are so crazy that it would be tempting to ignore them, to write them off as the delusional produce of fevered imaginations. After Tulia, it became impossible to ignore these stories. There were too many well-documented instances of Texas justice run horribly amok, and of lives ruined by overzealous prosecutors relying on the testimony of corrupt and/or racist law enforcement personnel.

My work has also taken me to tiny counties, like La Salle, in the deep south of the state where county commissioners signed dubious sweetheart deals bringing in private prison companies to operate prisons built using money raised, through issuing bonds, by shell corporations whose executives consisted of the local commissioners and the county judge. The deals always let the private companies walk away if business went sour, and they always left the counties at staggering financial risk if the prisons proved not to be moneymakers. My reporting has also landed me in impoverished, sparsely populated, and parched desert counties in the remote western reaches of the state, where local judges and commissioners have signed even worse deals with private prison companies than those committed to by the wise men of La Salle County, deals that result in vast federal and state prisons and immigration holding facilities being built that tap out the counties' meager water reserves and make it all but impossible for other businesses to come in. One particularly unpleasant judge asked me to see it from his perspective, to recognize that building for-profit prisons, and then using low-ball bidding to fill them up with out-of-state inmates, was nothing short of a "public service."[9]

In many ways, I've come to know Texas and its complex triple-tiered race relations through the geography of its incarceration system and the webs of cronyism that have facilitated the placing of so many private and public prisons and federal holding facilities throughout the vast spaces of the Lone Star State.

The road into Houston was crammed full of muscular sports utility vehicles and pickup trucks. In my rented Chevy Cavalier, I felt like a Lilliputian amid a race of giants cruising through life with an undiluted birthright to waste as much oil as humanly possible. I also felt like a foreigner in a very foreign land. Practically every one of these gas-guzzling monstrosities had either a Bush/Cheney bumper sticker or one of the eponymous W '04 stickers.

There were very strange billboards dotting this road. They advertised surgery to reduce sweaty palms (apparently when they say "everything's bigger in Texas," they're including sweat glands and the problems associated with glad-handing the crowds on a clammy summer's day). One urged drivers to acknowledge the fact that the Lord's Day was really Saturday and that the anti-Christ had changed it to Sunday. My favorite, however, was the one next to the dilapidated adult video store with its burnt-out neon lights and its plastic sign advertising the new Paris Hilton DVD, that said "Please: Stop the Porn, be Reborn—Jesus."

When I turned on the radio, the FM channels seemed to be all country music, and the AM all rant-radio and Bible-thumping shows. The ranters were busy telling their listeners that any criticism of a president during wartime was unpatriotic. And one of them was vigorously mocking John Kerry for courting the support of overseas leaders. "We're with you, John," the commentator sneered in what passed for a slimy caricature of a Middle-Eastern accent—the radio equivalent of the viciously anti-Semitic drawings that showed up as cartoons in Nazi Germany's newspapers seventy years earlier. Not long after this, a fundamentalist Jewish radio guest declared that the Old Testament tells us there will never be peace in Israel and that, because this was God's word, permanent conflict was a good thing and all moves to jumpstart the Middle East peace process should be broken off. It seemed apt, since I had just finished reading Michael Lind's book *Made in Texas*, in which he discussed the strange marriage of convenience between extreme Zionists and fundamentalist Jews and pre-millennialist Southern Baptists who believe that Israel's modern existence signifies the approach of a Messianic Age in which an apocalyptic era of destruction will be followed by Jesus's second coming and an age of permanent, and, of course, universally Christian, government.[10] Disconcertingly, given the power to wreak destruction handed to George W. Bush by his assumption of the presidency, the commander-in-chief and a number of his advisors apparently adhered to at least some parts of this package of lunacy.

All of this eye-poppingly awful chatter was interspersed with news reports on beheadings in Iraq—incredibly, inconceivably, almost commonplace in 2004, as if the French terror or the medieval crusades had suddenly reemerged to shock modernity out of its complacency—oil price spikes, and President Bush speaking about how liberated Iraq was now firmly on the path to freedom and democracy. Then, later in the day, obsessive coverage—minute-by-minute reality-TV-style coverage all through the night—of yet another Florida hurricane.

Houston proved frustrating. I was in town to talk with people at the already-mentioned job fair for ex-prisoners. But I arrived late, and several of the people I wanted to talk with had already left. So I spent most of the afternoon aimlessly wandering the almost empty streets of Houston's downtown. It was an ugly, soulless place, with unimaginative steel-and-glass skyscrapers on streets almost devoid of both people and trees, anchoring a sprawling, humid city that went on forever and was held together only by endless miles of concrete freeways tied in crazy knots at spaghetti junction intersections that made Los Angeles look rational. I hated it. It reminded me of an insipid version of Johannesburg or São Paulo, a city of grotesque extremes leaping out of the plains (the South African metropolis rises out of the flat mining land edging the great Karoo desert, São Paulo out of the flat Brazilian farming interior west of Rio de Janeiro), but with none of the vibrancy and street life and markets and music or, to be fair, the civil war–like levels of violent crime of either of them. Everyone seemed to be in their air-conditioned cars, which they drove to the endless malls before driving home to the endless suburbs. And, for those who couldn't afford the suburbs, the impoverished city communities lived in by poor blacks and Latinos looked and felt like nasty ghettos and barrios—like places where people live because they are trapped, where they do what they have to do to survive, which often involves ugly, violent crime (although not of the Johannesburg/São Paulo intensity); and where the younger residents are so alienated they have opted out, en masse, of the political process, either voluntarily deciding not to vote, or having that decision made for them by the state because they have wound up in the criminal justice system.

De Tocqueville believed American politics was unique because the highest and the lowest on the economic ladder all were simply individual citizens within the political process. Politics, he believed, belonged to the masses—for better or for worse—in America, instead of it being the purview of a small elite, as was the case in most European societies at the time. Even ignoring de Tocqueville's assumption that his readers would understand why he wrote only about white men when he defined democracy, his was probably always a rosy, somewhat naïve interpretation of American politics. But, in the early twenty-first century, it has become almost comically untrue. While much of Europe, Canada, Australasia, and the tiger economies of Asia have embraced a social democratic vision of society that eliminates many of the extremes of obscene wealth and utter poverty, and have, in doing so, created ever more inclusive polities, America is heading in the opposite direction: the wealthy are accumulating ever more riches and political power; the ghettoized poor are becoming ever more destitute, ever more circumscribed in their political and economic ambitions, and ever more likely to be literally expelled from the democratic process if they haven't already opted out and retreated into sullen, ignorant, apathy.

Webster's dictionary defines a ghetto as "a quarter of a city in which members of a minority group live especially because of social, legal, or economic pressure." It goes on to state that residency in a ghetto implies "inferior status or limiting opportunity." In a sick sense, the barrios and ghettoes and white edge zones of a major American city have the same political dynamic as do the decayed working-class neighborhoods in ex-Soviet states—where a formal commitment to democratic decision making has grown up in tandem with massive divides between those who have "made it" in the new social order and those who have been dumped onto the societal trash heap.

Those miserable, garbage-strewn neighborhoods, and the aimless, wandering, hungry-looking people meandering along their streets, crystallized my sense that the South, and, increasingly, the country as a whole as it has fallen under the sway of Southern conservative leaders, has decided to embrace Victorian England's harsh solutions to what German sociologists call *Lumpenheit* (lumpenness). Instead of committing itself to publicly financed social policies such as job training, transport infrastructures, and so on, that might eventually offer people a way out of their economically and socially impoverished states, it has chosen to accept *Lumpen-dom* and the appalling conditions lived in by the underclass, and to control the members of this underclass through an ever more punitive penal system. Then, to ameliorate the perceived dangers of uneducated *Lumpens* acquiring power and influence without the knowledge of how to use this power in a society based upon universal suffrage, it has fallen back on restricting the franchise again by simply removing large numbers of these individuals from the political process via catch-all felony and disenfranchisement codes. I wonder how different that is from the pious Victorian elite's decision to relegate Britain's underclasses, the losers in the country's rush to industrialization, to the workhouse while firmly resisting all attempts to extend the franchise to the working poor and to expand economic safety nets so that the poor wouldn't sink into destitution. Or, for that matter, how different is it really from the Chinese prison system of today?

American politicians, in failing to bring moral imagination and empathy to bear in crafting social policy and the country's current system of criminal justice, are responsible for a historic tragedy. Thinking only about scoring short-term points in a cutthroat environment, they have quite disastrously failed to come to terms with the ramifications of mass incarceration, with the long-term socioeconomic side-effects of creating a caste of criminal untouchables. By ignoring its impact on the voting process and on the numbers eligible to participate in elections, and, by extension, by ignoring what this disenfranchisement does to the broader culture of political participation, they have sown the seeds of a shriveled, mediocre version of American democracy.

I have no doubt that history will judge these misguided policies very harshly—perhaps almost as harshly as America today judges the creation of the brutal Soviet gulag in the middle decades of the last century, although a fundamental difference *does* remain, in that while the Soviets killed an unspeakable number of gulag occupants, America merely keeps millions in prison for absurdly long periods of time. The mass-incarceration policies that have failed to distinguish between violent predators whom society needs to incarcerate and nonviolent nuisances and addicts who could reasonably be diverted elsewhere will be looked upon as the irrational products of hysteria, paranoia, and demagoguery. And, unfortunately, they will also come to be seen by historians in future years as being central characteristics of late twentieth- and early twenty-first-century American culture.

Because of the policies of states like Texas, where the intersection of incarceration and political disempowerment is so potent, history might also make another comparison: between the Soviet gulag's excommunication of "enemies of the people," and the wholesale disenfranchisement of millions of prisoners and ex-prisoners in modern-day America. "After 1937, no guard used the word *tovarishch*, or 'comrade,' to address prisoners, and prisoners could be beaten for using it to address guards," wrote Anne Applebaum, in her Pulitzer Prize–winning history, *Gulag*.[11] Prisoners in the gulag, Applebaum continued, were not allowed to celebrate Soviet holidays such as May Day, and their prisons did not display portraits of the country's leaders. "Many foreigners were surprised at the powerful effect this 'excommunication' from Soviet society had on Soviet prisoners. One French prisoner, Jacques Rossi, author of *The Gulag Handbook*, an encyclopedic guide to camp life, wrote that the word 'comrade' could electrify prisoners who had not heard it in a long time."

The felon-labeled residents of the ghettoes that I was visiting around the country were, it seemed to me, pretty completely ex-communicated from the American political system and its participatory rituals.

Things in Houston stayed bad for another couple days. The man I'd hoped to interview about his work with felons in the Latino community did everything short of self-immolation in order to avoid being available. I got the distinct feeling he was leery of a gringo scaring away the people he was trying to get to register. Then Harold Dutton, the state representative who'd authored the 1997 law change abolishing the waiting period for voting, mysteriously failed to show for our 11 A.M. meeting, and, after I'd waited an hour in the parking lot of his office, I decided to leave and drive to my next set of interviews, 200 miles away in San Antonio.

I was supposed to meet a voting-rights organizer and one-time drug prisoner named Chuck Slaughter, along with four or five people he'd rounded up to be interviewed, at a Denny's at 4:15. I sat there waiting, getting more and more irritated, and, as I read de Tocqueville, I began taking out my frustrations on him. For the first time in the four months we'd traveled together, he began to seriously annoy me. First, he wrote that in the realm of agriculture, tenant farmers couldn't emerge in a democratic society—*pshaw! What about the hardscrabble tenant farmers who eked out meager existences on wealthy landowners' farms in the deep South well into the modern era? What about all the farmers forced to sell up to agribusiness concerns and to work as harvesters to these impersonal owners and to sell their produce at almost impossibly low prices because, if they didn't, the huge companies would threaten to take their business elsewhere?*

Then de Tocqueville began pontificating about how workingmen's wages in an industrial democracy would almost always rise, because "industrialists are very numerous; they have different concerns; thus they could not possibly reach any agreement or unite their efforts. On the other hand, workmen almost always have a few sure resources which allow them to withdraw their services when they are not awarded what they consider is the fair payment for their work."[12] I began scrawling indignant comments in the margins about the rise of the combines and trusts in the late nineteenth century, the battering of trade unions over the last quarter-century, the slashing of wages and health benefits by mega-companies like Wal-Mart, the abandoning of pension commitments by companies that find it easier to declare bankruptcy and screw their workforce by revamping themselves as low-wage, low-benefit employers than to admit to shareholders that profits might not be so high in coming years. Then I turned the page, and, of course, de Tocqueville had anticipated almost all of my objections with a long discussion about exceptions to his rules via the rise of what he called an "industrial aristocracy." He knew exactly how to take the wind out of my sails. He was like a chess master—a genius of analysis who could feint in one direction and then, effortlessly, do a U-turn to cover all his bases in the event of a sneak attack.

Chuck Slaughter finally showed up nearly an hour and a half late, with only one person in tow, a young man who'd almost killed someone in a gang shootout when he was sixteen, and who, now out of prison, turned out to have a story that really wasn't relevant to my book.

Trying to salvage the afternoon, I phoned an organizer, Henry Rodriguez, who had served time in prison for the murder of a white supremacist back in the 1970s before ultimately being pardoned. I had been told he was doing outreach in poor Latino neighborhoods with large numbers of ex-prisoners, but about all he was willing to offer me was an invitation to his sixtieth birthday bash in his son's house on a large lot backing straight onto a major highway. There would, he assured me, be lots of dancing and music. After debating the morality of skipping what might, it seemed, be my only chance to interview Rodriguez, I decided to play hooky and go to the beautiful San Antonio Riverwalk—a series of crisscrossing rivers, stone walls along the inner side of the walkways, the water barely a foot or two below on the other side, the whole scene illuminated by strings of dimly glowing lights hung from the low-lying bridges—for a late evening dinner.

People sat at outdoor tables sipping wines and beers and margaritas, watching the flatboats filled with tourists gliding by like gondolas. For as long as it took me to wolf down a chicken taco salad and a beer, at least, it felt like a mini-version of Venice. I could almost hear the mariachi music morphing into Vivaldi's *Four Seasons* and see the distant lights of hotels and office towers on the streets above the sunken river walks transmogrifying into the bell towers and exquisitely carved frontispieces of Venetian churches, palaces, and narrow, canal-front stone homes.

The next morning, I managed to track Rodriguez down. He was clearing up the mess left from the previous night's party, and he looked considerably the worse for wear. He wore a red Zapatista T-shirt; a bandana tied back behind his head, and blue jeans. His eyes drooped with what might have been fatigue or might have been a hangover, and his thick mustache practically twitched with exhaustion.

Rodriguez was rather disillusioned with his work. Latino ex-prisoners, he believed, weren't too concerned with voting, and, as a result, local politicians seeking to maximize the bang for their bucks avoided politicking in areas where high numbers had been through the criminal justice system. A year earlier, the Mexican-American Legal Defense and Education Fund (MALDEF) had reported that nearly 157,000 Latinos in Texas could not vote because of ongoing involvement with the criminal justice system.[13] This number was over 50,000 higher than the equivalent figure from California, and 30,000-plus more than that for Florida, the only other states to come even remotely close to Texas in this area. "Their [ex-prisoners'] main thing is to survive," Rodriguez said, with more than a hint of bitterness. "Voting is never an issue for them, hardly. The younger people don't vote—many of them because they're on parole or probation or have been told doing time disenfranchises them and they don't make the effort to find out otherwise." Rodriguez believed that, partly because of felon disenfranchisement, partly because of broader social factors, whites in the three most affluent districts in San Antonio turned out more voters each election than in the seven largest majority-Latino districts combined.

The birthday boy had had little luck registering ex-prisoners to vote. "It's like finding a needle in a haystack," he explained. "So many ex-prisoners hide the fact they've been to prison, and avoid contact with authority. A lot of them were sent down for petty stuff. Like because they like to smoke weed. It's stupid. Small crimes."

After hearing this depressing litany, there seemed to be nothing left for me to do in San Antonio except to visit the Alamo. I drove downtown, parked my car on Davy Crockett Street, and entered the enormous stone citadel. It felt like I was leaving the twenty-first century behind and stepping inside the portals of imperial Spain—which, in fact, is exactly what I *was* doing. The Alamo was monumental, the thick stone walls muffling sound, lush gardens and shaded pathways outside hinting at bygone days of glory. A sign at the door read "Welcome to the Alamo—the shrine of Texas Liberty," and a plaque next to it informed visitors that the site was managed by the Daughters of the Republic of Texas. Inside the main building was an exhibit on the Tennessee adventurer Davy Crockett, who championed Texan independence to the bitter end—the ex-congressman, along with over 180 of the soldiers under his command, was massacred inside the fortress by Santa Anna's vengeful Mexican army—and another on fellow mercenary Jim Bowie. There were cases full of rusting weapons unearthed by mid-twentieth-century archeologists. There were lists of the men from across the United States who had flocked to Texas to agitate for independence and who had died violent deaths inside the fortress, their bodies then burned by Santa Anna's troops. And there were posted warnings instructing visitors to show respect in what was, after all, a sacred space.

Outside, in the gaudy plaza adjacent to the Alamo—a plaza lined with Alamo souvenir T-shirt shops, a Ripley's Haunted Adventure, and a Guinness World Records museum—was a massive, impersonal, gray marble monument. It had been erected by the federal government in 1936 to commemorate the hundredth anniversary of Texan independence. On the side of the monument were carved bas-relief likenesses of the more famous Alamo warriors. On its front was an enormous Jesus-like figure, arms raised, two kneeling peons at his feet. Under this behemoth were the words "From the fire that burned their bodies, rose the eternal spirit of sublime heroic sacrifice, which gave birth to an Empire State."

Sitting at the foot of this grandiose monument, I realized something that I should have grasped years ago: America does not have a single narrative of the original War of Independence followed by decades of displacing native tribes and fulfilling Manifest Destiny. Rather, it has two entirely distinct Wars of Independence: the 1776–1783 war versus the British that took place on the eastern seaboard, and the War of Independence in Texas that took place in the 1830s, its roots dating back to the period when de Tocqueville was visiting and then writing about America.

The first of these independence wars was essentially about an established political culture declaring independence from an overseas master. (Whatever the many injustices against Native American tribes that took place in those years, the Revolutionary War itself was not a land-grab against Indians but a political power-grab against English kings and landed aristocrats.) The second war was really a campaign of conquest by Anglo settlers against an already-established, politically organized state and people. However much the Daughters of the Republic of Texas try to dress up Crockett and his crew as glorious freedom fighters, there's at least a partial truth to the counterargument that they were marauding land-grabbers—Anglo Protestant expansionists with a virulently racist ideology against not only Indians but also anyone who didn't speak English and worship a Protestant god. That, in addition, they were defenders of slavery who wanted to add to the U.S. vast tracts of land that permitted slave owning, so as to strengthen the South in the early days of what was shaping up to be the epic battle over the legality of slavery, a battle that would, of course, ultimately lead to the American Civil War. And it was this second war, Texas's war, that, in the long run, may well have shaped America's continental identity. After all, the agitation in the years following the Battle of the Alamo eventually resulted in the dissolution of Mexican power over its sparsely populated northern frontier provinces—over land that later became the states of Texas, New Mexico, Arizona, Nevada, Utah, Colorado, and California.

In 2004, with Texas, and Texans, dominating national politics, I wondered if the mythology of the Alamo and the martial ethos that accompanied it weren't at least as potent an image in shaping American policies and sense of country as that of the minutemen of Concord and Lexington resisting the British redcoats.

I indulged in a Texan daydream—an exercise in counterfactual history. When de Tocqueville visited the young America in the 1830s, North America south of the British-owned Canadian territories was divided between two newborn countries, each of which had, within living memory, thrown off a colonial yoke: the USA and Mexico. As it happened, by the time de Tocqueville visited, it was clear the United States was emerging as the dominant power;

it had a more stable, infinitely more democratic, political system; its economy was generating enormous, and widely distributed, wealth; and its culture was brimming over with self-confidence. By the time of de Tocqueville's visit, the philosophy of Manifest Destiny had already been formulated, and it was apparent to him, as well as to millions of ordinary Americans, that settlers were going to push ever-further westward, until the United States was finally a truly continental country.

But what if the reverse had been true? What if the postindependence United States had degenerated into a shambles while Mexico had accrued power and influence. At the time of de Tocqueville's visit, Mexico stretched from the ruined Mayan city-states of Chiapas in the south to the provinces of Texas, New Mexico, and California in the north. It was far larger, geographically, than the United States. What if some bright sparks in young Mexico had formulated a version of a Spanish-speaking, Catholic-Mexican Manifest Destiny, a mission to extend its cultural and political supremacy from Chiapas and the Mayan ruins of Palenque in the south to the Great Lakes in the North? And what if Mexican settlers had taken it upon themselves to settle sparsely populated frontier regions of the nascent United States? What if the Texan rebels had been crushed and the expansionist Mexicans had moved into Oklahoma and Kansas and Illinois and Missouri, even up into the Dakotas, Michigan, Minnesota, and Wisconsin? What if these Spanish-speaking settlers had then brought in armed compadres from the core regions of Mexico, declared independence, and forced the weakened U.S. government to fight for its land? And what if Mexico had won?

Well, today the maps would have a superpower-size Mexico stretching northward from Chiapas to Chicago, and westward to Los Angeles and possibly Seattle. And the United States would be a shriveled half-state, confined to the eastern seaboard, its far western borders in Ohio and Tennessee and Indiana. The border regions under Mexican control would have Anglo-Protestant descendants of the defeated pioneers living in impoverished conditions, their English language shunned by the Spanish-speaking majority, their job opportunities truncated, their life expectations often minimal. Many of them, in all likelihood, would turn to lives of crime, or would deal with their sorrows through indulging in the use of one illegal drug or another. And many of them, in consequence, would end up caught up in the burgeoning Mexican prison system.

An idle speculation. . . .

I ate a huge plastic cup of cappuccino ice cream and mixed fruit topped off by a healthy dose of whipped cream while sitting on a bench just outside the Alamo, then walked back down Davy Crockett Street to the parking lot in which I had left my car. I headed north to Austin—with its stunning state capitol building, its bohemian restaurants, and its dimly lit Irish pubs, in which great draft beers flowed in abundance, soft sounds of jazz music abounded, and University of Texas students gathered to discuss literature and surreptitiously decry the state of the world. I parked myself in a comfortable leather sofa at the back of a pub named after one of my favorite novels—J. P. Dunleavy's *The Ginger Man,* about the adventures of a ne'er-do-well American ex-pat in 1950s Dublin—and decided to make my peace with de Tocqueville.

The next morning, I drove north to Dallas. I passed the highway exit that would have led off to the Texas White House at Crawford, but I didn't have time to stop. I had to interview community organizers in Dallas about their voter registration drives, and then I had a flight to catch.

7
Waterloo Sunset

I flew into Des Moines, Iowa, on a hot, dusty, dog-days-of-summer afternoon, five days after the end of the Athens Olympics. That evening, President Bush was giving his speech at the GOP's New York convention—an oration larded with rhetoric about the spread of liberty around the globe; about emancipation, forged by American military triumphs, on a massive scale; about freeing 50 million people in Afghanistan and Iraq and unleashing democracy throughout the "Greater Middle East." (The phrase, Bush's personal imperial epithet, has always made me think of Lord Curzon and other late-nineteenth-century British statesmen, although I like to imagine that the Oxbridge-educated Victorian empire builders spoke English a good deal more elegantly than does George Bush.) Outside Madison Square Garden, the remnants of four days of energetic anti-Bush protests—overhyped to be the largest, most chaotic convention demonstrations since 1968—fizzled into the humid night air.

Perhaps it was hearing President Bush's whining, twanging voice all the time, that whine that sounded like the noise made by a bomb falling from an airplane bomb bay in an old World War II movie. Maybe it was just the endless coverage of the Republican convention. But, at a certain point in my Iowa stay, I realized that, while disenfranchisement affects people of all political persuasions and raises questions of fundamental fairness that transcend party-political allegiances, I could no longer keep my personal dislike of George Bush, and the conservative, Fundamentalist clique surrounding him, from influencing my analysis; nor could I keep at bay my suspicions that disenfranchisement was serving to push the country in a more conservative direction on a raft of social and economic issues than would be the case absent the restrictive franchise. Halfway across the country, every cell and every nerve end in my body was now crying out against the hubristic swagger of a president who sometimes gave the impression of being too stupid to wield the power of a junior corporate executive much less that of the most powerful man on earth. And while I've interviewed plenty of ex-prisoners who are enthusiastic Republicans—including some, such as Thomas Johnson in Florida and Mohamed Farrakhan-Bey in Washington, who have sued states to regain their right to vote—most of those I have interviewed have stated their support for the Democrats. This is not because they believe Democrats are "softer" on crime—in fact, few of the felons I've talked to have stated that crime policy is a top priority when they're making political choices—but because they feel the party is somewhat more responsive to the needs of poor people on issues such as health care, wage protection, and funding for education. Deprived of the vote in a polarized country where elections are increasingly decided by the slimmest of margins, these silent would-be voters make up one component part of the mirror image of Richard Nixon's famous, and conservative, "silent majority."

De Tocqueville may have heard about the Iowan landscape on the flat western prairie fringe of the known continent, although he didn't visit it. If he had, he would have considered it a wilderness, a place not yet tamed, not yet incorporated into the federal state structure of the early 1830s (it didn't gain statehood until 1846)—as a place where French and Anglo frontiersmen had created small communities far behind the official United States' border. He could not, however, have had any conception of the sprawling agribusiness farms, the giant silos, the plastic restaurant and motel signs soaring up into the sky, the cell-phone towers punctuating the flat farm landscape that would come to dominate this wilderness.

There is something utterly exhausting about being on the road for weeks at a time. Politicians running a six-month election campaign know this all too well. So do their minions and flaks who have to accompany them, organize their meetings, make their hotel reservations, arrange their speaker venues and media spots. (The scary thing is that, despite the accumulating exhaustion, political figures are then required to make on-the-spot decisions that impact the country and, by extension, the world, that involve life-and-death situations on an appallingly large scale.) So too do the journalists who tag along on planes and buses and trains and cars waiting for the breakthrough moment or the perfect sound bite. De Tocqueville must have felt this at some point in his nine-month sojourn as he rode horses and boats and carriages across landscapes far larger than anything he had grown up with in France. Certainly, there are passages in which the aristocrat seems to yearn for a life more sedentary, for a pace less frenetic than that conjured up by the new world he was chronicling, by a country and culture obsessed with its own democratic self-image, continually extending its frontiers westward, brutally and inexorably brushing aside all who stood in the way of its expansion.

Yet despite the culture of democracy at times jarring de Tocqueville, he recognized its extraordinary power and understood the strength he knew that it was acquiring—a force, he believed, that was more unstoppable than the fiat of a dictator or monarch, because it carried with it the moral authority of the beliefs and choices of the popular majority. In other words, because of political participation, people had a degree of trust in the state and its structures; because they felt a sense of ownership in those structures, they tended to be more enthusiastic participants in society. Participation provided the societal glue in a country such as

America, de Tocqueville believed, and wise rulers would, he hoped, do everything possible to encourage a sense of civic responsibility. Without such a glue, a country as mobile, as atomized, as huge, as impatient as America would risk becoming home to millions of people living only for themselves, lacking any understanding of the common good: "If an election accidentally divides two friends," he wrote in volume two, "the electoral system draws together in a lasting way a crowd of citizens who would have remained strangers to one another. Freedom evokes individual hatreds but tyranny gives birth to general indifference."[1]

I appreciated the Frenchman's slightly wary embrace of this new political culture, but it didn't stop the fact that by the time I arrived in Iowa, halfway across the country and somewhat under halfway through my reporting, two months before the election, I was drained. Drained from repeatedly getting up in the middle of the night to catch early morning flights. Drained from eating bad food in restaurants staffed by overweight and indifferent waiters and waitresses who on a good day called me "hon" and on a bad day sullenly thrust the plate of food under my nose as if I were a dog waiting to lap up my morning chow. Drained from living out of suitcases and traipsing from one motel to the next. Wherever I turned, there was something new to annoy me, to make me yearn for home.

And the thing was, it wasn't the Iowans' fault. They were gentle and stolid and generally seemed utterly harmless. Whether they were conservative or liberal, they all seemed sincere. Salt-of-the-earth types. Yet, for some reason, the state was just rubbing me the wrong way. Maybe it was just a few hundred miles too far from the nearest mountain and the closest ocean for my fancy. Or maybe because when the wind changed direction, I could occasionally smell the sour aromas of an old Southern approach to crime and punishment and race relations wafting up from beneath the surface bouquet of an inclusive society.

* * *

Technically, because it had a provision allowing for rights to be restored at the discretion of the governor, Iowa didn't have permanent disenfranchisement when I visited it. But the process of restoration was so burdensome that hardly anyone completed it, and thus most monitors considered it to be, in practice, a permanent disenfranchisement state. To get your vote back in Iowa, you had to complete your sentence and then apply for a pardon. If the Board of Pardons approved this application—and their decision was entirely discretionary—they made a recommendation to the governor. And if the governor approved this—and his decision was also entirely discretionary—you then got your vote restored.

Several months after my visit, in the aftermath of the 2004 election, Democratic governor Tom Vilsack issued a blanket reenfranchisement to felons who had completed all the terms of their sentences, belatedly removing many of the hindrances to voting that still bedeviled the state in 2004. But, important as this act was, it came too late to affect the closely fought 2004 presidential election.

Until 2001, applicants for pardons had to fill in a multipage questionnaire that asked everything from their social security number to details of their crime, their conviction date, and their sentence; the name and *current address* of the defense attorney, prosecuting attorney, and judge in the case; the name, address, and phone number of every employer they had had since being convicted; the applicant's marital status; and whether the applicant or any of his or her dependents were on any form of government assistance. The form also required a detailed, essay-like response as to "the facts concerning the crime," as well as "reasons why you believe you should be granted executive clemency."

Since many ex-prisoners are functionally illiterate, this form had the effect, in the words of one person who eventually succeeded in navigating the paperwork, of acting "as a gatekeeper's tool to discourage people from even applying for their citizenship." The form itself warned that after the applicant submitted it, the process would then take a year to play itself out.

By the time I visited, the application was down to one page, and the disclaimer said the process took only four to six months. Yet Iowans who had tried to get their rights restored told me that their parole officers were still providing them with the old applications instead of the new, pared down ones; that the Department of Corrections was stalling on providing all the necessary paperwork; and that they were bogged down in a seemingly endless waiting game with the various bureaucracies that all had an input in the restoration proceedings. Although Governor Vilsack, foreshadowing his 2005 decision to enact wholesale restoration of voting rights, had reputedly ordered the Department of Corrections to inform felons of the restoration process upon their release from custody, hardly anybody, whether felon or official, had a good handle on how to get one's rights restored going into the last few months of the 2004 election season.

In 2003, 385 Iowans had their right to vote restored. And that was a particularly good year. In 2002, according to numbers provided to Des Moines representative Wayne Ford by the Department of Corrections, the number was 227, and in 2002 it was 358.[2] And those numbers may well have been inflated. According to Paul Stageberg, a justice systems analyst with the department, in fiscal year 2003 there were 357 applications for clemency, but the Board of Parole recommended that only 263 of these be approved. Whatever the exact numbers, they were clearly unlikely to make a dent in the approximately 100,000-strong population of Iowans whom the U.S. Department of Justice calculated were prevented from voting at the start of the new century. And they were hardly likely to reverse the increases in disenfranchisement that will accompany an ever-larger penal system in the years to come. In 1983, the state had 2,650 inmates. By 1990, Iowa's prisons housed

3,300 felons. By 2003, that number had risen to over 8,300. And, that same year, the state's Division of Criminal and Juvenile Justice Planning predicted that Iowa's prison population would increase to approximately 12,000 prisoners by 2013.[3]

"I understand it's a procedure," stated Kelvin Briggs, a tall, middle-aged African American man with several teeth missing from beatings he said were administered by his mother when he was a boy and by fellow gang members in Chicago when he was a young man. "But they immediately took away my citizenship upon incarceration. Upon discharge, why don't they immediately restore it? They didn't hesitate to *take* my right to vote or hold office, but then when I terminate my sentence I have to now *apply* for my citizenship back." Briggs had applied to get his vote restored six months earlier, and he still hadn't heard anything back on this. "It has to go through the Department of Corrections, then through the governor's office, and where it may end up, only they know."

"It's terrifying to me to even think to try to fill the process out," explained one Des Moines woman, a recovering addict named Jackie, with several arrests and drug convictions in her past, sitting in a meeting of a support group for female addicts named Breadwinners' Circle. "It asks about *every* charge you had. I'm going to have to sit down and rack my brains and figure it out. I don't understand why I have to do that—they should automatically have all of that. Why make me jump through all of these hurdles?" It turned out she had been given the old application forms by her parole officer rather than the newer, streamlined version. Most of the women reported that their parole and probation officers had told them they had to have fully paid all court fees before they could even begin the process of applying for the vote to be returned to them; in fact, the new forms made no such stipulation. "It sucks," one woman burst out in frustration. "I feel as though I'm not part of anything. It feels like everything's passing you by and there's no control, no input into anything."

Kelvin Briggs claimed to know, both personally and through

his work at the Urban Dreams community center in inner-city Des Moines, a couple of hundred people in the Des Moines area who had lost their vote—and few, if any, of these men and women had managed to get their rights restored. They were, he said, "all living in the inner circle of Des Moines. The guts of Des Moines." In these neighborhoods, Briggs asserted, perhaps as many as half of the young black men had felony records, many of them for drug-related offenses. "I'd almost bet my pocket on that," said Briggs. "I played in the streets before I chose to change. I know what's going on."

In the 2004 presidential election, Iowa was considered one of those critical "swing states," having been won by Al Gore in 2000 by only about 4,000 votes—well within the margins created by legal disenfranchisement. Thus it joined Nevada, Florida, and New Mexico in the group of permanent disenfranchisement states where most observers who have looked at the numbers believe the result fell into the lost-voter gap. In fact, Iowa was so close in 2000 that Bush won the on-the-day vote only to have his majority disappear once the absentee ballots were counted. In 2004, the Republicans responded to the Democratic Party's absentee ballot strength by passing Help America Vote Act legislation that made it a serious misdemeanor for an absentee ballot voter to give their ballot (even if it was already inside a sealed envelope) to anybody else to mail. Hence, in one of those absurd twists that would be funny if it weren't so pathetic, an elderly lady in Iowa who orders an absentee ballot because she's too frail to walk to the polling booth, and hands her ballot to a friendly neighbor to put into the mailbox, is now risking criminal prosecution both for herself and for her concerned neighbor. How that can be considered helping America to vote has never quite been explained.

Iowa's senate races are also very competitive, with Democrat Tom Harkin holding onto a tiny, and shrinking, majority that could, ultimately, fall afoul of the state's rising disenfranchisement epidemic.

Generally, although not always, local election results are not so much affected by the erasure of large numbers of people from the electoral rolls, for the simple reason that most of the communities from which large numbers of people are removed into the prison system are so poor already that they return Democratic councilors and aldermen by large enough majorities that these Democrats are not at risk of losing even with high numbers of their constituents being removed. Thus, on the whole, it is elections for the country's president, Senate, and congressional districts, which incorporate a large number of disparate communities, for governors, and for citywide mayors' positions that are most concretely impacted by disenfranchisement.

Recognizing the importance of Iowa, the presidential candidates were boomeranging back to the state every few days during the summer and early autumn; two days before his acceptance speech in New York City, Bush was in Iowa for his sixth trip to the state in a little over a month. A few days before that, vice president Dick Cheney had stopped by. The evening after his speech, Bush was addressing a pumped-up crowd of fifteen thousand in Cedar Rapids, a mere twenty-five miles or so from where I was having dinner, in a Perkins restaurant on the outskirts of Iowa City, with the leader of Iowa's house Democrats—a middle-aged ESL teacher named Mary Mascher, who was busily explaining to me how she felt the Republicans were making ex-felons "jump through hoops" when they tried to get their vote restored in order to keep down the number of poor people voting in elections. The vice president and his wife were scheduled to arrive in Iowa for two days of picnics and golf on Labor Day. That same day, Elizabeth Edwards, wife of Democratic vice presidential candidate John Edwards, was dropping in for a visit to the state fairgrounds, following a mid-afternoon roundtable hosted the previous week in Iowa by Teresa Heinz Kerry—after which she had been briefly hospitalized with a stomach bug. And, to cap it off, John Kerry was penciled in for the following Thursday.

During the Democratic primaries, John Kerry, John Edwards, Howard Dean, Al Sharpton, and Dennis Kucinich had all stumped in inner-city Des Moines, making appearances at the Creative Visions community center in the heart of what passes for the city's ghetto, an impoverished neighborhood with an abundance of drug dealers, prostitutes, and homeless shelters dotted amid the slightly dilapidated-looking wooden houses. When the head of Creative Visions endorsed John Kerry, he did so in front of a great horde of newspaper journalists and television crews. Ironically, however, many in the audience were Creative Vision clients, ex-offenders who, in Iowa, generally cannot vote. In all probability, Kerry had no idea of this when he came to gather this endorsement at the center (with its outside mural depicting all the victims of gang violence, including a list of names of local murder victims—among them the founder's son—and the pessimistic tagline, "Sadly this is to be continued," as well as a painting on a wall of the ground-floor atrium of four famous black leaders and eight desperately running black figures, titled "Running Out of Time"). What Kerry did know was that Creative Visions had a big tie to the local black community in the River Bend area of Des Moines, and he was probably hoping the endorsement would translate to a sizeable boost in the Iowa presidential horse race. Yet Briggs and others who worked in the area believed that almost half of all the black men between eighteen and forty in this neighborhood were legally disenfranchised. And many more were utterly outside the political system, existing on the drug-and-gang margins of society, too strung out to vote, even if they hadn't yet formally lost their right to do so. In the projects of nearby Oak Ridge, in the back streets dotted with homeless shelters and rehab clinics, behind the closed doors and chain-link fences of the old wooden homes (selling price, about $50,000), political participation was now becoming the exception rather than the norm.

What once was considered a right, is now, in poor urban areas like River Bend, becoming an endangered privilege.

In the year leading up to the 2004 election, many Democratic legislators in Iowa, at the urging of the League of Women Voters, the Iowa Civil Liberties Union, and a handful of other organizations, began calling out for reform of Iowa's disenfranchisement provisions. They were joined by a small clutch of Republicans—legislators with impeccable tough-on-crime credentials who argued that disenfranchisement was both unfair and counterproductive, that it drove people out of the social mainstream rather than helping them find their way back in.

Representative Scott Raecker, a Republican representing the affluent Urbandale suburbs, eventually authored a bill that would have provided a limited form of reenfranchisement—returning the vote automatically, but only after felons had paid off their court fees and fines in their entirety. It wasn't a cure-all, but it would have certainly been a start. Raecker, a man with ramrod posture, cropped hair, and steely blue eyes—everything he wore, except the out-of-place plastic wristwatch on his left wrist, looked polished and classy—was the director of an organization called the Institute for Character Development. It was a motivational organization that sought to promote socially beneficial behaviors through cultivating what they termed the Six Pillars of Character: trustworthiness, respect, responsibility, fairness, caring, and citizenship. The ethical imperatives the institute advocated—based on beliefs in rehabilitation, human potential, and the possibility of people changing—spilled over into Raecker's politics; as a result, he wasn't afraid of speaking out on issues such as voting rights.

"It's not a partisan issue," the forty-three-year-old averred. "It's about doing what's right. I believe people that have been convicted of a felony, have served their complete sentence and paid their fines and restitution—in my mind they've paid their debt to society. I believe in second chances. I *do* believe there is a rehabilitation process that can take place in people's lives. They can have a change of heart."

But, in the end, the Six Pillars of Character weren't strong enough to reel in Raecker's colleagues. Unlike legislators in Nevada, New Mexico, Delaware, Maryland, Wyoming, and the other states that had at least doffed their caps toward reform in the wake of the 2000 election, Iowa's Republican leadership decided their best bet was simply to prevent change from being fully debated. House File 402 passed out of committee but then failed to secure a hearing on the House floor. (It's easier, apparently, to kill these bills in private rather than to go out in public and explain the pro-disenfranchisement positions. This has been the case in virtually every state that has preserved permanent disenfranchisement provisions in recent years. It's not that people will thump tables and loudly proclaim their defense of such laws; it's that they'll quietly kill reform using technical maneuvers and hope nobody notices.)

Another bill, sponsored by Democrat minority leader Mary Mascher, that would have limited "infamous crimes" and thus the collateral impact of lifelong disenfranchisement to class A felonies—the most serious violent crimes that generally result in a life sentence in Iowa—didn't even get a committee hearing. Apparently, the redemptive ethics of Scott Raecker's philosophy hadn't convinced most of his colleagues to jump aboard the second-chance train.

Forty-six-year-old Lance Horbach, chair of the Justice Systems Appropriations Committee, was one of those not convinced. Or rather, he claimed not to have heard of the reform proposals, but then made it clear he would have opposed them had he known of them. I was sent Horbach's way by Iowa Republican assembly speaker Christopher Rants, who himself declined to talk about why he had not allowed the reenfranchisement legislation to be debated. By now, this seemed to be fairly common practice: the

Republican senators in Nevada who had tried to scupper reenfranchisement legislation ignored all of my many phone calls. District attorneys who had staunchly opposed even the most modest of reforms declined to comment. Lobbyists for victims' rights groups emitted great shrieks of silence. Two ex–police officers now in the Iowa assembly, who opposed changing the reenfranchisement provisions, both did not return my phone calls.

And so I got in my little Chevy Cavalier and drove an hour and a quarter north of Des Moines to visit Lance Horbach. Horbach was a conservative Republican who sold insurance for a living and resided in a vast three-tiered ranch house surrounded by an expansive rolling lawn in a plush development outside the little farming town of Toledo. On the reddish-brown wooden exterior of his house, adjacent to the large Iowa State University flag, was nailed a sign reading "Let liberty ring"; inside, dozens of family photos dotted the thickly carpeted house, along with framed photos from golfing expeditions, reproductions of Norman Rockwell paintings, and chintzy Midwestern home comforts—such as the plaque over the kitchen sink that read "Welcome to my kitchen."

In 1998, Horbach was elected to the legislature to represent a rural district made up of 29,500 people. Although part of the district was affluent, another slice of it was populated by transient workers, many of them Hispanic, who manned the local beef packing plant and staffed the nearby Meskwaki Indian settlement casino. Many of these poorer residents came into contact with law enforcement, and many ended up accumulating felony convictions, thus removing them from the electoral rolls.

Horbach won the 1998 election by two votes. *Two votes.*

After three weeks of recounts and legal wrangling, he was eventually declared the winner over his Democratic rival by the slightly princelier margin of nine votes. While it would be impossible to prove from this distance, it's certainly not unlikely that had some of his poorer constituents been able to vote after serving out their felonies, Horbach would never have won the election and risen to become one of his state's most influential political figures. Now in a position to influence criminal justice policies in his state, Lance Horbach did not believe in automatic restoration of voting rights for felons who had successfully completed their sentences. Instead, he argued that if there was room for change, it should be in the direction of creating a discretionary system outside of the governor's purview in which correctional counselors, parole officers and victims' rights groups sat in judgment to determine whether individuals were rehabilitated enough to be entrusted with the vote. "Are they ready to have their rights reinstated?" he mused aloud, sitting in shorts, a T-shirt, and bare feet in the kitchen of his house, his cropped hair gelled down on his head. "To me, it's part of the sentence that the judge gives an inmate. And it doesn't have the same timeline that the incarceration part of the penalty has. You've got two separate parts of your sentence. It is something that's been done in Iowa and other states throughout my lifetime. It's no different to me than when a judge says you'll spend four years in prison and three years in community supervision."

Moreover, Horbach explained confidently, the prisoners he had encountered in his official capacity over the years were far more concerned about getting back their right to own a firearm so that they could go deer hunting after they got released than they were about their lost suffrage. "I talk to inmates, and I have never once had that come up as an issue," he said emphatically. "Not once. How many of these people voted before they went in? That'd be very interesting for you to know and me to know. My opinion is a lot of them do not participate in the events of society. If they had that ownership of their community, I don't think they'd be doing the things they did to get there [prison] in the first place. Voting rights is the least of those rights they are concerned about for reinstatement. The right to own guns is, without a doubt, their number-one priority."

Perhaps Horbach was partially right; perhaps some of Iowa's

prisoners *did* want guns rather than votes. Certainly the women at the Breadwinners' Circle acknowledged that many male felons they knew, including some of their own family members, were desperate to resume their hunting habits. Yet, despite National Rifle Association protestations to the contrary, America's political system relies on democratic participation rather than gun ownership to survive and flourish. Shooting deer may or may not be a pleasant and diverting pastime, a way to bond with brothers and fathers and uncles and friends, but it's hard to see how it is as fundamental a part of the nation's political system as casting votes on Election Day. It's also hard to see why it's an either/or choice, why just because someone wants to shoot deer with their dad that means they aren't independently concerned about voting rights as well.

On the other hand, perhaps Horbach wasn't entirely correct. When I took him up on his challenge and did start asking the felons whom I met in Iowa about whether they voted before being convicted and whether they wanted to vote now, many of them had voted before and most of them were desperate to vote now. Among women felons, large majorities of those I talked with said they had voted in the past. At the Breadwinners' Circle meeting, held in a conference room at the Iowa Lutheran Hospital a couple of miles from the center of Des Moines, ten of the eleven women present—a group made up of whites, Hispanics, and blacks, and one that didn't go out of its way to target particularly politically minded people as members—said they used to vote: seven said they had generally voted Democratic, three Republican. All ten wanted to regain their right to vote—and one of the three Republicans had since switched her sympathies to the Democratic Party. They talked about wanting to be able to vote for the school boards that ran the schools to which they sent their children; they talked about paying taxes and not having any say in who represented them in Washington; they talked about wanting to be a part of their communities again. "It's important to get people out to vote," one told the group, "on what happens on your block, in your neighborhood and your schools. It isn't just about the national election. It's a lot more than that."

"Before I went to prison," Jackie interjected, "I wasn't living right. I wasn't a good citizen. But during my stay, I changed. I grew. I came out wanting to be a part of my community. I feel it's a great slap in my face to not be a part of my country because I made bad choices. It's hard for me to want to be a part of my country when they're continually putting me down. If my country doesn't stand behind me, who will?"

Iowa is routinely touted as an almost laboratory-perfect example of small-town, hands-on politics in an age of mass-media images and billion-dollar campaigns. It has the nation's first caucus during the presidential season. And it has citizen legislators who plausibly claim to personally knock on over ten thousand doors during their election races for the state legislature. Yet at the time of my visit it had one of the most restrictive franchises in the country—disenfranchising all those convicted of "infamous crimes," which, as in almost all states that base disenfranchisement on such definitions, meant "all felonies." And, because of a particularly acute overlap of race and poverty in Iowa, it had a disenfranchisement problem even more tied into the issue of race than most other states. Fully one-quarter of all black men in Iowa could not vote—and that number was rising as the prison binge continued. Iowa incarcerates a higher percentage of its (admittedly small) African American male population than any other state—although less than Washington, D.C. In fact, while considerably less than 5 percent of the state's population is African American, about one in five of its prisoners are black.

Thus it is that one of the whitest states in the union now finds itself with catastrophic black suspension and drop-out rates from school, a level of black youth involvement with the juvenile justice system approaching 50 percent, and a black incarceration rate many times higher than the raw population percentages would suggest likely. These numbers have come about as a result of both high levels of despair in the black community and also a well-documented pattern of unequal treatment of blacks and whites by the different component parts of the criminal justice system.

With no end in sight to the years of high incarceration—a boom at least in part fueled by a particularly vicious, cross-racial methamphetamine problem and by meth manufacturers setting up shop in Iowa and siphoning off ammonia-based farm fertilizer from tanks in the corn fields in order to use the chemicals to make their drug—this is a problem with an increasingly cancerous impact on Iowa's democratic credentials.

Staggeringly, as of 2004, hardly anyone in Iowa's political elite had been prepared to touch this issue with a ten-foot barge pole. To me, it was simply extraordinary. Yet again, as I journeyed the back roads of the state, I was floored by the scale of the breakdown of participatory democracy. In Washington, I'd tried to imagine a scenario in which a quarter of white voters were removed from the process without anyone batting an eyelid, without citizens' movements screaming bloody murder about coups and tyranny, without legislators racing each other to the podium to denounce such an injustice, and I'd failed. It was virtually inconceivable. Yet, as in Washington, in Iowa, until recently, a blanket silence had greeted the extraordinary disenfranchisement of the state's black population.

Blacks in Iowa are concentrated in a handful of towns: Des Moines, Davenport, Waterloo, and one or two other locales. And it is in these towns that entire communities have been removed from the political process.

Waterloo is an old industrial town 130 miles northeast of Des Moines, on the banks of the Cedar River. It has a dilapidated-looking John Deere plant, some meatpacking factories, a tannery, a host of clapboard churches, streets lined with New England–style wooden houses, and a fair bunch of mom-and-pop businesses. And it is the county seat of Blackhawk County. About 27 percent of all state prisoners in Iowa originate from this county, according to local political figures.

Of Waterloo's 60,000 inhabitants, about 8,000 are African American—mostly the descendants of Holmes County, Mississippi, residents who, a couple of years before World War I broke out, were brought up to Waterloo by the Illinois Central Railroad as strikebreakers. Originally Waterloo's white folk wouldn't let them live in most parts of town, and so they set up house in boxcars and shanties on the outskirts of the little industrial city; from that lowly position, they began building up their own neighborhoods and eventually moved into previously all-white parts of the city. For a while, in the middle part of the twentieth century, black businesses in Waterloo flourished. There was even a black-owned newspaper. Then, the inner-city economy collapsed, and the black middle classes started to disappear. Where once there were large numbers of black-owned stores, today, along the main drag of East Fourth Street and the side streets running off it, there are only bars, liquor stores, a couple of beauty salons, and an abundance of hole-in-the-wall churches.

Nowadays, Waterloo's African American residents are mainly concentrated in the impoverished fourth ward, on the east side of town. Their ranks have been added to, in recent years, by migrants from such large middle-of-the-country cities as Chicago, St. Louis, Kansas City, and Minneapolis, families fleeing the poverty and violence of the ghettoes, looking for—but, according to local political figures such as forty-six-year-old Representative Deborah Barry, generally failing to find—a better life in Iowa.

By the summer of 2004, with the manufacturing sector shedding jobs seemingly every day and with no new industries coming into the region, there was upward of 20 percent unemployment in Waterloo, Barry estimated, and among blacks the figure was far higher. Many black teenagers spent their afternoons hanging out in desolate-looking fourth-ward parks, selling drugs to locals and to white outsiders who drove in to make their purchases. It didn't feel particularly dangerous—though I certainly wouldn't have wanted to be dumped there alone and at night—but it did feel lonely. Waterloo felt far away from everything: a barren little dead-end town with an awful lot of people whose biggest adventures in life would likely involve altercations with law enforcement officers and spells in the state prisons.

About 600 blacks from the Waterloo area were estimated to be in prison. Hundreds, possibly thousands, more carried with them felony convictions that impinged on their ability to find work, to find housing, to access government programs, and, of course, to vote and participate in the rough-and-tumble of political decision making. Representative Barry's own sister had a felony conviction related to drug use. Her secretary had a larceny conviction. Two of her nephews were in a federal prison awaiting trial on federal drug charges.

As we drove around the neighborhood in her white Lexus, Barry—a citizen legislator whose paid job involved working with at-risk kids in after-school programs—detailed the geography of disenfranchisement, a disenfranchisement rooted in the criminal justice system and magnified by the increasing de-involvement of family members and friends that accompanied widespread felony convictions. In one precinct, only fifty-five people would come out to vote in a typical election; in another, while close to four hundred were actually registered to vote, fewer than forty generally did so. And so on.

Trapped in a cycle of hopelessness, many ex-prisoners returned to drugs, to crime, and to lives on or outside the margins.

And the spiral into communal disenfranchisement and disempowerment continued. "It's a hustle," angrily declared one black Muslim preacher in Waterloo—an impeccably dressed, stiff-backed man who mixed conspiracy mongering and political critique into a hard-to-disentangle mass. "The biggest coup you could pull is to create the environment that would cause people to respond in a barbaric way, charge them with being barbarous, slap a stamp on them. They do their time, then they come out and can't get a job, can't integrate back into society. 'Felony' is the new N-word. They don't have to call you a nigger anymore. They just say you're a felon. In every ghetto you see alarming numbers of young men with felony convictions. Once you have that felony stamp, your hope for employment, for any kind of integration into society, it begins to fade out. Today's lynching is a felony charge. Today's lynching is incarceration. Today's lynch mobs are professionals. They have a badge; they have a law degree. A felony is a modern way of saying 'I'm going to hang you up and burn you.' Once you get that *F*, you're on fire."

Back in Des Moines, Representative Wayne Ford uttered similar sentiments. Ford was fifty-two years old and recently married. Four years earlier, he had been among those profiled in Dan Rather's book *The American Dream*. He was a huge man—330 pounds, he claimed—and, as if his size alone didn't announce his presence, he wore a flamboyant red cap and a vibrantly patterned shirt. When local newspapers and magazines wrote about him, they often called him by his nickname: Big Poppa.

Ford had grown up in a poor black neighborhood in Washington, D.C., had been in and out of trouble as a teenager, but had straightened himself out enough to get into college in Rochester, Minnesota, on a football scholarship. By 2004, he was a five-term legislator in Iowa representing a district of 23,000 people, about 5,000 of whom, he believed, were African Americans living in the heart of inner-city Des Moines. Ford thought that as many as one thousand of those African Americans had a felony conviction in their past.

Over the previous years, Big Poppa had proposed a bill in the assembly that would have restored the vote automatically to ex-cons who had completed their sentences and paid off all their fines, and another bill that would have required correctional counselors to inform releasees about how they could apply to get their voting rights restored. Neither bill had made it out of committee.

Angered by the state's seeming inability to integrate blacks into its economic and political mainstream—and by the terrifyingly high drop-out rates of black teenagers from high school, by the epidemic levels of juvenile and adult incarceration amongst blacks, and by the unrelenting poverty so many of his constituents endured—Ford was ready with some harsh words. "We have the highest percentage of blacks that can't vote in the country," he said with only marginal exaggeration, sitting over a large meal at the Holiday Inn just off downtown. "It's ironic we're number one in the election process and number one in the country in blacks who can't vote. This is the Midwest. This is the Bible belt. This is where we can call you a nigger and stand behind God."

8
Bluegrass Blues

I started heading south once more, taking a flight from Des Moines to Chicago, and another one to Louisville. I checked into a hotel not too far from the famous Churchill Downs racetrack—home to the Kentucky Derby, mint juleps, and some of the fanciest, most showy hats on earth—and set to work.

In the late 1990s, Kentucky's Criminal Justice Council—a group of experts and state government officials with a mandate to make policy recommendations to the governor and legislature—researched the problem of the state's lost voters. In January 2000, members issued a report that urged Kentucky's politicians to make it easier for ex-cons who had completed their sentences to get their vote back.[1] The Department of Corrections, the experts suggested, should generate monthly lists of felony offenders eligible to apply; the commonwealth attorneys in each county should receive notice of those individuals within the county's jurisdiction so eligible; and the monthly lists should then be forwarded to the governor's office. All told, they reported, these changes would cost the grand sum of $30,000—the amount needed to fund a low-level clerical position within the Department of Corrections.

To back up their arguments, members of the Criminal Justice Council polled eighteen commonwealth attorneys (Kentucky's version of district attorneys) and found that fifteen of them were not, in principle, opposed to such a reform.

Sometime after the 2000 elections, Kentucky's governor, Democrat Paul Patten, added his voice to the chorus for reform. Patten made it known that he was keen to reenfranchise any felon who had served his or her term, had paid the court-ordered restitution fees, and who applied for a restoration of rights. The Department of Corrections issued a binding policy memo stating it would inform releasees of the restoration process, ask them whether they wanted the department to begin this process for them, and, if they did, that it would initiate the paperwork. At the same time, following through on the Criminal Justice Council's recommendations, the legislature passed a law stating that there should be a presumption that applicants would get their rights back, and ending the largely symbolic $2 application fee.

Where between 500 and a little over 900 a year were having their vote restored in the latter 1990s, in 2003, 1,035 out of approximately 1,700 applicants gained back their civil rights. And all the policy statements emanating out of Frankfort, the state capital, suggested the trend would continue. For a brief period, it looked as if Kentucky was gradually easing out of existence a disenfranchisement code that dated back to the writing of the state constitution in 1891.

That 1891 constitution took away the vote from any felon and provided only one way for the vote to be restored: the felon had to apply directly to the governor for a partial pardon, and only the governor could issue that pardon. (Because it is so hard to amend the state's constitution, the Criminal Justice Council had had to argue for making the restoration process easier rather than abolishing outright the prohibition of felons voting without a gubernatorial pardon—a move that could only have occurred through passage of an amendment.) Yet nothing in the constitution specified when rights would be restored and when they wouldn't. In other words, the decision was entirely discretionary, with the governor having the final say-so and with no right of appeal built in should he decline to restore someone's vote. Nor did the constitution specify what kinds of information might be required by the governor's office of any felon applying for his or her restoration of rights.

Not surprisingly, given the history of race relations in Kentucky, many in the state feared that such discretionary power could be, and, in the past had been, utilized as a tool to limit black political participation come election time.

While disenfranchisement affected both blacks and whites, it fell particularly hard on the state's black population, and on the urban centers in which this population lived. Fully one quarter of the state's prisoners came from Jefferson County, of which Louisville made up the major part. And the inner core of Louisville, from which many of these prisoners came, was solidly African American. Only 7 percent of the state's population was black—a lower percentage than anywhere else in the South—but nearly 40 percent of its prisoners were.

The same issues that dogged most other Southern states played themselves out here: an underinvestment in the public education infrastructure, high levels of poverty, the ongoing existence of a large, economically marginalized black underclass, inner-city unemployment, rampant drug use, and a vast increase in the numbers entering the state's prison system over the past several decades. To cap it all, the state had virtually ceded control over its prisoner reentry programs to faith-based initiatives that seemed at least as interested in saving the souls of those fresh out of prison as in providing them with concrete help—such as accessing jobs and housing or applying for a restoration of voting rights.

At some point during my days in Kentucky, after I had interviewed several middle-aged African Americans who had lost their right to vote because of convictions for over $300 worth of shoplifting ($300 being the dividing line between a misdemeanor and a felony), the realization hit me that there must be many old men and women in the South who couldn't vote when they were young because Jim Crow disenfranchised them; who could vote for a few years after the Voting Rights Act; and who were then disenfranchised during the massive expansion of the criminal justice system in the 1980s and 1990s—people who, now elderly, once again could not participate in the political system. Given the numbers of people convicted of low-end crimes in the South, many of these old men and women would have spent years, even decades, disenfranchised for nonviolent, sometimes utterly insignificant, breaches of the law. It has an eerie parallel to the life stories of blacks born slaves in the antebellum years, presented with political rights for a few years during Reconstruction, and then cast out of the political system again during the early years of Jim Crow.

While America's felony disenfranchisement laws didn't originate in the post–Civil War South, it was in the South that the felony codes were first dramatically expanded with the specific *intent* of casting a wide net within which to snare freed blacks. It was in Dixie, in other words, that felony codes were first politicized—used as a pragmatic tool to achieve ends not related to the arena of criminal justice—so as to remove a group of people from the electoral process. Acts such as low-level theft, or stealing food to eat, that were previously treated either as misdemeanors or as felonies that didn't carry disenfranchisement as a collateral punishment, now became offenses that resulted in a person's permanent loss of civil rights. "Infamous crimes," which barred a person from the political process, were delineated by politicians who made no secret of their intent to hit black political power. Thus it was that several states made it an infamous crime to steal a pig or break into an outhouse, but neglected to declare murder—or, for that matter, voter fraud—infamous. Some of these bizarre distinctions remained on the statutes into the 1970s.

Because freed slaves were likely to be impoverished and to commit petty crimes in order to survive, and because law enforcement was overwhelmingly controlled by whites, this proved to be a particularly effective prop of the emerging Jim Crow system in the late nineteenth-century South: the poll tax, the literacy test, the property requirement, *and the felon codes.*

More than one hundred years later, the descendants of the post–Civil War generation were falling into a new trap of disenfranchisement—nowadays arrested not for crimes such as stealing pigs or breaking into outhouses, but, in many instances, for possessing or selling small amounts of drugs, for shoplifting, for committing an array of other offenses borne out of poverty and alienation. "It's a huge problem," Anne Braden, a feted seventy-something Louisville journalist and longtime civil rights advocate explained during a late-night phone conversation after she had returned home from a day and evening of back-to-back meetings. Braden is white; she and her husband achieved notoriety in post–World War II Louisville by acting as surrogate buyers for a black family that had tried, and failed, to buy a home in a white neighborhood. Subsequently, the home was bombed out, and Braden's husband ended up in prison on sedition charges. "You can't separate it from what's happening to a whole generation of African Americans. The prisons are just bulging with them. Society has decided that if you can't solve their problems, just put 'em away."

Braden's friend, a radical sixty-one-year-old Catholic priest by the name of Patrick Delahanty, agreed with this analysis. Delahanty lived in an old brick house, the inside walls of which were covered with artwork—black-and-white photos that he had snapped of Louisville residents down the decades, a quilt decorated with antiwar images hanging in the dining room, Mexican art, political posters, a cross in the center of the yellow living room wall. The priest had fine, delicate features, white hair, and steely blue eyes. He had worked on civil rights issues in Louisville for most of his adult life.

Was there a deliberate attempt to use the criminal justice system to dilute black political power? I asked him. He paused—an old man in shorts, sandals, and a T-shirt sporting a bicycle image and the words "anti-pollution device"—sipping from the coffee cup that, he said, he continually refilled throughout the day. "It's hard to tell if there's a *conscious* connection," he said cautiously. "But the end result is it is black people who are disenfranchised often."

That evening I headed to Baxter Street, a road lined with Irish pubs and promises of fine on-tap brews on the east side of town. I found one with a three-piece jazz combo in the back patio area and parked myself at a wrought iron table under lush green trees whose names I did not know; I ordered a pint of ale, opened my de Tocqueville, and read about the rise of mass culture in nineteenth-century democratic nations.

As the hours wore on, the tables around me filled up with chirruping, happy youngsters, beautiful people years younger than I out on the town the night before the Labor Day holiday. I read and I read, and, gradually, I realized that I was feeling a serious malaise. It wasn't that anything was wrong. To the contrary, the music was terrific—two bassists and a drummer wafting soft jazz into the velvety air of a Louisville night—the beer tasted great, and the plate of fish and chips was by far the best meal I'd had since hitting the road several days earlier. Moreover, de Tocqueville and I had been getting on particularly well as traveling companions throughout the past few days. But something wasn't right.

After a while, it hit me: I was sitting alone, unknown, unrecognized, surrounded by all the bustle of a holiday weekend. If I was lucky, the occasional bar patron would look over at me, probably wondering what I was doing reading such a thick book in a venue catering to the carefree. More likely, I would just go through the evening unnoticed. Nobody cared if I stayed or left, if I ordered another drink, if I got bitten to death by the aggressive mosquitoes doing the rounds of the outdoor tables, or even if I drank too much to drive back to my hotel safely. I could motor on over to the Ohio River, dive in, and swim across to Indiana, and nobody would have been any the wiser. In the pit of my stomach, I suddenly felt a wave of fear—a feeling of being utterly insignificant, of *not mattering*. The words of the Breadwinners' Circle women in Des Moines came back to me—their words on feeling unwanted and second rate, of feeling invisible in their own country. I remembered Ralph Ellison's book *The Invisible Man*, his description of realizing his invisibility, and the strange mixture of despair and exhilaration it unleashed: he was a nonperson, and that meant he could never get ahead in the regular community, but, at the same time, it gave him a sort of moral free pass to behave as an outlaw. Looked at in that light, it doesn't seem so surprising that ex-cons, locked out of civic society and declared politically invisible, so often revert to lives of crime. Why not? They've been told they are persona non grata anyway.

For just a few minutes, I felt like I could understand what it meant to be a noncitizen surrounded by hundreds of millions of citizens, to be disenfranchised in a society that places such a high premium on citizenship, on civic participation.

The next morning the *Courier-Journal* ran a front-page article on how Governor Ernie Fletcher was deliberately making it harder for felons in Kentucky to regain their voting rights.[2]

Fletcher, previously a U.S. congressman, had been elected the previous November, Kentucky's first Republican governor in decades, and in the nine months after his election he had reenfranchised absolutely no one. Perhaps with the state government paralyzed by bitter divisions between a Republican senate and a Democratic assembly, with the state operating by executive fiat without an agreed-upon budget, Fletcher was hoping to wield the tough-on-crime club to further popular support for his party and its leadership. Whatever the reasons, in 2004, somewhere in the region of 700 applications had piled up on his desk.

When I had requested information on this from the public advocate's office back in the late spring, I was greeted with months of runarounds as the office sought permission from the governor to communicate with me. The public advocate heads up all the public defenders in Kentucky, and, since 1996, the position had been occupied by a Democrat, Ernie Lewis. Lewis, a public defender in the small central Kentucky town of Richmond since 1977, was on the Criminal Justice Council that recommended reforming the restoration process, and he had always been extremely up-front in his belief that the disenfranchisement laws served only to handicap ex-prisoners and to undermine democracy in Kentucky. Lewis apparently wanted to talk with me, but, as a member of the executive staff, he had to seek permission from the governor's office, and the governor's office had asked him to hold off talking with anyone until a review of the existing policy was completed.

Finally, in midsummer, I'd been told a policy change was imminent and that they would allow Lewis to talk to me after the change had gone into effect. In late August, stage one of the "policy change" was revealed. In a one-off spurt of generosity, Fletcher restored the vote to about one hundred men and women who had been petitioning him for months. And then, the good deed done, he ushered in stage two, tightening the procedures even more and setting Kentucky on a trajectory at odds with the reforms implemented by many other states over the previous years.

Fletcher's office had decided that the old application form used by ex-governor Patten wasn't difficult enough, and so addenda to the applications were sent back to the felons, asking them to provide three personal references and also an essay addressed to the governor explaining how they had rehabilitated themselves and why they thought they deserved to get back the right to vote. "Describe in your own words the reason(s) you are seeking this restoration and why you believe your civil rights should be restored," the official letter, signed by the deputy general counsel and with the governor's name on its letterhead, stated. As I had found out in Iowa, questions like this can prove daunting, since most prisoners are undereducated or functionally illiterate to begin with, and since a great majority of ex-prisoners are intimidated by any contact with authority. And given all of this, it was hard to interpret Fletcher's move as anything other than creating a back-door literacy test for ex-prisoners seeking to regain their civil rights. "The guys who are not literarily savvy," explained ex-prisoner Robert Glenn, who was now working at a community organization named Visions for Hope, Inc. "They're shot in the water. If they don't have a ghost-writer, they're pretty much stuck."

Another man in Louisville who worked with ex-prisoners said that his clients were "not sure how to approach it. They are terrified of the system. This idea of sending a letter to the governor and exposing them to the system that has not exactly been friendly to them, it's a very terrifying process." So terrifying, in fact, that many either weren't filling in the forms, or they were starting to write out the answers but couldn't bring themselves to complete the questionnaire and mail it in, fearful that their answers wouldn't be good enough—that they would somehow be deemed to have "failed" in their responses. "I'm not finished with it yet," explained forty-eight-year-old Lillian Holloway, who had been convicted several times of stealing clothes from department stores in the quaint old town of Lexington—thefts she had committed to fund a long-term drug addiction. "I always wanted to vote. But being on drugs and stuff, I didn't get into it. Then I got out and found out I didn't have any rights and didn't like what was going on in the political system and felt my vote could make a difference. The problem is lack of education. People like me, we don't think our vote can make a difference. We should, but we don't. I had no idea."

"If it's based on the ability to articulate, then it becomes a literacy test, and then we're going to have to wrassle with that," said Lexington resident Jeff Coles. Coles worked with ex-prisoners at an organization named Emmaus Village, providing transitional services to them as they navigated the complexities of life on the outside. Five of the village's fifteen clients had recently told him that they were interested in getting their vote restored, but, scared off by the paperwork, none had so far completed their applications.

Now, the Labor Day edition of the newspaper was reporting that, in addition to the already imposed new hindrances, the governor was sending the applications, the references, and the essays to the commonwealth attorneys, giving them veto power over who ended up getting their vote restored. Felons, the governor's top attorney, John Roach, stated, would get their vote back only if the prosecutors approved of the measure. "We are relying heavily, if not almost exclusively, on the commonwealth attorneys," Roach told the *Courier-Journal*.[3] And, the subtext made clear, the governor's office was assuming that many of the commonwealth attorneys, despite their support for the Criminal Justice Council's recommendations four years earlier, actually had zero interest in seeing the vote restored to these men and women.

Ernie Lewis hadn't been told that any of this was imminent. Fletcher's lieutenant governor, a fellow Republican, hadn't convened any meetings of the reform-minded Criminal Justice Council since Fletcher had taken office. And no one in the executive office had sought to consult with a broad spectrum of experts before changing the procedures.

I phoned Ray Larson, the commonwealth attorney for Fayette County, in his Lexington office. Larson was a dyed-in-the-wool conservative, a man who would, according to witnesses, turn up at Criminal Justice Council meetings with a camera, photograph the participants, and then put their mug shots up on his Web site along with the information that these were the people recommending all these liberal policy changes. His Web site featured sensational "outrage of the week" pieces on criminals coddled and victims wronged.[4] And Larson took great pride in informing his readers that Kentucky couldn't afford to *not* put more people in prison. I had been told that Larson was a demagogue, and his Web site certainly looked to take its cues from the smear-and-rant politics of men such as Joseph McCarthy and Rush Limbaugh. It seemed that if anyone would want to speak out in favor of these new restrictions on voting rights in Kentucky, it would be Larson. In fact, the prosecutor had already told the *Courier-Journal* that he thought the move was "an outstanding decision. I don't think earning those rights back should be automatic or so easy."

Larson answered the phone with a heavy Southern drawl. I told him what I was writing and he asked who I wrote freelance articles for. I listed the *New York Times*, *Rolling Stone*, and the *Atlantic Monthly*, and the commonwealth attorney immediately cut me off. He called me a liberal—in a tone of voice that made it clear this was not a compliment—said he would have to check me out, and that I should phone back three days later. When I called back the following Friday afternoon, Larson's snarling voice was far from encouraging. "I have, in fact, investigated you and what you've done and what you've written, and, you know what, I'm not going to participate," he snapped. "I Googled you and I read what you're doing. I realize now you're one of the George Soros types [I had received a fellowship from the Soros-funded Open Society Institute a few years previously] and I have no interest in participating."

When the Criminal Justice Council had polled the commonwealth attorneys on making it easier for ex-felons to vote, they had also asked for comments. I had a strong suspicion that one of the three negative responses had come from Larson. And if he hadn't penned it, his policy stances were certainly aligned with its sentiments. "I oppose the new process for restoration of voting rights," the anonymous commonwealth attorney had written. "It is not the duty of the Department of Corrections to ensure that the maximum number of felons are voting. The [application] forms should be available for those who request them, and at that point the department's involvement should end. Any felons who care enough to obtain the forms and register will be demonstrating at least a modicum of initiative and personal responsibility. If they don't care enough to do so, the department will do the Commonwealth a disservice by adding them to the rolls."

I left messages with the governor's office, requesting an interview with Governor Fletcher; another with John Roach; and others with people in the executive branch who might have been able to explain their new policy to me. None of them phoned me back.

From his office in the state capital of Frankfort, and from his enormous red-brick home perched above the verdant banks of the Ohio River, State Senator Gerald Neal—a gray-haired man with a goatee beard and the air of self-confidence of someone used to being listened to—had been badgering the governor's office for data on disenfranchisement for months. His fear, and that of many community activists and voter-rights advocates, was that a deliberate policy was afoot to suppress the black vote in Kentucky. A few years earlier, the legislature had ordered a referendum on whether to expand municipal Louisville's boundaries to incorporate the surrounding suburbs, and the measure had passed by about 5 percent. The old Louisville was close to 40 percent African American, and four of its twelve aldermen were black. The new city, incorporating the white suburbs, was a mere 17 percent black, and the number of African American aldermen was now only six out of twenty-six. One of the first things the new city council had done was to emasculate the independent review process that had been set up a few years earlier to monitor allegations of police brutality in the city. That process had been set up after a number of young black male suspects were shot dead by the city police.

Then, in the November 2003 gubernatorial election won by Fletcher, the GOP brought in white poll watchers to monitor polling booths in the low-income, African American West Side, looking for signs of "voter fraud." In the wake of this, the ACLU filed two lawsuits alleging the monitors had been brought in to intimidate black voters. After all, while bringing in "monitors" might seem innocuous enough, you don't have to go too far back in Southern history to encounter white "monitors" armed with baseball bats and guns who would frog-march African American would-be voters out of polling stations, and, if they objected, beat the holy hell out of them in the process. Not surprisingly, black voters today don't take too kindly to even watered-down versions of the "monitor" tactic being deployed against them in Southern elections.

After Neal and community groups such as the Lexington-based Kentuckians for the Commonwealth filed open records requests, the governor's office admitted that from the time Fletcher had assumed office through July of 2004, not a single person had regained their right to vote in the state. It was in the wake of this that Fletcher had suddenly decided it might be worth his while to restore the vote to a token few people later that summer. Now, however, it looked as though the governor was going to make it all but impossible for Kentucky's growing number of felons to ever get their rights restored.

The state senator had a gentle voice that crescendoed into an outraged bass when he got excited. His district was a diverse one, home to affluent and poor, to black and to white, and he didn't fear that mass disenfranchisement was likely to cost him his senate seat anytime soon. Neither did he necessarily have great sympathy for individual felons. Instead, he said, he saw this as a systemic problem. "You have to talk about what's good government," he explained, sitting in his living room, where four figurines of jazz musicians were lined up on the mantle over his red marble fireplace. "What's good democracy. Kentucky is one of seven states that have this pardon requirement in this fashion. All the rest have automatic procedures for restoring rights. And here's Kentucky going in the opposite direction. We're out of step and we're going further out of step. The voting right is *so* fundamental to what this country is about, how can you even begin to think you can take this right away to begin with? Now we're sitting here with a reactionary policy that we haven't cleaned up. We're living in the past."

I drove down the Blue Grass Parkway, past lush green woods, small family-sized farms on gently rolling hills, and thoroughbred horse paddocks behind old wooden fences, all making up a landscape pretty if not exactly spectacular. As the lilac skies of a Southern sunset spread out from the huge, dull-red glow of a setting sun, I turned onto the Western Kentucky Parkway. And, hours later, with the lilac sunset replaced by a thick darkness, I pulled in to a hotel in the middle of nowhere and settled down to write. The next morning, I had a meeting lined up in Memphis, Tennessee, still close to two hundred miles to the south.

9
In Graceland's Shadow

I drove into Memphis through the impoverished northern African American part of the city. The streets were rundown, the lots full of garbage, the sidewalks chipped and uneven. A few people loitered about in the humid midday heat, in gas station parking lots, and near little convenience stores, some pushing shopping carts full of their life's possessions. Other than that, there was hardly any outdoor activity. Storefront blues bars hinted at a raucous night scene that I wouldn't have time to see. But, in the light of day, northern Memphis seemed rather eerily silent.

Perched on the eastern banks of the Mississippi, Memphis is one of the South's greatest cities; it was home to Elvis Presley, and it remains a center for jazz and blues. Yet it is also host to a frightening degree of race-based poverty, in large part a direct legacy of the era of slavery and undisguised racial oppression. When tourists drive in to visit Graceland, they park in a vast, fenced-in lot, walk through a museum and shopping area, and stand in long lines to go on tours of the King's carefully air-conditioned mansion. What they don't see is the surrounding squalor of a city from which the affluent have increasingly fled and within which drug use and despair run rampant.

In 2000, Bush had beaten Tennessee native Al Gore by 80,000 votes in the state. It was a moderate margin but less comfortable than the Republican victory in most other parts of the South. This time around, with Tennessee considered to be in play, the candidates were buzzing back and forth over the state like frenzied bees. A few days before I was there, Bush was out on the stump; so too, on different days, were Cheney, Kerry, and Edwards. They were slated to come back several times in the weeks following my visit as well.

While I guess it's conceivable that someone traveling through America's West, or its Northeast, or even its corn belt midriff, could somehow fail to see the connections between race, the criminal justice system, and loss of voting rights, once you get as far south as Tennessee, you'd have to be blind, deaf, and pig-headed just for good measure to miss this particular connection. It's simply impossible to ignore, like repeated rabbit punches to the kidneys. First, there's the obvious presence of all the ghosts of slavery—all the people alive today whose grandparents and great-grandparents were either born into slavery or, conversely, born to be slave-masters. Old men and women walk down the streets and pass other old men and women whose grandparents might have owned their grandparents. Then there's the world of circumscribed opportunities and carefully calibrated barriers to advancement that blacks faced from the moment of emancipation onward. There's the historical legacy that all of this has left, of high school drop-out rates, broken families, low job skills, low self-esteem, and so on—a legacy that the half-century-old civil rights movement managed to partially tackle but never to fully eradicate. Then there is today's covert discrimination. The good-ole-boy school of outright segregation, intimidation, and mob violence has largely given way to more subtle events, like blacks being pulled over for routine traffic stops more often than whites and having their cars searched; getting arrested more frequently for drug use and dealing; being less likely to be sentenced to probation than whites (only 36 percent of the state's probationers are black, whereas half of those in the prison system are). These things start adding up and eventually make it all too easy to see why so many African Americans end up with felony records.

Tennessee's population is 16 percent African American, yet

approximately half of its prisoners are black. And, while no one has done a definitive study on this, I'd venture to guess that because the restoration process for felons seeking the right to vote is entirely discretionary in Tennessee and puts a premium on an applicant's financial ability to hire an attorney, and then relies on the good will of district court judges, well over half of the state's disenfranchised population is probably black.

Not surprisingly, widespread black disenfranchisement in turn fuels cycles of antisocial behavior and despair among young and alienated African Americans. And so the downward cycle into criminalization and incarceration continues, and Tennessee is left with something approaching a diluted Jim Crow redux.

De Tocqueville feared that free blacks in America would continually butt up against the ugly realities of a privileged, and racist, white majority doing everything in its power to keep blacks from succeeding politically and economically. It was, he wrote, particularly intolerable because it was all done using the language of democracy. "In their treatment of the blacks," the Frenchman wrote, "they violated all the rights due to human beings. After that, they taught the blacks that those rights were precious and inviolable. They have opened their ranks to their slaves and then, when they tried to come in, they drove them shamefully away."[1] De Tocqueville also noted, somewhat smugly, that "in almost all the states where slavery has been abolished, voting rights have been granted to the Negro, but, if he comes forward to vote, he risks his life."[2]

To deny that history is powerful enough to impact current policies and current realities—even if today's politicians aren't responding to an intentionally racist agenda, and even if, which is generous to a point, one claims that no police officers are ever motivated by racist sentiments—is simply disingenuous. Anyone who has been into the large penitentiaries of the South—whether it be the Louisiana State Penitentiary on the old Delta plantation of Angola or one of the new, high-tech prisons that dot this landscape—knows that what you encounter is a sea of black faces in which the odd white face is a jarring apparition.

After the Civil War, large numbers of freed slaves in the old Confederate states were arrested on flimsy, oftentimes ludicrous, charges, sentenced to prison, and then leased out to farmers, mines, and railway companies as convict labor. Thousands of them died in work conditions little different from those of the Soviet gulags a half-century later, worked literally into their graves. In some states, such as Florida, the leasing system continued well into the twentieth century.

Today, the Southern penitentiaries are still places where vast numbers of blacks are incarcerated. And, while convict leasing doesn't exist anymore, in Alabama the chain gang—an archetypal symbol of humiliation—was briefly reintroduced in the 1990s at the urgings of tough-on-crime state politicians.

Like Alabama, Georgia, and a number of other rebel states, Tennessee reshaped its felony codes in the decades after the Civil War with the specific intent of using felon disenfranchisement as a prop of Jim Crow, as another way to legally remove the vote from large numbers of ex-slaves. Freed slaves permanently lost their vote for stealing food, or for committing an array of "morals crimes"; meanwhile, rebels who had actively fought to destroy the Union were, at most, only temporarily deprived of the vote for taking up arms against the government. Until 1973, only certain felonies—those deemed by lawmakers more frequently committed by blacks—merited disenfranchisement. Among the white (and thus somehow more "honorable") crimes that didn't merit disenfranchisement was murder; this was, I guess, based on a nineteenth-century worldview adhered to by Southern gentry that imagined the typical murderer to be a gallant white dueler rather than a scurrilous black gangster.

Those crude distinctions have long been leveled by politicians in the civil rights era who knew that if they didn't clean house themselves, the federal courts would intervene and start striking down their laws. But, in their place, a web of drug arrests has taken tens of thousands of blacks from the next generations down out of the political system.

Judge J. C. McLin, an African American who ran a mentoring program for ex-prisoners in Memphis, estimated that every single day, each of the city's ten criminal courts handed out between five and ten felony convictions, and the city's federal court handed out a number more. Between two-thirds and four-fifths of the convicted felons, McLin thought, were blacks. As of mid-2004, the Memphis area had more than 7,500 people on parole or probation, of whom more than 5,000 were African American, many of whom took plea bargains in order to avoid serving time behind bars—and many of whom picked up felony convictions without even knowing the implications that the label *felon* would have on the rest of their lives. "It's almost impossible to raise the numbers who are voting because of the numbers taken off on a daily basis," the judge calculated.

In the public housing projects in Memphis—rows of barracks-like two-story brown-brick structures evoking the bleak township slums of South Africa—voter registration advocates estimated that as the election neared, perhaps half the men could not vote. An entire generation of youngsters was growing up with no models to copy of adults participating in the political system and going to the polls on election day. Citywide, the NAACP and other groups I talked with believed that approximately one-third of black men were disenfranchised—*one-third of all black men in the city.*

After peaking in the 1980s, black political participation in Memphis began to decline. Older people talked of the apathy of the young 'uns, the kids who grew up after the civil rights years and don't appreciate the blood shed gaining civil and political rights. Yet mass disenfranchisement, while rarely talked about as a cause of this, certainly explained a large part of the drop-off.

In all likelihood, it is not the case that everyone who used to vote no longer wants to vote; rather, huge numbers of people who used to take part in elections, or who didn't use to but now want to, simply no longer have the right to vote.

State representative Larry Turner, who represents an inner-city district in Memphis and who had made voting rights one of his signature political themes, sorrowfully admitted that voting rates were now so low in the public housing projects that he couldn't afford to spend a lot of time campaigning in them during elections. "In those precincts," he said, "two hundred people turn out. In other precincts, fifteen hundred might go to the polls. I always concentrate where there's going to be a larger turnout." Turner felt that many of his constituents were disenfranchised in more ways than one. "It's more than just the ability to vote. It's economic. People who are disenfranchised don't feel a part of the system. They feel somewhat divorced from the system. Not being able to work the system also means you can't reap the economic benefits."

Jimmy Ellis, a self-possessed African American man, was working for Change Outreach Ministry when I met up with him. A decade earlier, as a teenager, Ellis had been arrested for selling drugs and had served a year in prison followed by three on parole. Since coming out of prison, he had stayed out of trouble and gotten a job with the ministry working with other young adults returning to the community from behind bars. Ellis wanted to vote, but he couldn't.

"Before I went to prison, I had no interest in voting. Ninety percent of us, when we go to prison, we have no interest in voting, because we don't realize what a privilege it is until it is taken away from us. By educating us through the prison system, we see it makes a difference. Every vote makes a difference. I have not regained my citizenship insofar as being able to vote. It doesn't affect you mentally, but you know there's something missing. Here you are, a grown man, in the United States, and you don't have the right to vote—because you made mistakes as a teenager. There's something wrong with our system."

With another presidential election nearing in which he could play no part, Ellis attached almost mystical importance to the ritual of voting. "If I could vote, it would probably make me feel more better to myself, or better to society. If I was to picture a moment of voting—I'd probably panic, or ask someone to come in and tell me what to do. I've never had the opportunity to vote, because I was convicted so early. I'd probably stand there freezing. I'd stand in awe in the booth all day long."

For twenty years, Representative Turner had tried to raise awareness about the growing pandemic of disenfranchisement. He routinely took bills to subcommittees of the State and Local Government Committee that would make automatic the vote-restoration process once a person had completed his or her sentence. And his colleagues routinely stymied the reform. Turner's bills rarely got out of subcommittees and they hadn't once managed to get out of full committee for a debate on the house floor. In the senate, similarly, no bills had ever been debated on this by the entire chamber. "Republican members of the assembly are very strongly against the legislation," Turner explained. "There are some Democrats, also, who are very strongly against it. In this state, a lot of things boil down to race. They hear the word *felons* and they think it applies to nonwhites, and the attitude is to lock 'em up and never restore their rights."

When a colleague of his, a woman named Henri Brooks, proposed a bill that suggested nothing more radical than forcing the Department of Corrections to simply inform prisoners who were being released of the *existing* process for applying for their vote to be restored, that bill, too, was killed in committee.

Turner was sixty-five years old when we met, a successful businessman and an elegant, soft-spoken, and self-confident member of the black middle class. He ran a local real estate company and had been a state representative since the mid-1980s. Yet, as we ate an early-evening dinner together in a restaurant on the banks of the Mississippi River, a strong, blustery wind blowing outside (the remnants of Florida's hurricane Frances), he told me that every black man knows people who are in prison or have felonies. Turner's now-dead brother got addicted to drugs and picked up a felony for shoplifting; two of his brothers-in-law got felony convictions—one for trying to cash someone else's check, the other on a drug charge; his own son, when he was eighteen years old, was charged with a felony marijuana offense, but the family successfully managed to plead it down to a misdemeanor.

"It's a rarity for a black male to grow up and *not* be in trouble with the law," Turner argued. "Unemployment in the black community is double digits. If you took a good count, you may have between thirty and forty percent. A lot of it is due to youngsters having felonies against them." In other words, trapped in poverty, many turn to crime, and convicted of crime, they then are barred from many walks of life and remain mired in poverty.

Felons in Tennessee, as in many other states, are barred from jobs that require a state license; they cannot teach in public schools or work in hospitals, and, even when they are not formally barred from jobs, employers increasingly utilize background checks to weed out from their workforce people with felony records. As a result, many have stories like that of forty-four-year-old Norman Redwing, a Memphis resident who had cycled in and out of the juvenile system from age thirteen, and who had been arrested in 1987 for carrying a deadly weapon. He had pled guilty, served no time in prison, and had stayed clear of the law since then. "I didn't know I had a felony as a result," stated Redwing, who had worked with the Urban Youth Initiative for the previous eleven years and also done volunteer work in local schools for five years. When he got a job as a family specialist working with "at-risk" youth in the city's school system—work he seemed well-suited for, given the stack of community service awards he had won over the years for his work with youth at risk of ending up behind bars—that felony came back to haunt him. Administrators did a background check, found out about his record, and promptly sent him a letter dismissing him from his new job.

Thus felons are pushed further and further outside of the political and economic mainstream, and the likelihood grows that, at some point, they will reenter the criminal justice system.

America is not deliberately, or even consciously, reverting back to an eighteenth- or early-nineteenth-century definition of democracy—one that defined the polity, and a citizen's right to participate in it, by property ownership and a certain degree of financial independence. But, in so dramatically expanding the scope of the criminal justice system, in handing out so many felony convictions, in placing such strict limits on what jobs felons can and cannot work in once they return to the community, and in further disenfranchising them, creating in effect a system that keeps large numbers of minorities and poor people from voting, it seems to me that *unconsciously*, largely without forethought, America *is* sliding back into such a constricted definition of citizenship and of democracy.

Change like this occurs incrementally. Americans are not going to wake up one day and find that the country is suddenly no longer a society that defines itself by universal suffrage. But, over decades and generations, the criminal justice system *could* serve to tip attitudes gradually in that direction. And, if this happens, it will be largely because of the overlap of nineteenth- and early-twentieth-century felon disenfranchisement codes in states such as Tennessee with late twentieth- and early-twenty-first-century arrest, conviction, and incarceration patterns.

It is bitterly ironic that Tennessee is at the forefront of such a move. After all, it was a Tennessean, President Andrew Jackson, who history credits with providing momentum to the populist philosophy that led to the modern understanding of democracy and suffrage in America. Of course, Jackson himself was a shamelessly racist man, yet he unleashed a democratic revolution that, over one and a half centuries, ultimately evolved into a glorious experiment in multicultural, multiracial, participatory democracy. And it is that experiment that is now increasingly at risk.

Tennessee's disenfranchisement code is not only discriminatory in its impact. It is also almost incomprehensible. It has been changed so many times over the years that even seasoned attorneys who have practiced law for decades have a hard time navigating it. For an average prisoner, coming back to the community with a low level of education, perhaps with problems reading and writing, and almost certainly lacking experience in interpreting complex bureaucratic documents, it's a maze from which there is no exit.

Since Tennessee has prosecuted many people in recent years for illegally voting—a class E felony that can, in theory, lead to several years behind bars and a hefty fine—many prefer to not risk taking a wrong turn on this maze and simply opt out of the political process altogether. It is, quite simply, the safest option, given the potpourri of rules and regulations affecting felons and the franchise.

Prior to 1973, the state adhered to one of those notorious late-nineteenth-century codes that made distinctions between supposedly white and black crimes. Tennesseans prior to 1973 lost their voting rights if they had been convicted of abusing a female child; arson and felonious burning; bigamy; bribery; burglary (including breaking into an outhouse); destroying a will; incest, rape, sodomy and buggery; or perjury. By contrast, they did not lose their right to vote if they picked up a murder or assault conviction. Thus, anyone in Tennessee in 2004 who was convicted prior to 1973 of any one of the crimes included on that list, could not vote; whereas those convicted prior to 1973 of crimes not mentioned on the list could vote.

From January of 1973 to May of 1981, the disenfranchisement code was suspended as legislators tried to come up with a newer version that was not so flagrantly race-specific. What that means is that there was an eight-year window when disenfranchisement was not a collateral consequence of conviction. Anyone in Tennessee today who was convicted during those years *can* vote.

Between May 1981 and June 1986, anyone convicted of any felony lost the right to vote. They were then given two ways of having that right restored: either get the governor to grant a pardon, or hire an attorney and petition the Circuit Court to allow them to vote. From July 1986 to July 1996, all felonies resulted in disenfranchisement, and the only way to get the vote back was to get the Department of Corrections to issue a document entitled a Certificate of Restoration. From 1996 onward, all felony convictions carried with them a loss of voting rights, and, as was the case between 1981 and 1986, felons could only get their vote back by seeking a gubernatorial pardon or petitioning the Circuit Court.[3]

Confused? You're not the only one. The law is such a tangle of dates and requirements and paperwork that the end result has been that, over the years, hardly anyone has applied to get their vote back. If Kentucky's system is a de facto literacy test, Tennessee's is a demonic slalom course down a mountain studded with legal obstacles. In practice, therefore, Tennessee is a state where the vast majority of felons either really are, or think they are, permanently disenfranchised.

Not surprisingly, rumors are rife on the street about con-artist lawyers hawking their wares who promise to get people's rights restored for $1,000 or $1,500 and then run off with the money. That the system is so stacked against applicants that there's very little point in forking over large sums of money to untrustworthy attorneys on the off-chance they'll get one's rights back adds a bitter twist to this urban legend.

In fact, though, in the year leading up to the 2004 election, there *were* a handful of lawyers, based mostly in Nashville and spearheaded by a dapper-looking commercial litigation specialist named Charles Grant, who agreed to work on applications pro bono. When black radio stations in the area—in particular a show titled *What's the 411?*—began publicizing this, and then helped to organize a rally at the Nashville courthouse, the attorneys were deluged with hundreds of applications from folks who, it turned out, were desperate to resume voting.

The attorneys put in long hours sorting out which applications stood a chance of succeeding and managed to convince local district attorneys not to hinder them in this process. Yet, despite the hard work, at the end of the day barely a couple of dozen people were successful in getting their rights restored. It seemed a huge amount of effort for a relatively small payoff.

From Memphis, I headed east toward Nashville to interview some of the men and women who had approached these attorneys.

Driving through Tennessee has a unique flavor to it. The highways are lined with endless side-of-the-road fireworks shops—big, flashy places jammed full of riotous explosives. On the interstates themselves, you pass one beat-up old car after another, their windows rolled firmly up, their drivers sitting stone-faced, puffing away at cigarettes, staring halfheartedly through the fug and out to the road.

I stopped for a late dinner at the Loretta Lynn Kitchen, built on a hill on the site of the singer's dude ranch, a place complete with hundreds of autographed photos of country music personalities, decked out in tight jeans, frilly shirts, and enormous hats. The food was some of the worst I've ever had—deep, deep-fried chicken so tough and dry it could have been used for bombs; green beans, corn, and collard greens all clearly out of a tin and probably lying in the open for days; greasy pulled pork; soggy fried bread. The waitress said, in a twang that could have broken wineglasses, "You have a good day now." It wasn't a suggestion. It was an order. I continued driving through the darkness toward Nashville.

Nashville, the state capital, is an interesting town. It is a place of dreams, nicknamed Music City, to which flock thousands of young men and women from around the country who hope to make it in the music biz. And it's a place that fashioned itself as the Athens of the West in the mid-nineteenth century and backed up this image during Tennessee's centenary year, 1895, by building a life-size replica of the Parthenon, situated in a beautiful park a couple of miles west of downtown. That Parthenon is still there, its huge pillars providing shadows for local lovebirds and late-night promenaders looking for a quiet place to drink some beers and smoke some cigarettes.

Behind the sham-glam exterior personified by the Grand Ole Opry and the neon signs of Broadway on the five blocks west of the river—honky-tonk blocks with the same anything's-possible-and-anything's-for-sale ambience as Hollywood Boulevard—Nashville is also a city with a large epidemic of disenfranchisement and a tough law-and-order leadership. The city has a teen curfew and large signs hung on lampposts downtown—above the pizza parlors, the country music saloons, the rockabilly and bluegrass clubs, the barbeque joints and kitsch-for-sale tourist joints—warn carousers that it will be strictly enforced. It also has numerous down-and-outs, the haven't-made-it flipside of the Music City's dream, who cycle in and out of local jails and state penitentiaries.

Out of an upscale office in a high-rise west of Broadway, Charles Grant had been busily reading the hundreds of applications he'd received, via the local NAACP chapter, from felons looking to get their voting rights restored. Many of these did not qualify because they hadn't completed their sentence—they were still on parole or probation, or they still owed fines and court costs. Many others, it turned out, were automatically eligible for restoration because of when they were sentenced and what they were convicted of; all they needed was a certificate of discharge, which had to be automatically granted once they requested it—but nobody had ever bothered to tell them this. About seventy-five, however, needed to go through the petition process.

In the months leading up to the election, Grant had twisted arms, curried favors and managed to line up several attorneys who agreed to do pro bono work putting the petitions together, taking affidavits from witnesses who could testify to the applicants' characters, serving federal and state attorneys with notice of the petitions (a legal requirement put in place to give prosecutors time to register an objection should they choose to do so), and then going into court to petition for restoration of rights.

Charles Grant had a good working relationship with the local DA's office and the federal office, and they both agreed to cooperate with him. He was advised to put the petitions on several judges' dockets rather than on that of a single judge so as to spread the political heat. In the past a senior member of the bench had told him that no one judge would risk being labeled as "soft on crime" for unilaterally taking part in a day of mass reenfranchisement. "When it comes to ex-cons," the immaculately coifed Grant explained, "they are persona non grata. They're political hot potatoes. To do anything for them is to be seen as coddling criminals. It's an absurdity."

Many of those who had approached Grant for help felt this sense of being persona non grata keenly. "Without a vote you're sort of walking on everyone else's ideas," said one twenty-six-year-old music business student at the city's Belmont University, a woman who had picked up a felony six years earlier after getting into a penknife fight with her boyfriend's lover. She had served no time in prison and three years probation and had been trying to get her vote restored ever since. "I voted when I was eighteen years old. It was exciting. It was the first statement to me that I had become an adult," she recalled, sitting in one of the gazebos dotting the pretty lawn around which were arranged Belmont's buildings. "My dad always encouraged voting. It would mean the world to me to vote. It's the one thing that will haunt me. It's cost me two elections. I couldn't vote in 2000 and I can't vote now. My fiancé laughs at me. He says, 'Well, you can drive me to the polls. It'll be like you voted.' Once you go through higher education, you understand the importance of voting. At eighteen, you don't understand the importance. Voting would probably be what I consider the most important thing that I lost. I can't even vote in small elections—for my councilman, my governor, my senator, different local government officials. I can't even pay attention to who's going to be my mayor. I will have missed eight years. November of 1996 was my first election, so I'll have really missed twelve years. And if I'm still working on it by 2008, I still won't be able to vote. And it can go on and on and on. Whatever I did is past history. Tomorrow, I start afresh, and tomorrow I need to be able to vote."

Thirty-one-year-old Emmette Barrow had picked up his felony nearly fourteen years previously, shortly after he'd turned eighteen. Barrow had been in a car with a friend of his who was selling drugs; the police had pulled the car over and found the drugs; and, since Barrow's friend wouldn't admit to being the owner, all the occupants of the car were charged with possession of a controlled substance. Barrow had had to choose between sixty hours of community service and paying a fine. He ultimately chose the fine. "The only thing I wasn't able to do was vote," he recalls. "I went to college, got my degree, bought a house." When I met Barrow, he owned a small taxicab business. Life had worked out well for him in the years since his conviction, and he was, with justification, proud of his accomplishments. "The last election made me think, How many guys like me can't vote? I'm a property owner. I own three cabs. I've taken care of everything else in my life. And

I can't vote. This present election, every vote counts. This is a pretty serious election. [But] I can't vote. I don't like to have political discussions, because they say if you don't vote you can't complain."

Told by the attorneys Grant had gathered to work on these cases that it was likely he'd soon be reenfranchised, Barrow was as excited as a kid in a candy store. After all, he'd never in his life been able to vote. "It will feel nice," he said, smiling, his voice disarmingly wistful. "I'm kinda excited now they're saying it's going to be restored. I'm thinking, *Yeah, I make a difference.* I'll be laughing all the way."

The next morning, slightly the worse for wear after a long night in one of the city's off-the-beaten-path jazz clubs, I met James Morris, an elderly man, tall and skinny, wearing a Stetson-style straw hat and a light gray suit the pant legs of which were just a fraction too short for his gangly limbs. He looked like an aged Duke Ellington.

Morris had joined the army at age seventeen and had remained in the service until he was nearly forty. He had trained in an all-black unit under a white commander, and had served in Korea and Vietnam. But the events he recalled most vividly occurred in the United States when he was stationed at Fort Benning, Georgia, a member of a unit whose primary duty it was to respond immediately should Martin Luther King Jr. be attacked. He'd been one of the soldiers who had been deployed to the University of Alabama in 1963, when Governor George Wallace stood in the university's entranceway blocking black students from entering. His unit, he said, was shot at by angry segregationist protestors. Perhaps as payback for their role in the conflict, black soldiers from the unit who crossed over the Chattahoochie River into Phoenix City, Alabama, to visits bars and nightclubs when they were off duty were often arrested and thrown into jail by the local white sheriff.

In his life after leaving the army, Morris had gotten a master's degree in public policy and criminal justice, and had subsequently worked as a senior criminal justice planner for the city of Nashville. Now, in his mid-seventies, he was retired and spending his time working with homeless veterans who were cycling through the local jails and the state prisons.

Many of these men, Morris believed, were suffering from post-traumatic stress disorder; many had gotten addicted to drugs while fighting in Vietnam, and many had not been successfully reintegrated back into civil society. "There are categories of people that are convicted felons that should never have been exposed to the criminal justice system. They should have been in veterans' institutions rather than jail." They were, Morris told me, "mostly black. Whites usually find employment of some type, and there's a double standard. Black veterans are usually put in a jail cell; white veterans are usually put in a program to deal with their addiction."

I headed east again, hundreds of miles east, into the heart of the conservative mountain culture of eastern Tennessee. Early in the twentieth century, this part of the world had achieved notoriety during the Scopes "monkey" trial, in which a high school teacher was prosecuted for the crime of teaching Darwin's theory of evolution to his students. By the early twenty-first century, it was still conservative, but its conservatism was partially balanced by the presence of a number of activist organizations.

The main activist group was named Save Our Cumberland Mountains (SOCM). Traditionally, it had focused on environmental issues—on pollution caused by local coal mining, on air and water quality, and such. Recently, however, it had also decided to launch a campaign to reenfranchise ex-felons.

I drove through the gateway town of Knoxville and thirty miles further, to the hamlet of Lake City, in the heart of Appalachia. The dense forests were showing the first hints of autumn colors, and the endless dumpy hills trapped light, oozed a sense of time standing still, of excruciating claustrophobia.

The communities nestled in these endless hills and mining ranges, are, historically, utterly self-enclosed, isolated little places. And, despite my cell phone and hotel Internet connection, I felt infinitely lonely, a world away from the climates and skies and cafés and people that I was familiar with.

Save Our Cumberland Mountains had embraced the suffrage campaign because they had been told about vast numbers of Tennesseans losing the vote, not just blacks in the western part of the state, but white methamphetamine addicts and dealers, and miscellaneous other felons, in the mountain towns. Now their members were talking about linking up with sympathetic legislators to push reenfranchisement bills over the coming years.

Unfortunately, their bark seemed to be worse than their bite. SOCM was, indeed, righteously outraged by the current state of affairs, but they hadn't yet gotten very far in crafting a grassroots campaign to change the laws. They couldn't find any felons to talk to me, since, they told me apologetically; the mountain people didn't talk about their criminal histories, and locals apparently were so politically apathetic anyway that a far bigger problem than felon disenfranchisement was simply convincing enough of those who were eligible to vote to cast ballots to make the democratic system endure in a meaningful fashion.

10
Appalachian Autumn

On the other side of the Appalachians from eastern Tennessee was Virginia. It was farther east—or rather, farther northeast—than I'd planned to go, but it did have somewhere in excess of a quarter of a million disenfranchised voters—people who, according to the state constitution, could only be reenfranchised by the governor himself and a vastly disproportionate percentage of whom were African American. The restoration process was so seldom used that, according to statistics generated by the secretary of the commonwealth's office, from 1938 until my visit in the fall of 2004, only 8,234 Virginian felons had had their rights restored by the seventeen governors who held the office during these sixty-six years.[1] During that same time period, many hundreds of thousands of the state's residents had, cumulatively, lost their votes.

Having gotten so close to yet another disenfranchisement hot spot, I decided it seemed a pity not to lurch just a little bit farther. And so I zigzagged eastward into the early fall and the oranges and yellows and reds of the forests coating the Blue Ridge Mountains and the valleys enclosed between them—endless armies of trees preparing to shed their leaves for winter.

I spent four days in the state trying to get used to the mountain chills and the night mists again, to the East Coast autumn that I had known for ten years before moving west to California. In the presidential election campaign the polls were still declaring a virtual dead heat, and debates were raging over both candidates' abilities to conduct a prolonged war on terror, their respective Iraq plans, abortion (and the controversy surrounding a number of Catholic bishops who had stepped into the fray and effectively endorsed Bush), stem cell research, the state of the economy, and the skyrocketing price of oil.

Some nights as I watched the news, I felt that I was seeing a particularly compelling, and gory, spectator sport being played out in front of me—like one of those boxing matches you hear about from the nineteenth or early twentieth centuries, fought with no limits, bare-knuckle fights that could go thirty, forty, even fifty rounds, until, presumably, one of the two combatants was literally beaten so senseless he couldn't even wave his bruised and broken hands in surrender. I heard about one of these battles on National Public Radio one day, as I was driving through the Virginia countryside—a nostalgia piece on an old ghost town in Nevada whose single greatest (if not only) claim to fame was that it hosted one of these bloody events back at the turn of the last century. Other times, though, the entertainment value suddenly disappeared, and I was overwhelmed by my sense that this was the most important election in my lifetime and by deep foreboding about the directions that the political discourse was taking—about all the noise drowning out the serious issues, about the poisonous sound-bite culture of the modern election. I kept getting a strange "warp" sensation, a feeling that things weren't quite right. I think part of it had to do with the endless intrusion of increasingly banal religious sentiments into the campaigning, juxtaposed against daily news of more atrocities committed in the name of religion by one terror group or another, either in Iraq or elsewhere around the world. I was starting to feel as if my modern, cosmopolitan world were being dipped into a toxic potion conjured up sometime between the tail end of the eleventh century, when the First Crusade was launched, and the Inquisition.

* * *

In the forests just outside the small town of Danville, perched on the state line with North Carolina, I met a middle-aged man named Lloyd Brown. He had a scraggly beard, bushy-but-receding long brown hair, a floral-shaped scar under his right eye, and a sizeable paunch beneath his orange T-shirt.

Brown lived in a crooked old farmhouse with sloping walls and a low ceiling, its porch home to several potted cacti, the surrounding grass somewhat chewed up by one of his neighbor's cows. The dusky wood-paneled interior looked like a cross between a ship's cabin and an art gallery. The walls were hung with paintings with a Southwest desert-and-horses motif. And the floor was crammed with overstuffed old armchairs, heavy old wooden furniture, and an iron chimney-stove next to an oversized TV. Above the fireplace hung a crossbow—to hunt wild turkey for a biannual turkey stew that he cooked for his friends, he explained, laughing. He used a bow instead of a gun because, being a convicted felon, he had lost his right to own or use firearms. Technically, he was supposed to use a bow and arrow instead of the more lethal crossbow, but he had produced a doctor's note saying he had a weak shoulder and couldn't pull back on a regular bow, and so he had been allowed to purchase the crossbow.

In the 1980s, Brown had started using drugs. Then, to pay for the drugs, he had started selling them. In 1988, at age forty, he was arrested after selling powder cocaine to some undercover officers. He was given a seven-year sentence, all but one year of which was suspended—probably because it was his first felony conviction. And he ended up serving about eight months in the city jail. After Brown came out of jail, he served one year on probation, during which time he successfully completed drug rehabilitation, and then had to spend the remaining five years on good behavior—a form of nonsupervised probation during which a criminal is not required to report to anybody but within which, if he gets in trouble with the law, he can be returned to prison to finish serving out the original sentence. Brown spent those five years drug-free and out of trouble.

In March 1995, Lloyd Brown's sentence was completed and he went to his old probation officer and asked him how he could go about getting his civil rights restored, particularly his right to vote. He was told he had to wait three years before applying to the governor. And so he waited.

In early 1999, Brown picked up the thirteen-page application form that Virginia required felons looking to get their rights restored to fill in, and began the time-consuming task of gathering certified copies of old court records, conviction documents, sentencing reports, notices proving he had completed his sentence, letters of recommendation from three people, a letter from his probation officer (Alan DeAndrea), proof of employment (he was by now a long-term employee at a local furniture store), and a host of other information. DeAndrea mailed the package to the governor's office in Richmond (the capital of the old Confederacy) and Brown waited. And waited. And waited. Two months later, he received a four-paragraph note from the office of the secretary of the commonwealth. Governor Allen, the letter said, was interpreting his constitutional mandate in a particularly conservative manner. He "has a strict policy regarding crimes involving drugs. In order for an applicant to be eligible for the restoration of civil rights, he or she must be free from any suspended sentence, probation, and parole for a minimum of seven years. Upon review of your petition, I noted that your probation did not end until March of 1995; therefore you will not be eligible for clemency until a minimum of seven years from that date."[2]

Allen's position wasn't surprising. His political career had been jump-started a few years earlier, when he ran for a U.S. congressional seat as a staunch law-and-order conservative and won by a few dozen votes. Like as not, he wouldn't have won that election had Virginia's franchise not been so restrictive. Allen had also championed the state's truth-in-sentencing law, which effectively removed the opportunity for parole for new prisoners entering the system in the early to mid-1990s. And he had been instrumental in the massive expansion in the number of prisons operating throughout Virginia, while also vetoing bills to create full-time public defenders' offices in cities such as Charlottesville. By the time Allen left office, Virginia was in the upper echelon of incarceration states, both in raw numbers and in the total percentage of its population that it imprisoned.

The letter from the secretary of the commonwealth went on to say that the office would keep Brown's application on file until the seven years were up, at which point they would automatically reactivate the file should Brown contact them again.

And so Brown waited some more. It didn't seem fair, but he didn't know what else he could do. Another presidential election passed in which Brown could not vote. Another gubernatorial election. Governor Allen ran for, and won, a seat in the U.S. Senate. The Virginia legislature went even more solidly Republican.

In June 2002, Brown wrote the governor's office and asked them to reactivate his file. But he didn't hear back about his application, and he began to get worried. A month later, he phoned the office and was told that his application would be reactivated, but that the office was short of staff and it would take at least a year for the office to get around to looking at the file and for the new governor, Jim Gilmore, to make a decision. Again, a frustrated Brown could do nothing but wait.

In June 2004, after nearly two years had elapsed, he phoned back again. By now there was yet another governor ensconced in Richmond, this time a Democrat named Mark Warner, who had promised to speed up the vote-restoration process, and was allowing some nonviolent felons—though not drug offenders—to submit a one-page application form instead of the complex old one that Brown had submitted years earlier. He had brought in staff to investigate these applications and to clear backlogs that had built up under his predecessors, and, to the dismay of a bevy of conservative legislators, he was promising to restore the vote to more people than had his predecessors. In fact, within his first year in office, Warner would restore the vote to almost 2,000 people, nearly one-third as many as his sixteen predecessors combined, though still a drop in the bucket compared to the total number who remained disenfranchised or were about to lose their vote because of new convictions. In response, a conservative legislator named Robert Bell—a onetime prosecutor in a small, rural county—had successfully introduced legislation to expand the number of crimes considered "violent," whose perpetrators would thus not be eligible to receive the shortened application form. At issue was not merely "a feel-good right to vote," Bell explained. He feared that felons who had had their rights restored could, in theory, sit on juries. "If you didn't have a job but were working as a volunteer or raising children, that would be okay," the delegate averred. "But if you've not paid restitution, not gotten a job, taken together we'd have less confidence that you have rehabilitated yourself and turned your life around so that we [would] want you to sit on juries of other offenders. Most of us law-and-order conservatives, Republicans, believe you can turn your life around, but we do believe a dose of skepticism is appropriate." Despite Bell's law, however, and despite periodic rumblings by even more conservative delegates about introducing legislation making it all but impossible for felons *ever* to get their vote restored, applications were being processed at a fair clip.

Unfortunately, in Lloyd Brown's case, there was a snafu. His file simply could not be found. Scores of boxes of unopened applications, sent in during the terms of Governor Allen and his successor, Governor Gilmore, had been discovered by Warner's staff when they came in. The files had been untouched, the applicants left with no word on the fate of their requests to be reenfranchised. When the new staff had finally gotten around to learning how to use the database software—an antiquated program written in 1995 and never updated—for tracking people who had applied to have their rights restored and began processing the files, some were so old that all the contact details on them were outdated and officials had no way of finding the prospective reenfranchised felons to inform them of their new rights. Scores more, the new staff theorized, had simply been misplaced, either thrown away or cast off into a basement storage space in one of Richmond's many government buildings. Apparently, according to the staffer Brown spoke to, the Danville man's must have been among them. "We've just not been able to find scores of hard copies in the files," explained Allen Brittle, director of rights restoration in the office of the secretary of the commonwealth. "Unfortunately, we've had some cases where we did get a whole lot of calls where people said they'd applied years before. We make no guess on what's happened to those things."

"What did I do?" Brown pondered. "I *didn't* break a bat on him or anything, but I wasn't very happy and I told him so. He told me that if I wanted to do anything he could send me a whole new package and I could start over again, start from scratch. Ground zero. At that point I kinda lost confidence in the political system and the governor's office and the way all this was handled. It'll be discouraging [on Election Day], not being able to vote. It doesn't give you a whole lot to look forward to, not being a regular citizen. It's sort of like I just exist. I don't have a real life in terms of being a part of the community."

The disenfranchisement of felons is built into Virginia's state constitution. But the definition of what counts as a felony has become ever broader over the years—from essentially capital crimes in colonial Virginia to the situation today, in which people convicted of $200 worth of shoplifting, $1,000 worth of property damage during, say, a graffiti episode or a negligent driving accident, the passing of $200 worth of bad checks, or habitual offenders who have committed three low-end crimes within a certain period of time (even including a third crime of misdemeanor shoplifting—for example, of a pack of cigarettes) pick up a felony and lose their right to vote.

In the 1980s, a then-Democratic Virginia legislature voted two years in a row to amend the state constitution to make it easier for felons who had completed their sentence to get their vote back. But when the amendment was put before Virginia voters as a referendum (to amend the state constitution, state legislators must vote in favor of change by a two-thirds majority twice, one on each side of a state election, and the population must then support the amendment in a plebiscite) it was defeated. More recently, when politicians like delegate Mitchell van Yahres, a Democrat representing the university town of Charlottesville, have broached the subject of bringing Virginia's suffrage laws closer in line with those of the majority of other states, they have received a barrage of irate e-mails from conservative constituents deeply fearful of the impact this will have on state politics. "ARE YOU TOTALLY INSANE!!!" read one such missive sent to van Yahres in early 2001. "These people have been convicted of crimes and you want to reward them!!! You are a disgrace to House of Delegates."

Over the decades, governors, quite possibly reflecting the will of many of their constituents, have been notoriously parsimonious in using their executive power to restore the vote to these people. In the year 2000, only twenty-six Virginians had their right to vote restored by the governor. The following year, fifty-five. And, as in Kentucky and Tennessee, the process is entirely discretionary, providing the governor with an avenue to distribute favors and also to wield the tough-on-crime stick. When a state senator named Robert Russell was convicted of embezzling money from a cycling club, Governor Gilmore promptly reenfranchised him while ignoring the applications of hundreds of other felons, including Lloyd Brown.

The results are all too predictable. Virginia is now one of the states in which likely over 25 percent of its black adult males are voteless.[3] When Ellen Ryan of the Charlottesville-based Virginia Organizing Project knocked on doors in poor parts of town looking to register voters in the run-up to the 2004 election, she found that between 15 and 20 percent of the people she talked to told her they couldn't vote because they were felons.

There was, according to Charlottesville's lead prosecutor, commonwealth attorney Dave Chapman, "a whole section of the community living separate and apart from the mainstream. Many times it's a lifestyle choice; many times it's the result of substance abuse; many times the result of inadequate education; many times the result of a combination of factors, including racism. One of the measures of that is participation in community, including political life. The greater the number of people who are disaffected from the mainstream, the greater the risk the gulf is so great it's either unbridgeable or very difficult to bridge. For a broad spectrum of crimes the process of completing a sentence should have among the goals re-enfranchisement. Suffice it to say, it should be flexible, efficient and relatively easy to achieve. At the moment, it's inflexible. Politicians still have a lot of mileage to make from beating up on felons. It's an easy mark to hold up. It's very popular in many communities—instead of looking at the complexity of an issue."

The rigidity of Virginia's reenfranchisement process wasn't unjust in just an abstract way. Like in other states where most of those who lost the right to vote in practice never regained it, in Virginia the hemorrhaging of voters from the political system had begun to affect election results in very tangible ways.

The old brick town of Lynchburg, named for a local Quaker bridge builder rather than in honor of the Southern practice of mob murder, is famous for two things: the enormous wealth local merchants of previous centuries generated by being one of the nodal points for the tobacco trade—a wealth the remnants of which can still be seen in the form of the grand old warehouses lining the riverfront—and the presence of Moral Majority leader Jerry Falwell's enormous church, property, and university empire. Falwell lives in a high-walled compound in a residential neighborhood on the south side of town. On Sundays, he preaches a virulent fire-and-brimstone theology from the pulpit at his Thomas Road Baptist Church—including an outburst after the September 11, 2001 attacks in which he blamed lesbians, abortionists, and other assorted enemies of Christians for bringing down the wrath of God on America. And, over the decades, he has nurtured Liberty University, a far-right institution that seeks to churn out an ultra-conservative born-again elite. Recently, Falwell has also started a law school in town, with the avowed aim of creating a cadre of "Christian lawyers" who, one must suppose, will eventually find their way into the higher echelons of the judicial system.

In addition to being Falwell's home and one of history's great tobacco centers, Lynchburg almost acquired another more socially progressive talking point in the 1990s: it came close to electing the first ever African American to Virginia's House of Delegates from a town west of Richmond and not dominated by a majority-black electorate. That it didn't is, at least in part, a result of mass disenfranchisement.

Gil Cobbs had been a teacher in the city for over thirty years when he decided that he wanted to get into local politics. In 1990, he ran for a seat on the four-person city council and won. Three years later, the district's house seat came open, and Cobbs announced his candidacy. He lost, spent the next couple years regrouping, and, in 1995, when the seat again became open—the man he'd lost to previously was now running for the state senate—he put his name into the mix a second time. This time around, it was a tight contest. Cobbs had the experience and the résumé. His opponent, Preston Bryant, a young white man hardly more than half Cobbs's age, had the support of the Falwell machine, and sound-bite conservative policies to match. He opposed affirmative action, supported drastic "reforms" of welfare, and opposed speeding up the vote-restoration process for felons.

A week before the election, polls gave Cobbs a seven-point lead among adults in the district. But, on Election Day, among those who actually turned out to vote, a narrow majority came out for Bryant. In a district with over 30,000 voters and nearly 100,000 residents, Cobbs lost by 766 votes. "I claim the disenfranchisement of so many people—especially African Americans—made a difference in 1995," Cobbs said excitedly. We were sitting in the lounge of a local hotel, torrential rain coming down outside, and Cobbs, by then in his early seventies, brought out scores of pages of documents to back up his claim—photocopies of newspaper articles, letters he'd written, letters he'd received from disenfranchised voters.

The district which Cobbs had so narrowly lost was about one-quarter black, meaning there were about 25,000 blacks of all ages living there; possibly about 17,000 of them were of voting age. Maybe 8,000 of these were adult black males. And yet one-quarter of black men in Virginia were voteless. Given these numbers, it was at least possible that Cobbs's belief that disenfranchisement robbed him of victory was true.

For the retired teacher, now dividing his time between a family real estate venture and attending a series of state panels on which he was a member, that possibility had hardened into a certainty. "You can say that any close election where someone wins narrowly and there's a lot of African Americans, the treatment of felons is a factor. You can work from that premise and go forward, in my view."

At the most local of levels, removing the vote from so many Virginians had served to cement a conservative lock on power in the state. And, indirectly, it had also allowed that conservative power to be leveraged upward, through the power of incumbency, to influence national elections and the makeup of the federal Congress. When George Allen, a take-no-prisoners conservative, first entered politics in 1982, he won election to Virginia's House of Delegates by only a couple dozen votes. When he won a special election to the U.S. Congress in 1991, his margin was also tiny. And, after a sojourn as the state's governor—during which time he pushed for an array of tough-on-crime measures, opposed relaxing the felon disenfranchisement laws, and created an informal ruling that he would not even consider anyone convicted of a drug crime for reenfranchisement until at least seven years after the completion of their sentence—when he ran for the U.S. Senate in 2000, he received 52 percent of the vote. It was a small margin of victory that could well have been facilitated by the large number of people who had lost their right to vote, or failed to get that right restored, during his watch as governor.

Allen had played a smart game: he had used his power to accumulate more power, and he had leveraged incumbency into a forward-moving career path up the state and national political ladder. Quite likely none of this subsequent career would have been possible had ex-felons been able to vote when he ran for office originally.

And Allen's career could, in many ways, be used to sum up the rising fortunes of conservative Republicans throughout Virginia. Perhaps not coincidental to the rise in disenfranchisement, it was at the same time that the modern Republican party, largely filling the race-baiting role on a local level previously performed by conservative, fiercely parochial, yellow-dog Democrats, began consolidating its control over the state's political machinery—winning the governorship, the senate, and, in 1999, the House of Delegates as well. It also gained control over the influential state electoral board. In the 1991 and 2001 redistricting rounds, following the 1990 and 2000 censuses, the Republicans used their increasing control to successfully gerrymander state districts, using sophisticated computer mapping technology to give incumbents virtual immunity from electoral challenge, thus making near-permanent their legislative majorities. And they then used this majority status at the state level to push through favorable redistricting that awarded them several more seats in the U.S. Congress and helped to consolidate narrow GOP congressional majorities in the first years of the new century.

A circle of power and disenfranchisement had been created: the denial of voting rights to so many low-income and African American Virginians helped, in practice, to shore up Republican majorities at the state level (and thus, through state power, to shore up the party's position at the federal level). The party then took advantage of these majorities to block any reenfranchisement measures that might ultimately undermine that majority.

In other words, whether through intent or convenient neglect, felon disenfranchisement in Virginia in an era of mass incarceration has served to help shore up Republican majorities that have then turned around and voted in increasingly tough-on-crime legislation that has served to disenfranchise even more voters and has, as a side-benefit, made it that much harder for the Democrats, or local progressives, to muster electoral majorities over the past couple decades. Mark Warner *had* gotten elected as a Democrat, but the rest of the political system was falling ever more solidly into the Republican camp.

11

The Mississippi Hustle

I'd gone too far east too soon. The Atlantic that was calling me wasn't the cold, damp eastern seaboard of Virginia but the glorious southern beaches and warmth of a mid-autumn Miami. I was counting on that sunshine to see me through the last days of the election, the final pages of my book.

So I turned around and caromed west through Tennessee again, all the way to Memphis. I turned left and headed south into Mississippi. And there, I began to drown.

Iowa had annoyed me; Texas had angered me; but Mississippi made me feel as if I had peeled back a democratic veneer and uncovered something just plain ugly. I spent the evenings in my hotel rooms, shuddering at the stories I'd heard and, even more, at the views people had expressed. There was the anecdote told me by a middle-aged toy store owner about how his housekeeper's husband, a worker in a local factory, had been sentenced to sixty-five years for dealing drugs to his colleagues. There were the stories of teenagers sentenced to decades behind bars. There was the sea of black faces inside the state's prisons. There was the state legislator who told me that—the U.S. Supreme Court ruling striking down state antisodomy laws notwithstanding—people who engaged in sodomy should be forever prevented from voting. "Homosexuality is a sin," Republican representative Gary Chism averred, a large, bald man in a green shirt and khakis, sitting in his office in the insurance company that he owned in the small eastern Mississippi town of Columbus, a framed portrait of

Confederate military leader Robert E. Lee hanging on the wall next to photos of Chism's sons playing baseball. "Just like any other felony is a sin. It's just as severe as these others. There're no big sins and little sins. They're all that way. If you've committed a felony you ought to jump through hoops to get your suffrage back."

In the mornings, I tried to scrub the previous day's dirtiness off with long, hot showers and bars of cheap hotel soap. It didn't work. I'd go off for breakfast in a smoke-filled Waffle House and practically weep into my instant coffee. Reading a pessimistic de Tocqueville—toward the end of his narrative, writing about how democracies contained within themselves a tendency for the population to withdraw from politics and to cede power to rather tyrannical central authorities who promised to protect their prosperity and safety—hardly helped my mood any. As the days went on, I felt more and more filthy, more and more appalled by what I was hearing and seeing.

I entered Mississippi from the north, from the Memphis area, a few days after the first Bush/Kerry debate, and interviewed Robert T., a man I'd been told had spent three decades behind bars for a crime committed as a teenager; I talked with him about how, even though he was now middle-aged and finally free, he still could not vote, and, in all likelihood, probably never would be able to.

Robert T. told me his version of his life story: he said he had grown up picking cotton in the Delta town of Greenville. He had moved to Jackson as a teenager to look for work, had fallen in with the wrong crowd, and, at the age of nineteen, was arrested for robbing a mom-and-pop store. Refusing to take a plea bargain, as his public defender had advised, he'd been sentenced to forty years in prison. He had served about thirty years: eighteen years, followed by a few months out on parole, followed by an arrest for violating the terms of his parole after he had missed an appointment with his parole officer, followed by twelve more years behind bars. It was, by any reckoning, an unfathomably long period of time. "At first it feel like the end of the world. Then you have to realize where you're at and come into reality and make the best of it. While I was there, I studied law. All I did was study law. I was successful in helping a lot of people get released through legal means, through the courts. I got a bunch of cases written up. Challenges to the conditions in prison. Challenges to different laws. That's what kept me going. What motivated me."

In 2001, when he was finally released, a strong but no longer young man, his hair now graying, with a fifty-dollar get-out-of-prison check (a paltry sum roughly equal to the amount he said he had stolen three decades earlier) Robert was in his late forties. He had been in prison so long he didn't even know how to cash the check.

When I met him, he was fifty-two years old. He was working as a self-styled paralegal—his clients mainly generated via a bare-bones Web site advertising his services—out of a crowded makeshift office built in the lot behind the wooden house where he and his wife lived in the little northern Mississippi town of Southaven. A computer printer was perched precariously on a filing cabinet, a microwave atop another cabinet, and an old RCA television sat on an industrial metal bookshelf. Over Robert's right eye he had an old scar, and under his right sideburn another; long, thin lines created by razors slashing his skin during fights inside Mississippi's notorious Parchman prison.

The Southaven resident was, I later found out, a controversial figure. Critics argued that he was using his prison-honed legal skills to somewhat dubious ends, apparently charging families to investigate their imprisoned loved ones' cases, even though he had no legal standing to help secure their release and even though paralegals are not allowed to offer legal advice to clients; one voting rights attorney in Jackson went so far as to say that he was "selling people hope for an outcome that doesn't exist." He wasn't a lawyer, nor was he in the employ of a law firm—although he did say he referred clients to an attorney based in the college town of Oxford. Robert himself, when I contacted him again for clarification, put it this way: "I do legal research, mostly post-conviction, looking for errors in procedure, in the conviction. The end result might be to get someone out of prison. [But] we don't want to give anybody the idea we're practicing law. We can't do that." Later, he e-mailed a further qualification, announcing that his office "cannot and do not [sic] practice law or provide legal advice, [but] we do perform investigations on fact finding or witness location as well as provide legal research on issues we are presented with."

I double-checked his story on why he had been returned to prison in 1989. It turned out that state legal records had him pleading guilty to a new crime of armed robbery in 1989. When I phoned him back to ask about this, Robert admitted he had, indeed, been convicted of a new crime in 1989, though he recalled it being a burglary rather than a robbery. It seemed that, after this conviction, he had ultimately served another twelve years in prison, some of it for violating the conditions of his parole, some for the new crime itself.[1]

Whatever the exact details of the 1989 conviction, what didn't seem to be in dispute was that Robert had flunked his shot at freedom, had bounced back into Mississippi's penal system, and had remained there into the new century.

The ex-robber did not seem entirely trustworthy, but the fact remained that he *was* finally free—Mississippi had deemed him rehabilitated enough to release early—and yet he still couldn't vote.

"My parents didn't vote while I was young. My mother might be voting at this time. My father, he never even spoke about voting. He died in seventy-one. That time, there wasn't much voting that was going on for the black people," Robert stated. "Not voting kinda makes me feel like I'm not a part of the system. But I also look at it that one vote not going to matter, one person not that important. But I'd like to be a part of it—for the simple reason I'd have something to say about who's put in office. If the person I voted for won, I could say I had a part in putting him in office. And if they didn't, I could say everything I could do I done and they just didn't win. I'd like to vote in the state elections. The federal elections I'm not all that much concerned about, because federal elections, I don't feel like they shape the laws of our state. The laws of our state come from the state branch of government. I wanted to participate this time around, but I won't be able to. I realize that now. Maybe next time, I been and get something done. I'm not a part of the process, and when you're not a part of something, you feel like an outsider. It feel very bad. If you wasn't strong, you'd probably give up on that. I tell myself I just have to keep on till I find that door."

I left Robert, with his "paralegal" office and his half-truths and his anger. His story depressed me: the crimes themselves, the extraordinarily long sentence he'd received as a teenager, the political rights he didn't have, and the "paralegal" interactions he now had with other desperate people. It was sordid and nasty and made me feel like I had bitter lemons in my mouth.

Would the world have been a better, fairer place if Robert T. could vote? Frankly, I wasn't convinced. But I did know that in releasing him, requiring him to pay taxes, and then telling him he was to remain a sub-citizen, we were shortchanging our own democratic ideals. "Democracy," Winston Churchill once said, "is the worst form of government . . . except for all the others." Clearly Robert was far from a model citizen; yet he *was* a citizen, living free in the community, with all of the obligations of citizenship—and therefore with a legitimate claim to the rights of citizenship as well. And I had to believe that democracy itself was strong enough to be able to absorb, and to survive the inclusion of, flawed characters like Robert.

* * *

I headed south, down Highway 61, the Delta road immortalized by blues singers as the central thoroughfare in the great black migration northward to Chicago. It is about as significant in the American story as is Route 66, and its old pavement has most certainly borne witness to a whole lot more pain and suffering. Millions of rural blacks migrated northward along this road in the first half of the twentieth century. I drove past the endless miles of cotton fields in full, spectacular bloom. The Mississippi River, unseen, was just off to my right, sometimes a few hundred feet the other side of the dense trees that bordered the cotton fields, at other times meandering westward, creating miles of soft, water-saturated dark earth between the highway and the storied river on which grew yet more acres of cotton. On the other side of the river was Arkansas, and, further south, Louisiana.

This was a place where a way of life developed that involved one group of people claiming ownership over another; that involved human beings bought and sold like cattle; that involved a resort to vicious retribution at the slightest hint of rebellion or insubordination; and that finally involved plunging a country into civil war so as to retain the "right" to own slaves. This was a place where a racial caste system as absolute and as unforgiving and as horrifying as any system on earth emerged and flourished. It was a place defined by slavery, and, after the Civil War, for over a hundred years it was a place defined by white attempts to preserve political and economic power using any and all means against blacks—and whites from outside the area—who tried to challenge their prerogatives.

There was a gentle beauty to the cotton fields, though, something almost painful in its contrast to the human saga of the Delta. It looked like rippling seas of creamy white, the cotton flowers hanging off skinny stalks, rising in endless rows out of the rich black Delta soil. A sea almost entirely devoid of humans—the cotton pickers of the past having mostly been replaced by huge mechanical reapers.

Other than that, there were a few casinos dotting the area, and billboards advertising the wonders of these casinos. There were marshy ponds with rotting tree stumps, like decayed brown teeth in an old man's mouth, pushing up from out of the murky, black water. Occasionally, Baptist churches rose up out of the fields and woods. When I passed houses, they were generally rundown wooden shacks or rickety-looking old mobile homes surrounded by ancient rusting cars. The larger towns, really no more than glorified villages, were a strange mixture of fast-food outlets promoted by gaudy plastic signs larger than the restaurants themselves, little stores that looked like something out of *To Kill A Mockingbird*, gas stations, and tiny wooden homes with crumbling porches. Almost all the residents in these towns were black.

Just shy of two hours south of Memphis, I arrived in Clarksdale, one of the great centers of blues music and home to a large museum dedicated to the musicians of the Delta. There were steel guitars and regular guitars and banjos played by Howling Wolf and other legends; there were old 45-speed records, and audio presentations featuring blues performers talking about why they had left the South and headed on up to Chicago. Clarksdale's old streets were lined with crumbling, tiny, one-story brick buildings—some abandoned, some housing blues clubs. In a ramshackle sort of way, it was a pretty town. W. C. Hamby, the so-called "Father of the Blues," lived here at the turn of the last century, in a small white-brick house now converted into a barber's shop.

The U.S. congressman from this area was an African American Democrat named Bennie Thompson. I stopped at his office and explained to the volunteers there what I was doing and asked if they knew of any felons who were unable to vote. They were polite and kind, and adamant that they knew nobody. I stopped in at the NAACP office—run by a near-stone-deaf eighty-year-old lady who swore blind she also didn't know any felons and couldn't introduce me to anyone. It was the same story at the local legal services office. And when I called various Delta attorneys and community activists, I either got promises of help and then no follow-up, or my messages were left unreturned.

It wasn't that there weren't felons in abundance in the Delta—all the statistics suggested involvement with the criminal justice system among residents in the Black Belt counties was endemic, perhaps higher than anywhere else in the country, certainly as bad as in any large inner-city ghetto. About one in three young black men in Mississippi have felony records, and, in small, impoverished, Delta towns, it's possible that the numbers are even worse. In fact, out of the nearly 25,000 prisoners in the state, more than 16,500 were African American; 12,000 of the state's approximately 21,000 probationers were black, as were about 1,300 of the 2,100 parolees in Mississippi. (It was true that there were plenty of poor whites who had also lost the vote in Mississippi; but it was also undeniable that a far higher percentage of blacks were trapped within this web of laws and rumors.)

Rather, the lack of cooperation was more to do with a deep-rooted distrust of outsiders—a powerful reluctance to talk to strangers, even if those strangers came with introductions from voter-rights workers in the state capital of Jackson. It was understandable. No other state has had such a sordid history of voter suppression and intimidation, of political fancy footwork to avoid complying with the Voting Rights Act, of ongoing tricks such as whites impersonating Department of Justice personnel and standing guard at polling booths in black neighborhoods supposedly to watch for "voter fraud."

In a very real way, the use of felon codes to reduce the voter rolls is but the latest ongoing example of these practices. Blacks and whites in Mississippi eat in the same restaurants and attend the same schools these days, and, on occasion, even intermarry. Because of the creation of all-black political districts in the decades after the passage of the Voting Rights Act, Mississippi has more black politicians in the legislature than any other state. And organized violence against blacks who try to participate politically is a thing of the past. Yet only a fool would claim that the state's unfathomably conservative political machinery does not still create obstacles to black advancement. Today, with felon disenfranchisement, there's a sort of now-you-see-it-now-you-don't trick regarding voting, a suffrage version of the three-card-monte scam that was practiced all over New York by young hustlers when I first moved to the city in the early 1990s.

Mississippi was the first state in the South to craft a constitutional provision specifically targeting "black crimes" for disenfranchisement, rather than all felonies. In 1890, legislators enacted a constitution of which Section 241 denied the vote to anyone convicted of "infamous crimes" such as bribery, burglary, obtaining money or goods under false pretenses, theft, and bigamy, as well as a host of other crimes involving "moral turpitude." The lawmakers apparently thought that these were crimes for which blacks were more likely to be brought before the courts. Excluded from the law were more traditionally "white" crimes, such as murder and rape. In 1896, the state's supreme court heard a challenge to this statute, ruled that there was indeed a racial intent behind it "to obstruct the exercise of the franchise by the Negro race," and then proceeded to declare that that was an entirely legitimate goal. So successful was the law in removing blacks from the electoral rolls that in 1901 Alabama followed suit, crafting a constitution that followed Mississippi's model, adding felon disenfranchisement into the Jim Crow arsenal. Within five months of the Alabama constitution's passage, only thirty registered black voters remained in the entire city of Birmingham.

Other states followed suit; and, for two-thirds of the twentieth century, felon disenfranchisement laws performed the same role in Dixie as did the poll tax and the literacy test—laws that the U.S.

Supreme Court had upheld in 1898. In the 1960s, Mississippi's law was modified, supposedly to purge it of its racial intent. A number of violent crimes, including murder and rape, were added to the list, and some of the "moral turpitude" crimes from the original collection were removed. In the 1980s and 1990s, the law was further tweaked to expand the number of crimes that resulted in the loss of voting rights. When the law was challenged, in a case known as *Cotton v. Fordice*, the expansion of the disenfranchiseable offenses was enough to convince the Fifth Circuit Court of Appeals that the law was no longer racially motivated.[2]

By the time I drove down Highway 61, the list consisted of murder, rape, bribery, theft, arson, obtaining money or goods under false pretence, perjury, forgery, embezzlement, and bigamy. Earlier court rulings had found that armed robbery fell under these broad categories. And more recently, the attorney general had issued a ruling declaring that felony shoplifting also was included. In 2004, voter registration forms explicitly said felons could *not* vote if they were convicted of any of these crimes. There was nothing on the forms saying that felons convicted of other crimes could vote, leaving a powerful, albeit unwritten, impression that anyone with a criminal conviction ought not to consider filing official paperwork to register to vote.

Yet, in fact, that wasn't strictly true. One of the interesting side effects of this law was that Mississippi was the only state in the country that still didn't treat all felons equally regarding voting rights. While the original 1890 list of disenfranchiseable offenses had been amended and expanded several times, many felonies still did not technically result in loss of voting rights. In fact, theoretically though not in practice, a felon still in prison on a nondisenfranchiseable crime had the right to cast an absentee ballot in elections from behind the bars of the penitentiary.

Among the crimes that didn't explicitly result in the loss of voting rights were drug crimes, which generated more prisoners than any other class of criminal activity. When I visited the state a month before the November 2004 elections, fully one in three of the state's 25,000 prisoners were serving time on drug convictions.

The right of some criminals to vote in Mississippi, at least in theory, was a source of angst to the sixty members of the Legislative Conservative Coalition, many of whom favored permanent disenfranchisement for all felons. Gary Chism told me, somewhat improbably, that Mississippi's constitution was "not stringent enough. I guess I am saying it's too liberal." He also announced, contemptuously, that there were black political "advisors," trawling black neighborhoods trying to convince felons to vote. And he stated that it was high time the Voting Rights Act was ended and "Big Brother" was removed from Mississippi's shoulders.

At the same time, the selective disenfranchisement law was a source of somewhat bitter irony to slightly less conservative legislators—with the exception of a few African American lawmakers, the political gamut in the state seemed to run from ferociously conservative Republicans to moderately conservative yellow-dog Democrats—many of whom were convinced that if all their colleagues realized that there were some felons who could vote, they'd fairly quickly get around to doing exactly what Chism wanted and make Mississippi's laws even more punitive. A former prosecutor-turned-house-representative named Jeff Smith, who worked out of an ornate law office in downtown Columbus that, with its peacock-patterned wallpaper and wrought-iron frontispiece above the stairwell, looked like something out of a William Faulkner novel, joked that on this front "ignorance is bliss." Smith had a bright red face adorned with a carefully curled mustache. His cream-colored shirt cuffs were monogrammed with his initials in gold, and his forehead was wonderfully wrinkled.

He looked, and sounded, like a larger-than-life Civil War colonel, or, at the very least, like a figure who had leapt off the pages of a Southern literary classic.

Smith was currently serving as chairman of the Judiciary B Committee in the state House. This meant that anyone wanting to get their vote restored had to rely on Smith's goodwill. The vote-restoration process in Mississippi was so ludicrous that it would have been funny if it hadn't had such severe consequences. The only way a person convicted of these infamous crimes could get their vote back was to ask their local state representative or senator to sponsor a legislative bill specifically restoring their suffrage. If it passed out of the Judiciary B Committee that heard the arguments, and if it was then passed by a vote of the entire legislature, it would go to the governor for signing. The system only worked if hardly anyone used it; had thousands of people begun applying to have legislation passed to reenfranchise them one at a time, Mississippi's legislators would have become full-time suffrage debaters.

Smith was a self-described "Northern Mississippi Democrat; it just means 'conservative.'" He was a decent man, well aware of the implications of disenfranchising so many people via the criminal justice system, and equally aware that blacks were particularly likely to end up in prison because, being poorer, they were more likely to be given overworked, harried part-time public defenders who often did little more than convince their clients to plead guilty. (These attorneys were paid only $25,000 a year for their work as public defenders, so it was hardly a surprise that many treated their clients as impersonally as a factory farmer might treat his chickens.) Seventy-nine of Mississippi's eighty-two counties, Smith exclaimed in disgust, had no full-time public defenders, even though the state could properly staff a statewide public defender system for a relative pittance: somewhere in the region of $11 million, he estimated. "If a guy had to do five hundred appendectomies a week," the legislator said, "he'd miss some. He'd cut off your pecker or something." The lack of a proper public defender system in Mississippi, and the effect this had on impoverished, often black defendants, was nothing short of "an atrocity."

But Jeff Smith was also a realist. Because there was so much opposition to restoring the vote even to the few ex-felons who bothered to ask for a legislator to sponsor a reenfranchisement bill for them, and because the Judiciary B Committee had some of the most conservative legislators as members, Smith had recently proposed a "compromise" that, he hoped, would end the practice of legislators blocking suffrage bills. It was, at best, a sorry solution: the house wouldn't even consider a suffrage bill for any nonviolent criminal until at least five years after their sentence had ended; and, for violent criminals, the waiting period would be ten years. But, without this compromise, it was more than likely no one would have their vote restored—as was the case in 2003, when conservative senators blocked all but one suffrage bill that came before them. "It's hard to explain how overwhelmingly people in the legislature don't like suffrage bills," Smith said. "It's hard to explain how conservative the legislature is. My guidelines were not philosophical, they were practical. You've got a very conservative governor, a very conservative senate. The senate thought the house was being too liberal, too reckless."

In reality, though, the conservative outrage was directed at a straw enemy. The nuance of the disenfranchisement law wasn't just lost on many state politicians; it was also lost on the overwhelming majority of Mississippians who came into contact with the law. In the run-up to the 2004 elections, voter-rights workers found that parole officers, probation officers, correctional officials, and even judges had repeatedly warned felons of all stripes not to attempt to vote—threatening them with up to ten years in prison if they did. It was a pattern of on-the-ground disenfranchisement that went back decades. Election Protection Project attorney Amanda Alexander recalled that, when she was in high school in the early 1990s, the teacher in her government class taught students that all felons forever lost their right to vote in Mississippi. "If you have a felony, you cannot vote," one thirty-seven-year-old man recently convicted on a drug charge told me definitively. "I've heard it in circulation. Years ago. I didn't think anything about it. Now I'm in a position I can't vote, I think about it." The man was still free while he appealed the conviction, yet he was sure he could not vote in the upcoming election. "I'd really like to vote. I'm worried I'm going to feel pretty lousy."

And few of the tens of thousands of people who really *were* disenfranchised were trying to get their vote restored through the legislature: in 2001, the state senate approved a grand total of four suffrage bills and killed two; in 2002, it approved thirteen and denied eight; in 2003, it approved one and killed twenty-four—including an application by an old man who had been convicted of burglary in Hinds County in 1954, and who had been unable to vote since then. In 2004, it passed thirty-four (including, at last, the elderly onetime burglar rejected the previous year) and killed seven. In other words, over a four-year period, fifty-two people in Mississippi had their right to vote restored. Most of those seemed to be personal friends of the state legislator who sponsored their suffrage bill, and a suspiciously large number of this depressingly small number were white.[3]

"I got in trouble [in 1963]. I got with the wrong bunch of guys and we broke into a place or two. Stole some things—gasoline to put in the car. Just nothing spectacular. Household items. I was only seventeen," a white man in his late fifties from the tiny town of Coffeeville recalled. "I served about a year and a half. No problem after that. When I first got out, I was doing plumbing work. Now I work as a trucker." The man told me that he'd been voting without any problem for decades, but that, at some point, he'd wanted to formalize the process. He asked an attorney about it, but the attorney told him there was nothing he could do. So he continued voting anyway. Finally, he contacted a friend of his who was a state legislator, and the man agreed to sponsor a reenfranchisement bill. "I didn't have to make any kind of sworn statement or anything. He knew me well enough to know I was telling the truth. It [the bill] didn't get passed [in 2003]. I'd all but given up on it and then out of the blue I got a letter from the courthouse in Grenada with the governor's signature on it. And the speaker of the house had signed it too. Like I said, I was voting all along anyway, even though it wasn't legal. Nobody was checking. But, like I said, I did want to get one hundred percent legal."

Jeff Smith told me the story of a sixteen-year-old he'd prosecuted in the 1980s, who had been charged with rape by his aunt. The boy had claimed it was consensual sex, but, faced with his aunt's testimony, he was convicted. Before a judge could sentence him, however, the aunt recanted her testimony. The sex, she admitted, had indeed been consensual—and, she implied, she had cried rape after her husband had found out about the incestuous affair. Because the alleged victim had withdrawn her testimony, the teenager served no time in prison, although his conviction was not formally overturned. Smith came to believe he was truly innocent of any crime, and when, a decade later, the defendant—now a preacher in his late twenties—had come to Smith asking him to sponsor a suffrage bill on his behalf, Smith had gladly agreed. He even received encouragement in this from the aunt herself. The bill passed in the house. It passed in the senate. And, then, when it went to the governor's desk for a signature, the governor vetoed it. As of 2004, the preacher still could not vote.

Because those who can't vote are, almost by definition, marginalized people, there's no real political pressure to restore felons' voting rights. Rather, politicians feel they have far more to lose than to gain by touching the issue. When state senator Bennie Turner, an African American attorney based out of the little town of West Point, introduced legislation to provide automatic restoration of voting rights after full completion of a sentence—legislation modeled on the law passed in Texas in 1997—the bill was killed in committee. The second time around, he tacked it on as an amendment to another bill and forced a floor vote: all the eleven black senators in Mississippi supported it, and only four of the forty-one white senators did. Again, the bill died.

Opponents of reenfranchisement swore their stance had nothing to do with race. Black legislators, on the other hand, were persuaded otherwise. After all, segregation in Mississippi is still too deeply ingrained in the population's consciousness to be able to think about such laws without thinking about race. Senator Turner could remember accompanying his nervous parents when they first registered to vote (with federal voter registration people taking the registration forms of blacks because local whites wouldn't) in 1965. He could also remember how, when public facilities were ordered integrated, local politicians decided to fill in West Point's Olympic-size swimming pool rather than bear the indignity of blacks and whites swimming together. "The town leadership decided it was better to bust the walls off the pool and fill it up with dirt and cover it over," Turner told me, his voice still filled with wonder at such craziness.

At the very least, the *results* of disenfranchisement in contemporary Mississippi played out in a racially skewed manner. In Parchman, the state's oldest and largest prison, four in five prisoners were black. Statewide, more than two-thirds of Mississippi's prisoners were black. Blacks had made up the bulk of Mississippi's prisoners for generations. And, by extension, they made up the vast bulk of those who cycled back out to the community but spent their lives as political invisibles.

And these results showed themselves in a state where racially charged events, racially motivated voter fraud, and oil-poured-on-fire statements remained commonplace. Mississippi's voter rolls were still not computerized by the 2004 election season, and there was virtually no effective way to share voter information between counties. Advocates believed that people frequently registered to vote in more than one county. And in some, such as Holmes County, because the dead were not removed from the electoral rolls, there were more names on the rolls than there were people living in the county. In some rural districts, I heard rumors of ballot boxes that disappeared down abandoned back roads for prolonged periods of time on route between the polling station and the counting house every election night—time enough, I was told, for extra ballots to be mysteriously stuffed into the box. White poll "observers" at recent elections had stood watch over blacks at some polling stations as they came in to cast their ballots; and voters in some black districts had complained that strangers, whom they said were impersonating Department of Justice officials, sometimes stood guard at voting spots.

A couple years before I visited the state, one of Mississippi's two U.S. senators, Senate majority leader Trent Lott, had made a speech at South Carolina senator Strom Thurmond's one-hundredth birthday bash. America, Lott told the crowd, would probably have been a good deal better off if Thurmond had won the 1948 presidency when he ran on a Dixiecrat segregation-or-die platform. Lott was an old-school Mississippian with widely alleged ties to his state's "prowhite" Council of Conservative Citizens—the heir-apparent to the violently segregationist Citizens Councils of the 1950s and 1960s, which in 2000 boasted thirty-four members of the Mississippi legislature among its members.[4] And while his speech had ultimately attracted enough negative publicity to force his resignation as Senate majority leader, he remained an extremely popular figure in his home state. Two years later, the week I was in Jackson (a state capital in which the old rebel flag still flies) protestors were gearing up to picket the upcoming state fair, because the state, led by Republican governor Haley Barbour, had, for some inexplicable reason, decided to allow a white supremacist group to set up a table at the festivities.[5]

The results also played out against a background of stark poverty. The slums of Jackson look almost like the underside of a seamy Central American city. Many of the bare-bones wooden-plank houses are boarded up, yet clearly lived in, and there is an almost total absence of legitimate economic activity. Not surprisingly, large numbers get caught up in crime from a very young age. And, in response, Mississippi throws the full might of the law at its underclasses. Defendants as young as sixteen are routinely prosecuted as adults, and, when convicted, deprived of the right to vote before they are old enough ever to have exercised that right in the first place. And if they aren't formally disenfranchised, chances are pretty good that, lacking access to reliable information, they nonetheless believe they are.

In 1998, when Human Rights Watch and the D.C.-based Sentencing Project issued a report that found 7.4 percent of adults in Mississippi and fully 28.6 percent of the state's African American male population had lost the right to vote, in theory those numbers overstated the case—since the researchers were deeming all felonies to be offenses that cost a person his or her suffrage.[6] In practice, however, because so few felons in Mississippi are aware of the subtleties of the law, the criminal justice system in Mississippi does serve as a sinkhole down which vast numbers of potential voters fall in precisely the way documented by the Sentencing Project's researchers.

"People that want to vote don't know they can vote. If they knew, I'm almost sure they would vote. But they just don't know they can," a forty-four-year-old African American woman named Willa Womack, who had cycled in and out of jail and prison on drug charges from her teenage years into her thirties, explained. Womack had been out of prison for nearly a decade and now owned a copy shop on historic Farish Street, in the heart of Jackson, just down the street from Miss Peaches' famous soul food restaurant. It was quite an achievement for a woman who had fled a violent home at age fourteen, had ended up homeless and on the streets, and had spent years surviving—illegally—literally beyond the margins of society. "We were told we didn't have the right to vote on anything. I never knew how important it was to vote. I thought that way for a long time. The subject came up and I said 'I don't think I can vote.' Anybody tells you something, it spread like wildfire. How long you think it take if someone tells you you can't vote before it spreads? It's been years and years people telling you you can't vote. You live in a slum area, you're not counted. So all this plays in the same way." In the late 1990s, voter registration people from the Southern Christian Leadership Conference (SCLC) convinced a skeptical Womack that she *could,* in fact, vote—and she finally agreed to fill in the registration form on the sidewalk in front of her shop. "I got a voice now," she told me proudly. "I can decide who will be my governor, who will be my president. I have a vote now. You feel like somebody. It's a feeling of relief from where I came from—that I'm actually somebody."

Womack also explained that many people on welfare in Mississippi were scared of voting, worried that any little thing they did to bring attention to themselves might put their food stamps and measly cash payments at risk. "I've been out there with them," Womack continued. "Nobody's going to do anything that'll interrupt the little money you are getting. If you stay quiet, nobody will know who you are." At first I found this hard to believe. *Not being able to vote because you were on welfare? That doesn't make any sense.* And then I remembered some of the other things I'd heard around the country: people who thought they couldn't vote because they'd spent a few days in jail on a misdemeanor charge; the waitress I met in Texas who thought she'd lost the right to vote because she had some unpaid parking tickets.

Throughout Mississippi, as the 2004 election geared up, voter-registration workers encountered numerous people too scared to register. People convicted of crimes as minors. People convicted of crimes as adults. Overwhelmingly, black people scared of any form of contact with authorities they saw as looking for excuses to reincarcerate them. In neighborhood after neighborhood, the grandchildren of the civil rights pioneers from the 1950s were as scared to vote, because of prisons and the threat of prisons, as their grandparents were half a century ago because of the threat of the lynch mob.

"They just don't believe they can vote," explained Nshombi Lambright, of the Jackson ACLU. "They've been told very strongly that they can't vote. Mostly, parole and probation officers are telling them this—but also judges and correctional officers. People aren't even trying to get their vote back. It's hard just getting them to attempt to register. They're terrorized. They're so scared of going back to jail that they won't even try it."

The combination of true disenfranchisement and street rumor stoked by correctional officials and judicial authorities had indeed served to decimate Mississippi's electorate—removing more than enough voters to swing close election results. In 1999, the race for governor was eventually won by Democrat Ronnie Musgrove by slightly more than 1 percent. Although most analysts believe a majority of ex-felons would vote Democratic if given the chance, it is possible that Republican Mike Parker might have been able to win had Mississippi's large number of disenfranchised been able to vote.[7] Four years later, the tables were turned when Haley Barbour, an extremely conservative Republican, won the governorship by 60,000 votes. It was a not insignificant margin, but, at the same time, like the previous gubernatorial race, this one was also one conceivably within the margins of doubt created by the disenfranchisement epidemic.

That same year, Gary Anderson ran for state treasurer. Anderson had previously been the state's fiscal officer, rendering him well qualified for the job. He was also African American, and, had he won, he would have been the first African American elected to a statewide position in Mississippi since Reconstruction more than 130 years earlier. But Anderson didn't win. He was defeated by a few percentage points by Tate Reeves, a political novice and a staunch conservative who had the advantage of being white in a state where many whites still wouldn't cast their ballot for a black man and where many blacks had seen their political weight dramatically reduced by modern-day disenfranchisement.

The night of the Cheney/Edwards vice presidential debate, I stayed in Bennie Turner's town, West Point. It was now only four weeks until the election, and, after the previous week's presidential debate, the polls showed the candidates were in a dead-heat again. I'm not a religious man, but I have to admit I was praying Edwards would pummel Cheney; that he would expose the rotten hypocrisies at the core of the Bush administration. After several days in Mississippi, I wanted conservative blood to be at least metaphorically spilled during the candidates' confrontation.

As staged television debates go, it wasn't a bad show. The two men jousted on the war in Iraq, terrorism, health care, jobs. Amazingly, neither of them, nor the presidential candidates the week before, talked about crime, about being "tough on crime," about building prisons. Terrorism had quite convincingly, and arguably for far better reason, replaced run-of-the-mill crime as public enemy number one. It was a world away from the central themes of elections in the 1990s, when every politician running for office spent much of his or her time out-toughing opponents on the crime issue.

But the legacy of that era of hysterical, ill-thought-out responses to crime, to drugs, and to the collapse of social order in many impoverished neighborhoods was still playing itself out all too clearly all around the country. There were still two million incarcerated Americans. And while politicians might not have been proposing reams of new legislation that would ramp up the size of the prison system still more, they were also extremely reluctant to discuss redressing some of the excesses from the 1980s and 1990s, for fear of opening themselves up to charges of being "soft on crime." Crime, and prisons, had, in a sense, become invisible topics. The prison system had entered a period of stasis, with the total number of prisons and prisoners neither rising nor falling by much. And there were, because of permanent disenfranchisement laws, many millions more who had been removed from the political process over the previous decades. In a state like Mississippi, mass incarceration had, by 2004, served to undo a good part of the legacy of the 1965 Voting Rights Act.

"People that don't want you to do something," Willa Womack mused, "have a knack of leaving something open. 'If I were you, I wouldn't do that because you may get yourself in trouble.' To me, that's intimidation. You don't actually threaten a person. You just leave something open and they can figure out what you're talking about. When something's being repeated time after time, it spreads. It's lack of education. People are not educated. They're not making people aware that they can vote. When you let 'em sleep, they sleep."

12
The Governor and the Pot Smoker

I crossed into Alabama just east of Columbus. For a few hours it seemed like normalcy reigned again. Suddenly the radio waves had stations on them. My cell phone got reception. There were decent cafés and nice restaurants in the heart of Birmingham. And, for a while, I could see why, one hundred years ago, the town had been nicknamed the "magic city." It seemed vibrant, full of life. But then I started interviewing people, and my mood rapidly sank once more.

Seventeen years earlier, Governor Guy Hunt—the state's first Republican chief executive since the Reconstruction era—had diverted about $200,000 from his inaugural fund into his own pocket, using the money to buy cattle, make home improvements, and even purchase a large lawn mower. Hunt's activities came to light some years later, and in 1993, a few months after he had gained national attention by ordering the Confederate battle flag to be flown above the state capitol building, he was prosecuted and convicted of violating state ethics laws. Although he was not sentenced to prison time, the felony conviction was enough to have him removed from office.[1]

Over the next several years, the disgraced politician appealed his conviction in state and federal courts. But none of the courts were willing to reverse it. Finally, in May 1997, Hunt took his case to the state's Pardons and Parole Board. He probably calculated he'd have a better shot of success in front of a three-man board, two of whose members he'd personally appointed.

Hunt's gamble paid off. The board promptly recommended he be pardoned, and then-governor Fob James—a man who would later achieve notoriety by threatening to use National Guard troops to defend a judge's Ten Commandments display in the face of a federal ruling that it violated the separation of church and state—promptly followed this recommendation. The following year, 1998, five years after he had been removed from office, Hunt ran for governor again, the latest in a long line of Southern political figures to have fallen afoul of the law and then to have resurrected their careers. He came in third, with 8 percent support—not enough to win, but a far remove from the dog days when Hunt not only couldn't run for office but didn't even have the right to cast his own vote.

Six years later, another of Alabama's ex-governors, Don Siegelman, would be indicted on federal felony charges alleging that he helped friends rig bids for state contracts.

Perhaps Hunt was just lucky in getting his political rights restored so easily; or, perhaps, in a state renowned for crony politics and crooked back-door dealings, in a state that, like Mississippi, had a long history of making it easy for whites to vote and difficult for blacks, he knew the right people and had the right color skin.

As late as 1981, when a congressional committee investigating abuses of the 1965 Voting Rights Act conducted field hearings in Alabama, several counties in the state still had open voting, with voters having to cast their ballots in a public setting rather than in the privacy of a voting booth. It was largely because of Alabama's abuses that Congress amended the original Voting Rights Act in 1982 to include a "results test"; no longer did plaintiffs have to prove that a particular policy or action was intended to be racially discriminatory. They now only had to prove that the results of the action were discriminatory. Well into the 1980s, cities and counties in Alabama held what were known as "at-large elections." In an at-large election, if a city had, for example, seven councilmen, the entire city would vote for all seven officials, rather than having the seven districts each hold their own election. The result of this process was that the political power of black neighborhoods was diluted. In cities where, for example, three of the seven districts were majority black, at-large elections would often result in the election of deeply conservative all-white city councils. In 1985, advocacy groups successfully sued over 180 districts in the state, forcing them to end this practice. As a result, majority black districts were created, and the number of black elected officials soared.

But, despite this, Alabama's legislature remained, as did the population, majority white, and, given the realities of Southern politics, that meant it continued to be dominated by a mixture of conservative yellow-dog Democrats and conservative Republicans. In many ways, the state was still wrestling with the legacy of slavery, and with the legal mechanisms set in place during Jim Crow that were designed to minimize black access to the political system. Governor Hunt's decision to fly the Confederate battle flag might have looked inept to a national audience, but, on the ground, a majority of the Alabama electorate apparently supported the move.

Like other parts of the South, Alabama's disenfranchisement problem in the early twenty-first century had its origins in the state constitution passed by the architects of Jim Crow a little more than one hundred years earlier, in 1901. Article VIII, 182, of that document provided for the disenfranchisement of felons and also of those convicted of any crime, including misdemeanors, deemed to involve "moral turpitude." Specific crimes listed in the constitution included bigamy, adultery, sodomy, miscegenation, and crimes against nature, as well as more obvious crimes such as murder, rape, robbery, arson, and perjury. More vaguely, however, the definition of a crime of moral turpitude was not defined, intended as a catchall category designed to allow local election officials to remove people from the voter rolls at their discretion. At the constitutional convention, speaker after speaker averred that this was intended as a *legal* method of barring blacks from voting; and, when the constitution was ratified by a popular vote, its selling point was precisely that fact: that the document was successfully circumventing the post–Civil War provisions intended to ensure blacks access to the rights of citizenship. It was a series of nudges and winks, a set of provisions that talked about criminal justice when everyone knew it was really referring to race and to the disenfranchisement of blacks.

An act of moral turpitude, the Alabama supreme court declared in 1916, adding its imprimatur to the issue, meant something that was "immoral in itself, regardless of the fact whether it is punishable by law. The doing of the act itself, and not its prohibition by statute, fixes the moral turpitude."[2] In other words, it was pretty much whatever the electoral registrars said that it was.

In 1985, sixty-nine years after the Alabama supreme court had upheld the law, the U.S. Supreme Court heard a case titled *Hunter v. Underwood,* brought by people convicted of misdemeanors who argued that Alabama was disenfranchising them in a way that violated the Equal Protection Clause of the Fourteenth Amendment to the U.S. Constitution. In a unanimous decision, the court found that laws reflecting "purposeful racial discrimination" were unconstitutional, and the state was ordered to change its system. As a result, the "moral turpitude" provisions were dropped, and Alabama adopted a uniform disenfranchisement system: anyone convicted of a felony lost the right to vote, and only the governor could, at his discretion, and on the advice of the Pardons and Parole Board, restore that right. Nevertheless, despite the cosmetic changes, the effect of the system remained the disproportionate disenfranchisement of Alabama's African American population.

When a black legislator named Pat Davis was convicted of using her office to sell political favors to the tune of $19,000 in 1995, she was sent to prison, stripped of her right to vote, and barred from ever holding elective office again. When Davis came out of federal prison in 2000 and applied for a pardon so that she could vote again, legislators lined up to denounce her; newspapers in Alabama editorialized against pardoning her; and, after briefly considering her case, the board held that she was not a fit candidate for a pardon. One newspaper editorialized that "a pardon would have allowed Davis to run for office again, if she so desired, and that's simply not acceptable. An elected official who violates the public trust never should be eligible to run again."

Undeniably, Davis had behaved appallingly. She had slid from being an upright politician to violating the public trust and becoming a crook. But it was quite a leap to go from there to saying that, even after she completed her prison sentence, she should never again be allowed to vote—especially since Hunt had been pardoned for crimes involving ten times as much money. "It's a terrible feeling, being disenfranchised," said Davis. "It takes so much away from you. My parents left the South in the fifties because they didn't have the right to vote. For me, now, not to have the right to vote, it's like starting all over again. You lose everything."

The campaign was into its final few weeks now. November 2 was looming on the horizon, a great obstacle at the end of the road. Unlike almost everywhere else in the country, Alabama was still registering voters. That, however, was about the only concession the state, whose motto is "We dare defend our rights," had made to encourage voter participation.

Across Alabama around 250,000 people had lost the right to vote over the course of two decades of rapid increase in the number of people convicted of felonies—as many as those disenfranchised in California, a state with ten times the population of Alabama but with only a temporary loss of voting rights for felons. "I met person after person that had been disenfranchised," recalled thirty-one-year-old state representative Merika Coleman, an African American antipoverty activist, about her 2002 campaign in Birmingham. "Just knocking on people's doors. 'I'd love to vote for you, but I can't vote.' Some would tell and some wouldn't. I met a man in his mid-forties. He was a minister. After I'd done my whole spiel, he let me know he couldn't vote. Because of something he'd done when he was young. He was a man of the gospel, a taxpayer, and he couldn't vote."

After staying out of trouble for at least three years following the end of their sentences, felons in Alabama then had to jump through a series of hoops to get their vote restored. They had to fill in a multipage form, travel to the state capital of Montgomery to submit DNA samples for a state database, convince the three-person Pardons and Parole Board to recommend a pardon, and then hope that the governor agreed to follow their advice. Hardly anyone successfully made it through every step of this process.

In 2004, about half of the voteless were white and half black—which, since the state's population was only one-quarter black, meant that African Americans were dramatically over represented in the criminal justice system. And the situation had been worsening in recent years as more and more young African Americans were swept into the prison system during the "War on Drugs." By the end of 2004, over 60 percent of the state's prisoners were black; thus, down the road, as the numbers of disenfranchised ex-felons increased, Alabama's voteless population would be increasingly African American. Best-guess estimates had it that one out of every three adult black males in the state was, to all practical intents, already permanently removed from the political process—the same shocking statistic that I had already encountered in Memphis. "We were very successful in changing the election system," Jerome Gray, the field director of the Alabama Democratic Conference, explained, in his law office a few blocks east of the imposing, but coldly austere, architecture that makes up the government district of downtown Montgomery. "But the one thing none of us were paying attention to were the laws being passed that were disenfranchising blacks faster than they could register to vote. We were looking at the old barriers; few of us were paying attention to the criminal laws that were disenfranchising people."

"Before I realized I was disenfranchised," a one-time drug felon and voting rights activist named David Sadler explained, "I didn't vote because I didn't think it mattered. Once I knew it was taken away from me, it became my mission to vote. It's a right the poorest person in the country has and the richest person in the country has. Once they take it away from you, that's when you want it most."

Disenfranchisement, tied in to an expanded penal system, has had a huge impact on Alabama's political makeup. It's likely that there is no state in the country where so many crucial elections have been affected by the removal of low-income and minority voters from the political process.

In 1996, Republican Bob Riley narrowly won U.S. Congressional District Three. The district was 30 percent African American—a higher percentage than all but one other congressional district in Alabama. Until 1996, it had sent Democrats to Washington, but, as more and more of its population was removed into the prison system and then returned to the community voteless, its eligible electorate had become more Republican.

Six years later, Bob Riley was elected governor, beating incumbent Democrat Don Siegelman by a little more than 3,000 votes out of over 1.3 million cast statewide.[3] (When he was secretary of state, in 1982, Siegelman was the only white official in the Alabama state government to support an expansion of the Voting Rights Act.) Riley's victory can be attributed at least in part to the fact that so many low-income and African American citizens had lost their right to vote; it can, however, likely also be attributed to the allegations of corruption surrounding Siegelman—allegations that later resulted in a felony indictment. That same year, District Three returned another Republican, this time by just under 4,000 votes. At the same time, Alabama's two black supreme court justices were defeated in their reelection bids, leading to the creation of an all-white court.

There is nothing wrong, in and of itself, with an election being closely fought and narrowly won. All other things being equal, close elections are signs of a vibrant, healthy democracy, indicative of debate occurring and incumbents being kept on their toes. But there *is* something wrong when the population as a whole leans in one direction while the eligible voting population leans toward another political party because significant numbers of potential supporters of one party have had their vote taken away. When elections are tipped by the votes or nonvotes of a fraction of a percent of the electorate, as occurred when Riley won election in 2002 (and as occurred with the presidential election result in Florida in 2000) and when over 7 percent of a state's voting-age population has been disenfranchised (as is the case in Alabama, many of them for low-end crimes committed years or even decades earlier), then close election results cannot but be controversial, cannot but have question marks as to their legitimacy.

It struck me—as I drove through Alabama from Birmingham south to the state capital of Montgomery, from Montgomery southeast to Dothan, and from Dothan west along back roads cut through a forested landscape scoured by recent hurricanes with fallen trees everywhere and houses and trailers with walls and roofs destroyed—that I was witnessing a terrible paradox: on one level, America in 2004 was more democratic than it had ever been before. People were standing for election, and voting in elections for everything from the local school board on up to the presidency, as the signs on front lawns, even in remote rural corners of Alabama, and the bumper stickers on cars testified. Numerous states had embraced an initiative process that, increasingly, was bypassing legislators and handing critical decision-making power directly to citizens. California's voter guide, which I had recently received in the mail and set aside to read before casting an early absentee ballot, was the size of a small book, containing detailed descriptions of propositions that would affect the state's criminal justice system, mental health services, stem cell research, casino industry, local-state government relationships, the funding of emergency services, and a host of other issues. If I was bored with getting my news from the papers and television stations and radio shows I read and watched and listened to, I could always go online and browse literally millions of Web sites on virtually every topic ever conceived. The Internet was practically a modern-day Athenian agora, a space of public debate unparalleled in its immediacy. And this cornucopia of information was, interestingly, forcing political candidates to be more focused in their attempts to reach out to voters: in the months and months of presidential campaigning that were drawing to a close, the candidates had crisscrossed the country ceaselessly, jumping from town hall meeting to railway station gathering to stadium rally day in and day out, all instantly conveyed to audiences of tens of millions by the breathy coverage of the twenty-four-hour news networks.

Yet, at the same time, millions of people were being internally banished—were being told they could not take part in politics—and this was fueling a cycle of political disinvolvement and a spiral down into enforced apathy.

In other words, for the enfranchised, relatively affluent, majority, it was possible that things had never been so democratic. Yet for the disenfranchised, relatively impoverished, minority, for those living in the grim, economically destitute, drug-infested back streets of towns like Birmingham and Montgomery, at no time in modern, post–Jim Crow American history had participation been more illusory.

De Tocqueville came to believe that there was nothing more intolerable to the democratic mind-set than the creation of rigid ingrained differences between supposedly equal citizens. Nothing, he wrote, was more antithetical to the spirit of democracy than the imposition of some form of political caste system. Yet laws like Alabama's that permanently bar one set of citizens from political participation lead to precisely that kind of legislated social hierarchy.

Since the late 1990s, an African American representative named Yvonne Kennedy had sponsored bills to make vote restoration easier in Alabama. Every year, the proposals were shot down. Finally, in 2003, the black caucus in the Democrat-controlled state legislature convinced their Democratic colleagues to link passage of a Republican-sponsored Voter I.D. law to reenfranchisement legislation. Having secured this commitment, they pushed for a bill that would make the vote-restoration process slightly easier, although still leaving it one of the most restrictive in the country. The proposal would have listed a series of offenses the perpetrators of which would be eligible for fast-track reenfranchisement once they'd applied for a certificate of eligibility. (Excluded from this process would be those convicted of murder, rape, treason, impeachment, possession of obscene material, and sexual crimes.) It would have expanded the Pardons and Parole Board to seven members, appointed to reflect the "racial, gender, and geographic diversity of the state," on the assumption that an expanded body would be less likely to wilt under "tough-on-crime" pressure than a panel of three, would be more likely to make fair recommendations, and, because of the larger number of people involved, would be better able to speedily examine applications. It would have mandated that the board issue recommendations within fifty days of a person's filing to get their vote back. And it would also have created a presumption of eligibility, limiting the governor's ability to arbitrarily deny the vote to people who had fulfilled all of their sentencing requirements. Voting rights activists voiced their support of the measure by holding a large rally on the steps of the statehouse.

Despite the Republican leadership's agreement to support this, freshmen GOP legislators tried to filibuster. When that proved unsuccessful, and a majority of legislators voted in favor, Governor Riley promptly vetoed the bill, perhaps leery of bringing more people onto the voter rolls who might turn around and help vote him out of office. Led by the Reverend Jesse Jackson and members of the state's black caucus, hundreds of people rallied on the statehouse steps again, this time in protest.

Only afterward, when Democrats threatened to withdraw their support for the governor's tax-reform legislation—urgently needed to keep the state from sliding into bankruptcy—unless he came out in favor of reenfranchisement legislation, did Riley withdraw his opposition. In September 2003, a limited reform, containing similar language to the earlier version, was signed into law.

But, as with other states that had halfheartedly moved away from permanent disenfranchisement, Alabama did so without spending any money to publicize the move, without making any effort to educate voters in poor neighborhoods about the change. Thus while many did try to get their voting rights restored, tens of thousands of others likely had no idea this was even a possibility.

Moreover, the Pardons and Parole Board began stonewalling, not issuing certificates of eligibility to applicants within the fifty-day timeframe mandated by the 2003 legislation—and thus rendering them unable to register to vote in the November election—and not sending out the legally required letters to applicants who had been rejected because they hadn't paid off all their court-ordered restitution fees explaining why they had not been issued their certificates and how they could make themselves eligible. As a result, by the time I arrived in Alabama, with less than two weeks left to register to vote in the state, only about 1,600 felons out of the over 200,000 disenfranchised had managed to get their rights back. Many hundreds more had applied and were awaiting word from the board, and many more still had been rejected because they hadn't paid off every last cent of their fines and restitution fees.

"I've written to Montgomery three times to try to get my vote restored," one Birmingham woman exclaimed in a fury. "And I have not gotten a reply." The woman had slipped into drug addiction in the early 1990s, and had used her position as an employee of a local bank to create phony bank accounts under false names, from which she had then withdrawn thousands of dollars using ATM cards she had issued to herself. By the time she was convicted three years later, however, she had gotten clean. She served her time without any incidents and had come off of parole several years before I interviewed her; in the years since, she had become increasingly active in her local church and increasingly interested in politics. Unable to vote, she planned to spend Election Day driving elderly neighbors to and from the polling stations.

In all likelihood, the Pardons and Parole Board had simply neglected to tell this woman they weren't restoring her right to vote because she hadn't paid off all of her restitution—which, given the amount of money she'd stolen to fund her addiction, she was unlikely ever to be able to pay off. In practice, this lady had committed a crime that she would never be able to fully repay and which would, therefore, serve to forever deprive her of the right to vote. "At first I felt it was a backlog, paperwork piled up. I made excuses for them. Then, after a year had passed, I began to get irritated. It kind of pisses me off. Even though I've done what the judge said I had to do, I've completed all of that. When I got ready to leave the facility I was in, you have to meet the warden and the officer in charge of your case there. They said I'd been a model inmate, no discipline, no trouble, nothing. If I've done all I'm supposed to have done, how can I get my life right when the system won't let me?"

In Montgomery, I met a fifty-five-year-old African American man named Clinton Drake. Drake had been arrested in 1988 for possession of marijuana. Five years later, he had been arrested again, this time for having what he claimed to be about $10 worth of the drug on him. It was, he remembered, enough to roll about five joints with. Because it was the second time he'd been caught with pot, under Alabama state law the DA had the option to charge him with a felony carrying enhanced sentencing. And this he did. Facing between ten and twenty years in prison, Drake, a Vietnam veteran and, at the time, a cook on a local Air Force base, took his public defender's advice and accepted a plea bargain. In exchange for pleading guilty, he would *only* have to spend five years behind bars. *Five years for $10 of pot. One year for every $2 worth of the drug.* He was sent to the Ventress drug treatment prison facility, where, presumably, the state "cured" him of his liking for pot; he was then moved to Staton prison, then to Red Eagle honor camp, and finally to the Montgomery work release facility. Even given the rock-bottom services provided by Alabama's backward prison system, Drake's five years behind bars on a $10 pot charge would have cost Alabama over $50,000.

In some ways, though, Drake was lucky. Until Alabama's budget went into the toilet at the start of the twenty-first century and it began to look for ways to cut its bloated correctional budget, nonviolent habitual offenders could be sent to prison for life on a marijuana charge. In 1999, I interviewed several middle-aged men in the prison at St. Clair who were all serving precisely this sentence. None of them were eligible for parole.

Drake didn't see it that way. He was enraged by what had happened to his life. When he was arrested, Drake had had a good job at the Air Force base. Now, he drifted from one construction job to another and was, when I met him, unemployed. At least as painful to him, he was going to have to sit out the upcoming election, unable to cast a vote in a wartime election, despite the fact that his eldest son had served in the first Gulf War and his youngest son was, at the time, serving in Iraq, in the aftermath of the second Gulf War. And, unless he could somehow scrape together $900 to cover his outstanding court costs—a fortune for an unemployed man in a state with benefits as measly as that of Alabama—he would never be able to vote again.

"I put my life on the line for the country," Drake said bitterly, a tall man in an Adidas baseball cap, T-shirt, and jeans, with most of his upper front teeth missing and his goatee gray. "To me, not voting is not right; it lead to a lot of frustration, a lot of anger. My son's in Iraq. In the army just like I was. My oldest son, he fought in the first Persian Gulf conflict. He was in the Marines. This is my baby son over there now. But I'm not able to vote. They say I owe nine hundred dollars in fines. To me, that's a poll tax. You've got to pay to vote. It's 'restitution,' they say. I came off parole on October 13, 1999, but I'm still not allowed to vote. Last time I voted was in '88. Bush versus Dukakis. Bush won. I voted for Dukakis. If it was up to me, I'd vote his son out this time too. I know a lot of friends got the same cases like I got, not able to vote. A lot of guys doing the same things I was doing. Just marijuana. They treat marijuana in Alabama like you committed treason or something. I was on the 1965 voting rights march from Selma. I was fifteen years old. At eighteen, I was in Vietnam fighting for my country. And now? Unemployed and they won't allow me to vote."

I drove southeast to Dothan the next morning, through the beautiful forests of the southern part of the state. I saw buzzards coming out from the tree cover and snapping at the rotting flesh of animals killed by speeding cars. They'd tear at the red meat, and only lazily, begrudgingly hop off to the side of the road just before my car arrived at their feasting spot. The ghastly birds seemed an apt metaphor for some of the excesses of what passes for that state's criminal justice system. It's unfathomable to me that lives can be held so cheap.

Dothan was a small town perched just above and just to the west of the Florida panhandle. Its center was crisscrossed with broad avenues lined with malls, with motels, with chain restaurants of varying degrees of quality. Its residential streets were lined with rinky-dink wooden houses, many of which looked no bigger than the third-class booths on old steamer ships. The town felt about as far from anywhere as any middle-of-nowhere place I've visited in America over the years.

John Thomas lived alone in a cluttered little house on the edge of town. He was one hundred years old and blind; but his mind was still sharp and his memories vivid. The centenarian was a pale-skinned African American man, with a shaved head, a slight mustache, and a gray suit. Hanging in Thomas's living room, behind the chair on which he was planted, was an old sepia photo of Robert E. Lee. It was the second time in a week that I'd seen Lee's face staring down at me. Unlike Gary Chism, however, Thomas volunteered information on why he had the man's image displayed on his wall. He claimed, nonchalantly, that the famous Confederate general was his great-grandfather.

Thomas said that he was in his forties or fifties when he cast his first vote—he couldn't recall the exact year; that he was the first black man in Houston County to vote; and that it had cost him what must then have been the princely sum of $45, paid in the form of a poll tax, to be able to do so. "It was rough on some folks," the old man said simply. "You know, they didn't qualify to vote—some didn't want to, and some didn't know how. They were turning all coloreds down. You had to pay them tax up before you could vote. To the clerk down the courthouse. You had to learn why do you want to vote and answer them questions. Blacks would meet two times a week to learn why you want to vote. Books stated the reason why: the only way to be a citizen in the country you live in is to be able to vote." And, he went on, for those who could pass the literacy test and pay the poll tax, there was the always-present fear of the lynch mob. "You might get killed," he said. "Hung up a tree or something. I seen people hung. I see that up here in Newville. I'd been to Georgia. I had my daddy with me and two twin sisters. Big tree right there and a man hanging from the neck. He'd been shot everywhere. Looked like meat hanging off him." Now, he told me, things were different. "Doesn't cost nothing now," he said. "Everybody ask you now to vote. Now, anyone running for office, they're all going to ask you to vote, ask you to vote for them."

I wanted Thomas's version of political history to be right—the bad old days, followed by a time of calm and universal political participation. But it was too pat. Of course, Thomas was correct when he stated that blacks weren't beaten or lynched for trying to vote these days; many of his neighbors, though, still *were* legally prevented from casting ballots at election time.

There was the mentally ill army veteran who had picked up a low-level drug conviction in 1997 and still couldn't vote. "It make me feel like I'm missing a part of being a responsible adult. I'm an adult and that's one of my rights," he explained. "My responsibility to be a part of society is missing." There was the forty-three-year-old owner of a janitorial business who had recently graduated from college with three associate degrees (in electric technology, industrial electronics, and computer electronics), still disenfranchised as a result of two drug convictions from the 1980s. The man had filled in the application form and had submitted his DNA sample two years previously, and still hadn't heard back from the Pardons and Parole Board. "I voted once, but I ain't never been a regular voter," he explained. "I try to keep up with politics, what's going on in society, now. I guess I feel more valuable now. I've been solid a long time. Once you have a reason to feel like you *do* count, then you get involved in more things." And there was Lorenzo Jones. Jones was in his early forties, and, until he hurt his back and had to have surgery, he had had a job with the Houston Paper Company. After his surgery, he'd had to go on disability. He was a long-time volunteer with the local Boys' Club, coaching their sports teams and counseling teenagers to help them stay away from drugs. He was also one of Dothan's many voteless citizens.

When Lorenzo Jones was eighteen, he voted for the first and only time in his life. Some time shortly afterward, he had gotten drunk and wandered into a stranger's house. He claimed not to have even known why he did this. True or not, the lady of the house, who was home at the time, was not amused. She called the police, and Jones was arrested and charged with breaking and entering. He spent three hours in the county jail and was then released. When his case subsequently came to court, he was told that he could go to prison for between three and ten years. Instead, with the Boys' Club and other groups vouching for his character, the judge sentenced him to three-to-ten years of probation.

But the felony conviction carried the same collateral penalties, regardless of whether he went to prison or not. "The state told me I don't have any rights," Jones recalled, a generation later. "The probation officer told me I lost my rights to vote. I couldn't bear a firearm and I didn't have the right to vote." Until he was notified by suffrage activists in mid-2004 that he could apply for a Certificate of Eligibility, Jones believed he had forever lost his political rights. "Everybody have different stories about it," he explained. "You got to pay this much to get your rights back, you got to do this. I believed it."

When he found out that he could apply to get his vote restored, Jones immediately filled in the paperwork and sent it off to the Pardons and Parole Board. As the election approached, he still had not heard a word back. Come November, he would be, once more, sitting on the sidelines. He had been sitting on the sidelines every election since he was eighteen.

It seemed to me that Jones was a forgotten person, a man whose past was forever trumping his present, a man whose past would likely forever dominate his future. That evening, Bush and Kerry were to debate each other once more. Watching them on television would be the closest Jones would come to participating in an election everyone and their uncle was declaring was one of the most important votes in decades. "I regret it every day," he declared, talking of his drunken felony from nearly a quarter century earlier. "I had goals in life. I had dreams."

13
The Name of the Game Is Total Control

Two days before Halloween, I set out on the final leg of my journey. I flew in to Orlando, into a futuristic terminal with a podlike transport machine whisking fresh-off-the-plane vacationers to the baggage claim area, and immediately was almost knocked down by a surge of adrenaline. I was in Florida. I was in the epicenter. I was exactly where I wanted to be in the final days of one of the most important elections of my lifetime.

I stopped to buy a paper, and saw that John Kerry was delivering a speech in town, at the Expo Center, ten minutes later. I jumped in my rental car, tried to navigate the roadmaps while heading in what I hoped was the right direction, and, of course, found myself lost on the one-way streets of central Orlando, stymied by the repetitive glass skyscrapers and the palm-lined sidewalks. I finally found the Expo Center just as the speech was wrapping up, and, momentarily deflated, drove off to a meeting with staff at a Latino voter-rights organization working to bring out thousands of new voters on Election Day. Within minutes, my sense of deflation had been replaced by a sense of glee—the whole state, it seemed, was awash with politics. There were posters and banners everywhere and innumerable cars were decked out with bumper stickers and impromptu political slogans. It didn't matter that I'd missed the rally. I still felt like a kid in a particularly enormous candy store.

Later on, as I interviewed lawyers and community activists, Kerry traversed the brilliantly sunny, humid state, whipping up supporters from Orlando down to Miami. Bush was following hot on his footsteps, slated to be in Orlando the next day, then in Jacksonville and Gainesville and Miami. Then Kerry was due back in the state for a series of Sunday rallies, and the vice presidential candidates were also jetting in for last-minute speeches further north. Providing what the Democrats must have hoped would be the musical equivalent of a shot of pituitary gland extract, Bruce Springsteen was giving a huge pro-Kerry concert in Miami over the weekend.

As if all of that weren't enough, this was also the day Osama bin Laden got into the fray, with a long video broadcast on the al-Jazeera network. It was an extraordinary day, two days before Halloween, with everything up in the air, and the insanity of the modern world in full throttle. Four days from then, George Bush would either stay as the most powerful man on earth or be preparing to head back to Crawford ("Crawford, Tx, misses its village idiot," read one evocative cardboard banner I saw that weekend), his tail between his legs. Likewise, Kerry would either be the Big Kahuna or a has-been senator valued on the campus lecture circuit as a curiosity item rather than an arbiter of world affairs.

At the two campaign headquarters in Orlando, there was an almost feverish energy; posters and banners and flags and balloons were everywhere, and tired, nerves-frayed volunteers were walking around too fast and snapping at each other, while huge TVs blared the latest news and volunteers wandered in and out picking up posters, collecting tickets for the day's rallies, or just looking for confirmation of their hopes from fellow party workers.

Florida was awhirl with rumors, with a smoglike muck of conspiracy and paranoia floating hazily over the state. Puerto Rican organizers in Orlando recycled rumors they'd been told by friends in Colorado that the GOP was busing in hundreds of volunteers from Colorado whose job it would be to slow down the voter lines and thus presumably prevent people from voting in poor

Democratic precincts in Orlando. The Republicans were already telling all and sundry that they had reason to believe 925 ineligible felons had already cast their ballots, and were preparing to send out "poll watchers" to challenge ineligible voters on election day. An e-mail surfaced, written on May 4, 2004, from a Florida Department of Law Enforcement officer responsible for providing the felon data used in constructing the purge lists to his boss, indicating that experts within the secretary of state's office had suggested to the governor that the list was inaccurate and disproportionately affected African Americans, but that Jeb Bush had brushed the concerns aside. "Donna, Paul Craft called today and told me that yesterday they recommended to the Gov that they 'pull the plug' on the CVDB [the Central Voter Database], primarily because they weren't comfortable with the felon matching program they've got," Jeff Long wrote, referring to his contact at the secretary of state's office. "The Gov rejected their suggestion to pull the plug, so they're 'going live' with it this weekend."[1] The governor, of course, had speedily denied these charges.

Meanwhile, immigrant-rights groups were decrying a registration form in Florida on which voters had to mark two times that they were citizens. Those who marked it only once had, in some counties with Republican elections officials, not been registered. African American activists were denouncing an early-polling system that, they said, was resulting in early polling places opening in affluent white areas but not in impoverished black districts in many counties. Lawyers up and down the state were getting ready for fierce legal triage work and emergency lawsuits, on Election Day and afterward. Ion Sancho, the election supervisor in Leon County, based out of a courthouse across the street from the state capitol building in Tallahassee, was telling any reporter who cared to listen (and many did; Sancho's cell phone was ringing off the hook as he patrolled the lines of voters outside his courthouse, a sun-tanned middle-aged man, in blue jeans, a white shirt, and a bolo tie held in place by a stars-and-stripes pin) that he feared civil unrest and possible rioting should Republicans try to stop African Americans from voting in Florida.

A few weeks earlier, when I had first phoned Sancho to get his take on the felon purge list, he had delivered an extraordinary critique of the Republican Party and their manipulation of the voter rolls. He told me the felon purge lists going back to the late-1990s were rife with errors and "false positives"; that election supervisors around the state knew they were inaccurate, told administration officials so in a series of meetings, but that a politicized secretary of state's office had tried to force them to use these lists anyway. "The only conclusion I can draw is that they did have another agenda," the Leon County supervisor blurted out. "And that was ensuring that the largest possible net had been thrown out to disenfranchise individuals, not because they were felons but because it was part of a policy to disenfranchise voters, particularly African American voters. Florida, in my opinion, was simply a chess piece in a much larger strategic political game being played out across the nation." His state, Sancho told me, became a laboratory for purging voter rolls, a laboratory opened up by an executive and legislature entirely Republican controlled by the late 1990s. It worked in 2000, and so, he said, the Republicans had tried to play the exact same game in 2004. "The game of politics in Florida is played in just as hard-ball a manner as anywhere in the country. The name of the game is total control."

And playing this game created a miasma of rumor and innuendo. The radio stations I listened to as I started driving up and down the state were full of tales, largely unsubstantiated, of vote fraud, of voter intimidation, of a misuse of poll monitors in Florida and Ohio, of lines so long people were having to leave for work without casting ballots. In Miami, the grapevine had it that Republicans were going to vote and then stand in line again, just to create chaos and slow the process down to a crawl. There was also talk of bucket-loads of unsigned absentee ballots making mysterious appearances. One activist in the small central Florida town of Ocala even told me a rumor he'd heard that poll watchers affiliated with David Duke and the Ku Klux Klan were being sent to "watch" voters in some black precincts in the northern reaches of central Florida. On CNN, Walter Cronkite was explaining that it was fairly likely we wouldn't finally know who the president would be until the spring of 2005.

It was, in a way, sick. It was also wonderful. This was the political and legal carnival de Tocqueville glimpsed, the full force of mass culture, the overlay of politics, instant media and lawyering, that he foresaw and shuddered at, but which he saw to be irresistible. It was, after the meanness and blandness and drabness of Alabama and Mississippi, like a mid-autumn Mardi Gras. This was where all the most antidemocratic forces that had been unleashed in modern American politics and politicking had come together; and, to counteract this, it was also the place where American democracy had most vividly come back to life, where cadres of activists and citizen associations—de Tocqueville's beloved private groupings that he believed were necessary to keep the democratic system from sliding into a centralized tyranny—were patrolling the back alleys of the system, trying to make sure that even the lowliest of citizens was allowed to exercise his or her right to vote.

I loved it. I felt the same rush I used to feel when I had done political party grunt work in England as a teenager, knocking on doors, canvassing, trying to convince those who seemed to be wobbly—who seemed to almost want someone to knock on their door and convince them of a cause—learning when to cut and run when the person was clearly not going to be swayed. I was good at it back then, but I'd been out of the fray for over a decade.

Now, in Florida, I was a political junky getting fix after fix after fix straight into the bloodstream. Here was democracy in action—warts and flaws and incompletions and corruptions and all. There were merely a handful of hours left in this campaign now, and all over the country lines were forming with people trying to vote early; voter registration was up by millions over the last election. In city after city in Florida, lines hundreds of people long slowly snaked their way into early voting sites. Nobody wanted to leave. Nobody wanted to risk waiting till Tuesday and then finding there was some sort of chaos that prevented them casting their votes.

It was shaping up to be an incredible finish. All the more ironic that, given this feverish political interest, millions were forcibly removed from the process. In these final days, the candidates really were scraping the barrel—given the law of diminishing returns, they must have been spending thousands of dollars on advertisements and mailings and rally organizing for every swing voter they were convincing at this point in the game—and yet there was still an enormous pool of untapped, unsought-after citizens. It was like trying to solve the energy crisis by opening up Alaska to oil exploration instead of moving toward a hydrogen fuel cell economy—or something like that.

I had taken three cross-country flights (two overnight and one late evening) in eight days, had chronically underslept for the past week, and was seriously on edge. All I could think about was the upcoming election. All I could talk about were the possible permutations. Luckily, everyone I was interviewing seemed to be just as obsessed. It didn't seem hyperbolic to say that America's future was at stake—that questions as to the country's fundamental national character were being voted on: whether we were a democracy or an empire. Whether we were inclusive or exclusive. Whether we were to be governed by secular or religious institutions. Perhaps in the cold light of day these would seem to be rather too grandiose framing terms; but in the waning days of the longest, most expensive presidential campaign in history, they felt apropos, possibly even understated.

On the Sunday night before the election, Halloween, I stood in line for two hours to attend Kerry's final large Florida rally, in a park in downtown Tampa, sandwiched between a multistory parking lot ringed with gigantic palm trees and a museum, on the other side of which was the city's river. After watching people all over the state standing for hours waiting to vote, it seemed like the least I could do was line up to hear a barnstorming oration. There was something strangely wonderful about standing in the crowd surrounded by young people dressed as witches, goblins, and other Halloween ghouls, while Kerry soared to his (admittedly limited) oratorical heights, telling the crowd how vital the election was, promising he would work to make America respected in the world again.

When I checked my voice mail afterward, there was another anxious message urging me to look into the story of the KKKer doubling up as a "poll watcher" to prevent felons and other ineligible voters from participating in the upcoming election.

In a way, Florida had never had time to calm down after the 2000 debacle. It had lived through the lawsuits and the bitterness and the sense of growing mutual suspicion for four years, its political mechanism—the underbelly of the system that was usually hidden from view—exposed for all the world to see. Like a house the front of which has been knocked in by a wrecking ball, the wires and pipes and rafters all askew were painfully visible to the naked eye. And, at the forefront of this rancor was the issue of voting rights for ex-felons.

In the late 1990s, momentum had begun building in the legislature to make it easier for Florida's growing number of felons to get their vote restored. There were news articles in 1998 and 1999 suggesting that reform was imminent. But, despite the growing support for change, attempts at changing the law were killed off in committee. As the state's legislature and executive and administrative machinery increasingly fell under the sway of conservative Republicans, so any move to expand the voter base ran into more and more opposition. And so, going into the 2000 election,

Florida had had a larger disenfranchised population than any other state in the country, with the possible exception of Texas. It had also undergone a more aggressive "purging" effort of potentially ineligible voters than any other state.

But going into the 2000 election, few people were paying attention to what seemed an esoteric, almost technocratic, problem. *Felon disenfranchisement? Come on. Surely there are a million bigger issues to worry about.* News organizations neglected the story until after the tied-election outcome. And even then they spent far more time and energy analyzing hanging chads and butterfly ballots than detailing the issue of hundreds of thousands of people not voting in the first place because the state had barred them from doing so.

I wrote articles on this hidden scandal, and a handful of others also began pushing the topic.[2] Gradually, over the following years, a critical mass of attention developed; civil rights groups, human rights monitors, the congressional black caucus, and numerous other organizations started talking about mass disenfranchisement.[3] Ultimately, going into the 2004 election, the loss of suffrage experienced by upward of 7 percent of Florida's adults became one of the most widely reported stories of the political season.

A number of developments had forced the issue to the fore, not least of which was a lawsuit filed before the 2000 election, *Johnson v. Bush*,[4] which evolved into a lengthy legal battle that bounced between state and federal courts throughout the 2000 to 2004 period, picking up media attention each step of the way.

Thomas Johnson was originally a New Yorker, from Brooklyn. He was fifty-five years old when I met him in the conservative northern Florida town of Gainesville, where he had resided since 1995 since coming off his last stint of parole in the Big Apple for a series of drug-related crimes. A tall, powerfully built African American man with a thin, graying mustache and a kindly smile, Johnson had spent much of his adult life spiraling further and further into drug addiction. Heroin, crack—if it gave him a rush, Johnson wanted it. By the time he was in his forties, Johnson was bouncing between prison and New York's streets. He'd lost his job and he'd lost his home. All he had left were his drugs.

And then, somehow, something inside him told him to stop. And he did. Since the 1990s, he'd turned his life around in a dramatic fashion—he claimed in the wake of a born-again experience in a church ministering to the downtrodden somewhere in Manhattan. He was now a devout, and extremely conservative, Christian; he ran a faith-based reentry program for ex-prisoners that he called House of Hope, supported by the goodwill of local Gainesville businesses and churches, and he had become a familiar figure on the redemption-via-God circuit in Florida. Johnson counted much of Florida's political elite, including Governor Jeb Bush, among his acquaintances. Newspapers around the state frequently wrote articles on Johnson and on the clients he worked with—they were tacked up on the walls of his living room–cum–office, alongside the motivational Jesus Loves You–type posters and the various certificates of achievement Johnson had picked up along the way. Churches and schools invited him to give lectures. In many ways, the displaced New Yorker had become a poster child of redemption.

But when Johnson tried to register to vote in Gainesville, he was told he couldn't—even though his crimes had been committed in New York, a state that automatically restored felons' right to vote after they'd completed their prison and parole sentences. It didn't seem constitutional; states didn't have the power to ignore, or nullify, the suffrage provisions of other states. And so Johnson contacted some attorneys, and they decided to sue. Because so many Floridians were affected by disenfranchisement laws, the attorneys had it classified as a class-action lawsuit.

A couple of years after Johnson launched his litigation, he received a letter in the mail from the Office of Executive Clemency, informing him that—mysteriously—his rights had been restored.[5]

On September 11, 2002, Alachua County issued Johnson his voter registration card—number 981473358, precinct 68C. Not long afterward, the state agreed that it did not have the power to remove the vote from people who'd been reenfranchised in other states and who had then moved to Florida. The broader issue of disenfranchisement for Florida felons still remained—and, because of this, the Johnson lawsuit continued—but at least one group of citizens, making up over 100,000 people, would now be getting their suffrage back.

Ironically, given the Republican Party's hostility to reenfranchisement, Johnson—a staunch opponent of abortion and gay marriage, a man morally opposed to welfare, and in favor of lowering taxes on businesses—was going to cast his first presidential vote for George W. Bush. His front yard was studded with Republican posters, and his old minivan was, by late October, essentially a motorized GOP advertisement. Johnson told me about the anger this political choice of his aroused among many of his friends and relatives. He did an impression of a cousin of his—"a Christian woman"—practically clawing him in the face in fury when he informed her how he intended to vote. But he didn't care. What was important to him was that he now had the right to exercise his political choice again.

At some point, shortly after the 2000 vote, the governor's office admitted that well over 400,000 people, by its own conservative count, who had fully finished their sentences and were living in the community again, remained disenfranchised.

Lawyers from the Florida Justice Institute (FJI) then filed another lawsuit, *Florida Conference of Black State Legislators et al v. Michael Moore* [the then-secretary of the Department of Corrections], asserting that the Department of Corrections was failing in its statutory duty to help felons coming out of prison and off parole or probation begin the process of applying to have their rights restored. Between 1992 and 2001, the lawsuit claimed, just under 125,000 felons had not been given the application forms they were supposed to have received. (Randall Berg, FJI's lead attorney on the case, claimed that the then-attorney general for Florida, Bob Butterworth, subsequently phoned Berg and admitted to him that the cabinet had known about this problem but had chosen to ignore it because they lacked the manpower to rectify it.)[6] In 2002, a circuit court in Leon County ordered the Department of Corrections to make a good-faith effort to contact these 125,000 people and send them application forms, and by November 2004, about 22,000 of these men and women had gotten their vote restored.

Yet it seemed that however many lawsuits were lost or settled by the state, the disenfranchisement scandal simply wouldn't go away. Shortly before the 2004 election, the *Miami Herald* reported that over 200,000 felons had been denied clemency by the Office of Executive Clemency over the previous few years.[7]

Finally, fueled by the work of a Democratic state senator named Mandy Dawson, momentum gathered for a ballot initiative that would make it easier for felons to get their vote back. While not enough petition signatures were collected to put it on the ballot in 2004, activists were using the 2004 election as a springboard to gather signatures for the following election cycle.

The thing that really pushed the story into the headlines, however, and kept it there was the secretary of state's extraordinary decision to repeat, in 2004, the practice pioneered in 2000 of using private companies to merge various state databases and create lists of "possible felons" to be removed from the voter rolls. The action attracted so much scrutiny, and aroused such a high degree of outrage, that the secretary of state's office was ultimately forced to scrap this purge list-redux—but not before a whole lot more damage had been done to the state's already fragile political reputation.

For months, I'd been trying to get interviews with the key

players in the disenfranchisement saga. ChoicePoint had refused to permit conversations about the chaos of 2000. Now, lobbyists and executives for Accenture, the Bermuda-based company with numerous ties to the Republican Party hired to repeat the purge in 2004 through the creation of a central voter database—though mandated to use tighter matching criteria, negotiated during the settlement to the *NAACP v. Katherine Harris* lawsuit, than that in place in 2000—ignored numerous phone calls from me.[8] The closest I got to an interview was with a public affairs spokesman, based out of Reston, Virginia, named Peter Soh, who told me the development of the purge list was the responsibility of a business unit with the rather Orwellian name of Accenture E-Democracy Services. As ChoicePoint had stated, Soh also argued that if there were flaws in the product, those flaws were the fault of Florida's secretary of state's office. "They provided all the information," he averred. "They have to. We're a vendor. We don't maintain lists."[9]

Accenture might well have had partisan political connections—and they had, it is true, subcontracted out part of the database-compilation work to a company named Election.com, whose owners, *Newsday* reported,[10] included a group of anonymous Saudi businessmen, presumably somewhat favorably disposed to seeing a continuation of the Bush White House—but they were correct that much of the blame did lie with the secretary of state. In essence, both DBT/ChoicePoint and Accenture had been given deeply flawed, outdated, and haphazardly collected lists of names, and had then been asked to set up a tracking mechanism based on these criteria. Not surprisingly, in making the tracking system more efficient, they had, in essence, made it easier to remove from the electoral rolls the "wrong" people.

When I phoned state agencies and senior political figures to get their comments on this problem and on the broader issue of mass disenfranchisement, they also sealed their lips. The secretary of state's office, now under the control of a Republican operative named Glenda Hood, declined to talk about it. The Office of Executive Clemency, I was told by a spokesperson, didn't discuss their clemency deliberations. I left numerous messages with the house majority leader and the speaker of the house, both dyed-in-the-wool Republicans. Neither returned my calls.

I guess it wasn't too surprising they didn't want to talk. The list was a scandal—a massive series of blots on the country's democratic credentials large enough to double as a Jackson Pollock painting. Every major urban area—Miami-Dade, Orlando, Gainesville, Jacksonville, Palm Beach—had thousands of voters removed. Almost half of these lost voters were African American. Hardly any of them were Cuban American—the one Hispanic grouping in America reliably prone to voting overwhelmingly Republican. (Only sixty-one Hispanics of any background showed up on the list of over 47,000 people.) And policy analysts who delved into it further found that nearly 60 percent of those on the list were registered Democrats, while fewer than 20 percent were registered Republicans.

But regardless of whether the flawed list hurt Republicans or Democrats more, the one undeniable loser was the democratic political process itself. At the end of the day, this was a question of fairness, and, because of the shoddy ways in which the list had been constructed, there was precious little of that commodity on display.

Somehow a name-matching database system had been created that failed to identify almost all Hispanic names—largely because the Florida Department of Law Enforcement's electronic database didn't have a field to input "Hispanic" under the category of "race," and the matching software developed by Accenture wouldn't generate a match unless the "race" of the suspected felon tallied with the "race" of a voter with the same name. When I requested more information on this strange omission from the Florida Department of Law Enforcement, I received an e-mail brush-off that I was, by now, all too familiar with: "As you know from widespread media accounts, the Secretary of State discontinued using the list after some technical glitches arose," wrote the department's public information administrator, Tom Berlinger. "Since that time, the issues surrounding the list are currently under review and audit by the Office of the Inspector General within the Florida Department of State. Out of respect to that active and ongoing process, we will be withholding any further comment on the matter. In that light, neither Mr. Long [the employee who had written the e-mail alleging the governor knew the list was flawed] nor anyone here at the Florida Department of Law Enforcement will be available for interview when you visit Tallahassee. Thank you for your understanding."[11]

My understanding? My understanding was that the bizarre exclusion of Hispanics had removed from the purge list a huge pool of Cuban Americans who might have been expected to cast their vote for Bush. At the same time, if "race" *was* delineated, despite the reforms supposedly implemented in the wake of the NAACP's lawsuit, it generated overly broad matches that could sound the alarm bells if there was only a partial overlap of a suspected felon's name—or a similarly spelled name—date of birth, social security number, and race against a person on the electoral rolls. Whites and African Americans showed up on the lists while most Hispanic felons did not; and, since African Americans were already vastly more likely to end up with criminal convictions in Florida than were other racial groups, this had the effect of magnifying an already powerful social problem and further undermining black participation in Florida's political process.

Even if this was, as defenders of the concept of a purge list claimed, all the product of perfectly innocent incompetence, at the very least it created an impression that the list was intended to be covertly partisan, that it was designed to hit some groups harder than others. And that impression was serving to sap confidence in Florida's electoral machinery.

"It's ludicrous to think you'll mix these lists and get a perfect list," Kay Clem, elections supervisor from Indiana County and outgoing chair of the Florida State Association of Elections Supervisors, explained to me. "They're just tools. The list is just a tool. We know it's not accurate." Clem had this demonstrated to her most dramatically when her own neighbor turned up on the felon list; apparently he had been convicted of a crime years earlier, but his record had since been sealed and expunged. "To say I had little confidence in the list is an understatement," Clem continued. "We've all learned from 2000, when there were many counties that took the list, said 'This is the best we can do,' and processed it that way. I don't have full faith and confidence that it is accurate. There are too many variables. You can't take a bad list, a bad list, and a bad list and make it a good list."

Forty-five-year-old Sam Heyward, an African American man from Tallahassee who'd been convicted of receiving stolen furniture in 1980—he'd bought some hot household goods on the cheap from a local fence shortly after he'd left the military and returned to his hometown, had been convicted, and had had to do some community service work as punishment—found out the truth of this maxim a few months before the election. A friend of his from the Bethel AME church, who worked for the liberal watchdog organization People for the American Way, was investigating the lists being sent out by the secretary of state's office; suddenly he came across Heyward's name. Investigators from People for the American Way came out to his condo a couple miles east of the state capitol to talk with him. Heyward had lost the lower half of his left leg to an infection a couple of years earlier, and, while he did get out of the house when he had to, it was easier for him if they came to interview him at his home—the walls of which were covered by Mediterranean-style paintings, a taste he'd acquired while in the army, stationed at a base in Italy.

"I told them I did have a felony back in 1980, but since then it had been expunged off my record." Heyward had copies of the document, signed by Governor Graham, in January 1986, granting him clemency and restoring his civil rights. He'd been voting, unchallenged, ever since then, and was fairly astonished that he'd now shown up on a purge list. "I was just as surprised as anybody else. Why did my name show up all of a sudden? It was never a problem. I was never turned away at all of these elections. Now, in 2004, I'm told I'm on a purged felons list and may not be able to vote."

When he got out the clemency document for the People for the American Way investigators, it had his prisoner ID number and his date of birth, but his last name had been slightly misspelled. The document granted clemency to Samuel L. Haywood, instead of to Samuel L. Heyward. While the exact reasons for Heyward having been included on the list were never provided to him, it's more than likely a state clerk's sloppy spelling eighteen years earlier had something to do with the error.

Heyward contacted attorneys working on voter rights issues, along with CNN and other media organizations who were suing the state to make public the names on the purge lists. And, in short order, he managed to convince the elections supervisor there'd been a mistake and he should never have been on the purge list. He was lucky. He lived in a county where the supervisor already distrusted the lists, and he was aided by having his story reported on by national media outlets. But, as 2000 had shown, for many others, simply being told they were on a "purge list" was enough to keep them away from the ballot box and send them into defeated apathy.

Because of the ugliness of the 2000 process, many county elections supervisors flat-out said they wouldn't use the lists in 2004—despite an initial May 5 memo from the secretary of state's office ordering them to do so without any modifications or further investigations. Yet many supervisors *did* send out letters to people from their areas who had shown up on the purge list.

In July, faced with overwhelming evidence the list was inaccurate—Heyward's story was by no means unique—the state had to respond to CNN's legal challenge designed to force Florida to make its felon lists public. Rather than publicize the list, the state chose the least bad option, and, kicking and screaming, decided to scrap it entirely and to allow the elections supervisors to fall back on their old relationships with the county clerks to get their lists of ineligible voters. The secretary of state's office even sent out a memo to elections supervisors informing them they could not use the purge lists in any way. "The felon matching component should not be used to commence any investigation of a voter's eligibility status and should not be used to confirm a voter's eligibility status," the August 13 memo stated.[12] In plain English: the list should be discarded.

Of course, by then at least fifteen counties had already sent out letters to people whose names had appeared on the list informing them they would be removed from the voter rolls unless they could show, by proving there had been a name mix-up, that they weren't felons—and there was no guarantee that follow-up letters telling voters to ignore the previous "You're ineligible to vote" missives would be received, read, or even understood.

In late August, I e-mailed a questionnaire to every elections supervisor in Florida, asking about their use of the purge list, whether they'd been pressured to use the list by the secretary of state's office, how they'd double-checked the accuracy of the lists, and so on. Nine of the supervisors responded: their answers were, at best, confusing. One supervisor wrote that, in using the 2000 list to remove voters in 2000, not a single person had been wrongly disenfranchised. Indeed, he went further and said not a single person from his county had a felony conviction that would prevent him or her from voting. But in the next answer he asserted that he had then contacted people who had been wrongly disenfranchised to tell them that they could, in fact, vote. Another wrote a long note saying she had not used the 2004 list because she feared it was inaccurate, but that she believed "the entities that are responsible for this process are not sinister in their motives, but are being asked to do a job (by statutory mandate) that is next to impossible to perform without a degree of error." Another simply wrote, disarmingly, "You asked these heavy questions at a very bad time, we are a week away from our state primary and up to our ears in alligators."

Yet, that wasn't the end of it. As the days wound down to the election, Florida was facing all kinds of allegations of voter suppression, of which the felon purge lists were but one part. There were stories of police "investigations" into "voter fraud" in black neighborhoods that involved uniformed officers storming into the homes of elderly get-out-the-vote volunteers. There were stories of people being unable to register, or having their registration discounted because they'd missed one tick on the registration form. Finally, about a week before the election, when it looked as though Republican Party poll observers might try to launch large-scale challenges against voters in Democratic neighborhoods, Secretary of State Hood sent out a final memo to elections supervisors. Buried in a footnote was the decision that supervisors *could* use information contained in the discredited purge list as long as it was supported by other backup information. "She did it at the last minute so it was difficult to launch any legal challenge against it," said Miami attorney Thomasina Hood, the Florida counsel in the NAACP lawsuit.

To many, it seemed all too similar to the chicanery that used to go on in the old South before the Voting Rights Act supposedly ended all of that nonsense.

By 2004 disenfranchisement in Florida had come full circle. In the post–Civil War period, the Southern states built felon disenfranchisement into their constitutions specifically as one of the

Jim Crow props designed to remove blacks from the political process. Then, when this ceased to be legally or morally permissible in the wake of the Voting Rights Act, Southern states that maintained felon disenfranchisement claimed it was a law with very limited, and specific intents: it was simply to remove felons from political participation, with no broader ties to a given socioeconomic-racial agenda. Now, in Florida, in 2004, with felon disenfranchisement being viewed by party operatives as part of a package of voter suppression—along with "monitors" in black neighborhoods, the use of the police to intimidate elderly voter registration volunteers, the twofold citizenship question on voter registration forms and so on—and with the utterly arbitrary nature of the Office of Executive Clemency hearings, the issue had once more become embedded in a broader pattern of politicking over access to the ballot.

The day before the election, I snaked down the Gulf Coast of Florida, from Tampa south to Naples, then east across the flat swamps of the alligator-infested Everglades to Miami. It was hot—very hot for November—and the sky, made huge by the dwarfishness of the mangrove trees, alternated between a menacing humid gray and a gorgeous blue.

The road was fast, a ninety-mile-per-hour speedway, and I drove it to the soundtrack of last-minute radio election coverage. The swing states were supposedly still too close to call. The president was talking about national security and the sanctity of marriage. Kerry was talking about a fresh start for America. Both candidates were so hoarse they could hardly croak out the platitudes.

And then I reached Miami. I'd made it. Five months on the road, and here I was, more than three thousand miles from Seattle, the drizzle and mists and jazzy hues of Washington replaced by the Indian summer of southern Florida, by the fast, multilane highways, the skyscrapers, the Cuban music pounding off of the radio, the pastel colors and the fierce tropical sun.

I spent the afternoon interviewing a teacher who'd been a heroin addict and repeat offender in the 1970s, who had voted without hindrance until 2000 and had then been "purged" from the voter rolls when Florida got serious about removing felons from the political process. The first time she heard anything about this was when she went to vote on Election Day and was turned away by apologetic poll workers. She hadn't yet managed to get her vote restored, and was planning to console herself by spending the following day driving people to and from the polls.

And I spent the evening talking politics with state senator Frederica Wilson at an expensive, dark wood–paneled steakhouse in the heart of downtown Miami. A flamboyant woman, the senator turned up for dinner in a sparkling blue straw cowboy hat, a tight jacket with a fake-gold flower on the lapel, and a stylish skirt. Wilson, an African American, had been pushing the suffrage issue for years. I'd interviewed her in 2001, when she was a state representative practically spitting blood over the 2000 election outcome in Florida. A couple of years later, she had introduced a bill that would have made the vote-restoration process far easier. It never made it out of the Ethics and Elections Committee. Now, on election eve, Wilson was almost spilling over with enthusiasm. The election, she believed, was turning in Kerry's favor. The dirty tricks that had been predicted were being stymied by a massive voter protection grassroots effort. A day from then, she expected Florida to have given its electoral votes to the Democrat, and, she said, she was convinced the country would do likewise.

It was an expensive meal, but it was worth it. I felt rejuvenated. Wilson's enthusiasm was infectious. Election Day was about to unfold and I was sitting with a cowboy-hat-wearing suffrage champion who was bareback riding into the election on a wave of optimism and hope. Perhaps, despite the millions of people who'd been removed from the voter rolls because of criminal convictions, despite attempts to cast the disenfranchisement net as far and wide as possible, perhaps after all of this the election would still produce a result that, after the richness of this meal, didn't give me heartburn.

14
Heartburn

I stayed in Miami Beach on election eve, in a little old blue-and-white hotel on Collins Avenue, half a block from the sand. It was the kind of place that New York snowbirds must have puttered about in their Hawaiian shirts and oversize sunglasses back in the 1950s, with external walkways along its four floors, the room doors leading off these walkways; and it smelled vaguely of raw fish and seagulls.

I got up early on Election Day, watched the news, checked the online headlines, and treated myself to a leisurely walk over to the ocean. There really wasn't much else to do. After the months of frantic reporting, my journey, like that of the candidates, was over. It was already over eighty degrees, and the lush sand was, at intervals, dotted with sunbathers. Briefcase in hand, formal work clothes on, I walked to the water's edge, and put my hand in the frothy blue water as a young couple just down the sand giggled at me. It was perfect: the breeze was blowing the palms back and forth, the art deco hotels and curvy, swirling glass and pastel-colored skyscrapers and neon-tinted towers and restaurants and bars stretched north and south along the shore. On any other day of the year, I'd have felt I was in paradise, would have returned to the hotel, put my trunks on, and gone for a prewinter ocean dip. But that day, I was too nervous to swim.

I walked back to Collins Avenue and went to have an over-priced, leisurely breakfast at a sidewalk table at Jerry's Famous Deli. Then I drove to downtown Miami, where I went into a strikingly beautiful office tower, took an elevator up to the twenty-eighth floor, and spent a couple of hours talking with a civil rights attorney while looking out the windows onto the sun-drenched, Mediterranean-styled central city below.

Afterward, I drove to Liberty City, a poor black neighborhood in north Miami, and jumped between precincts talking with poll monitors and attorneys who'd flown in from around the country to make sure the much-heralded Republican dirty tricks campaign didn't succeed in driving voters away from the polls. There'd been lines at the precincts that morning, but, by early afternoon, there were more observers than voters at many of the sites, the attorneys identified by blue baseball caps, the various monitor organizations by a slew of different T-shirts. It was overpoweringly hot, and many of the observers had retreated to little patches of shade to drink sodas and wait for whatever action might develop. I found one story of a person who'd been told by precinct workers that he couldn't vote because his name appeared on a felon watchlist they were using, who denied he was a felon and who'd had to wait one and a half hours on hold with the Miami-Dade election department before being able to cast a provisional ballot. The attorney at the precinct had had him fill in an "incident report," and he'd gone on his way. One story in an afternoon of interviews. It hardly indicated systemic on-the-day vote suppression. Then again, the pro-disenfranchisement brigade had done a pretty good job of keeping hundreds of thousands voteless and away from the polls in the first place.

And then there was nothing to do but wait.

At seven o'clock, when the polls closed, I was standing outside an elementary school-cum-polling place in the heart of Liberty City, waiting to go inside to watch the preliminary vote count with a bevy of journalists from around the world, local monitors, and international observers. I'm not sure what everyone was expecting to see. I'm not sure what I was expecting to see. The blue linoleum floor, the children's crayon paintings tacked to the walls, the rows of electronic vote machines in the center of the floor—that's about all there was. That, and a host of flustered-looking poll workers waiting to start teasing out the secrets contained inside the machines. If there were going to be problems with the electronic voting machines, they were going to be at the microchip level, and certainly not visible to the naked eye of a non-techno-literate observer.

As I waited for the poll workers to start counting the vote, I began getting phone calls from friends in New York. The exit polls, they told me, all suggested the night was Kerry's. The numbers coming out of the swing states were particularly favorable to the Democrat.

By 7:45, the votes at my precinct still were not being counted, and I was getting itchy feet. I wanted to be somewhere with big televisions blaring national information, and with a group of people fired up and ready to cheer. After months on the road, alone, driving for hours with only my thoughts for company, I wanted to be in a crowd. And so I left. I got back in my car and drove twenty-five miles north to the Florida Democratic Party's shindig in the Fort Lauderdale–Broward County Convention Center. There were balloons everywhere, a platform filled with TV crews from around the world, huge televisions broadcasting CBS and CNN coverage of the election, and healthily stocked bars toward which snaked huge lines of overdressed, desperately nervous Democratic party workers. When Pennsylvania's results started to come in, showing that Kerry had won the state handily, the crowd cheered wildly. When Southern states came in for Bush, they booed heartily. When Florida precincts started reporting, they watched the TV screens and saw what they wanted to see and ignored the news that wasn't so good. Gradually, as more and more votes for Bush began piling up in Florida, the crowds began ignoring the numbers altogether—waiting for better news from

Illinois, from California, from New York. The cheering got more desperate. The lines at the bars got longer. Four hours after I'd arrived, I was ready to leave. It was clear that Florida was heading straight into the Bush camp by several hundred thousand votes. And it was also clear that Bush was going to get more votes nationally than Kerry. What wasn't yet clear was whether he was going to win Ohio and end up with more Electoral College votes than his opponent. Ohio was, said CNN, "too close to call."

I returned to Miami Beach. Drinking beers in a largely deserted watering hole, I watched CNN into the small hours. Ohio quickly disappeared. Because of the question of uncounted provisional ballots, the networks weren't going to call it for Bush that night; but it was clear that, by the next day, Kerry would have to concede.

I had one day left in Miami Beach. Judging it more than likely that Florida 2004 would end as chaotically as Florida 2000, I'd kept a day free postelection to report on possible riots, lawsuits, disputed votes, dirty tricks. Instead, there was nothing. Just a subdued silence and a whole bunch of *What the hell happened?* questions hanging in the tropical air.

And so, the day after the night before, I found myself sitting on the sand at South Beach, watching the waves gently hit the shore, and pondering the Florida and national outcomes.

The Grand Old Party's strategy had worked. Although voter turnout was high, it was high largely because a huge number of evangelical Christians had been mobilized. In Democratic strongholds, the vote was up, but not up by as much as was needed—and, at least in part, that was because huge numbers of citizens from demographic groups generally sympathetic to the Democrats had lost their right to vote. The Democrats *had* raised their turnout, but they had hit their limit—unless reenfranchisement legislation was passed, it was likely that they'd never be able to get more of their base out than they had in 2004, and, as the world was realizing, that was just shy of being enough to win an electoral majority.

Ironically, Ohio, the state that ultimately proved most important to Bush given the way the Electoral College math had broken elsewhere, had seen a huge push in recent months to inform ex-felons of their right to vote. Weeks before the election, pro-suffrage activists in Ohio had won a major legal victory, forcing the state to expand its voter education efforts and to send out letters to tens of thousands of recently released prisoners informing them of their voting rights.

But Iowa had gone Republican by a mere 13,000 votes, and it now had over 100,000 disenfranchised, a considerably higher number than was the case four years earlier, when Gore had won the state by a nose. Nevada, which no longer had permanent disenfranchisement, but which was still dealing with the perceptions associated with it, stayed narrowly Republican. New Mexico, which had also recently ended permanent disenfranchisement but was similarly affected by ongoing assumptions that a felony conviction permanently removed a person from political participation, went from being narrowly Democrat in 2000 to being narrowly Republican in 2004. Had those three states gone to the Democrats, the Electoral College vote would have ended up tied, at 269 apiece for Kerry and for Bush.

In Florida, the other critical big-ticket swing state without which Bush would have found it difficult to cobble together an Electoral College majority, well over half a million people remained voteless. And, while Bush's margin of victory in Florida in 2004 was large enough that felon disenfranchisement alone couldn't explain it—in contrast to 2000—the hemorrhaging of voters had certainly helped the Republicans in other ways. In its U.S. Senate race, Betty Castor, the Democrat running to replace

Bob Graham, who was retiring after three terms, lost to a conservative Republican by barely more than 1 percent, or 80,000 votes out of over 7 million cast.

And Florida wasn't alone in having had important nonpresidential races directly affected by large-scale disenfranchisement. In Kentucky, Republican senator Jim Bunning, who'd run one of the most inept and bizarre reelection campaigns in recent memory—one in which he'd announced that he hadn't even read a newspaper in six weeks—won reelection by only 20,000 votes, or about 1.5 percent. And in Washington State's gubernatorial race, an election the Democrats had been expected to win handily came down to a couple of hundred votes after the initial tally. After weeks of recounts, the Republican candidate came out even more marginally ahead, declared the winner by all of forty-two votes. Finally, after yet more recounts and legal wrangling over the validity of provisional ballots, the Democrat was declared the winner, by a sliver. As with the presidential election result in Florida in 2000, so close was this margin that if even 1 percent of the state's disenfranchised voters had been able to, and had exercised their right to, vote, the result could, depending on how they aligned themselves, very easily have been different.

Sprawled out on the warm sand, I took out de Tocqueville one last time. I'd finished the actual text of *Democracy in America* a couple of weeks previously, but, like a chocolate lover hoarding that last little bite, I'd been saving two essays that he'd written on traveling in America for my final day on the road. *Two Weeks in the Wilderness* and *Excursion to Lake Oneida*.

"In America," de Tocqueville wrote, while searching for a wild land at the outer reaches of the 1831 frontier, "only one society exists. It may be rich or poor, modest or brilliant, engaged in commerce or farming, nevertheless it consists everywhere of the same elements. The level of an egalitarian civilization has been laid upon it . . . and the spirit of equality and republicanism has spread an exceptionally uniform coloring over the personal habits of life."[1]

I hoped de Tocqueville was right. But, after months traversing a continent, I'd become somewhat cynical. It seemed to me that equality—if it ever in fact existed in America—was in serious trouble. And it struck me that the "habits" of republicanism had been at the very least eroded by the competing "habits" of incarceration and disenfranchisement.

I shut de Tocqueville's tattered covers and headed for the airport.

Postscript

Two weeks after the election, I received an e-mail from Jamaica S., the woman in Tennessee who had wanted so desperately to become a full citizen again. The attorneys who had filed to get the vote restored for a handful of ex-felons in the Nashville area had managed to expedite her case, and, with literally hours to spare before the election, she had received word that she would be allowed to vote.

After hearing from one proponent of disenfranchisement after another that "these people" wouldn't vote even if they could, it was, to say the least, a refreshing e-mail:

> My hearing was Wed. Oct. 27th, before Judge Brothers in the 6th Circuit Court. He was having a trial that day but agreed to have our hearings at 5:00 P.M. The hearing was horrible. The D.A. didn't contest my petition but I had to answer a lot of questions under oath about what happened etc. I felt like I was being tried twice! The D.A. and Judge were actually pretty pleasant but I was humiliated. Any confidence or enthusiasm that I had built up going in was completely undermined by the process. The state was judging me on whether I am a good person or a bad person, have I redeemed myself? Do I deserve to have the same rights as other Americans or do I deserve to be condemned and voiceless? I don't know what criteria is used in deciding to grant or deny restoration. Is it just their gut instinct? The uncertainty made me feel unbearably anxious. The

fact that I have to grovel for my basic rights to be restored makes a statement about how the public/government feels about ex-felons.

Anyway, the judge granted my petition but it still wasn't a sure thing that I would be able to vote in this election. The court clerk's office was closed for the day so I would have to come back the next day and hope that the order had been processed because Oct. 28th was the deadline for the election commission to receive a copy of the order. I went back to the court clerk's office and got a copy and took it to the election commission. It had to be verified by the county and state election commission before I would be able to vote. They said they would know on Monday, November 1st. I talked to them on Monday and they said it was completed and approved. They would send a note or call my polling location to let them know I can vote. I was still apprehensive because I expected more glitches, and I was correct. I went to the poll on Tuesday morning, Nov 2nd, and they hadn't been notified. I knew it would be nearly impossible to get a call through to the election commission office on election day so I was afraid that I would have to cast a provisional vote, which I was concerned wouldn't even count. The fail-safe worker tried a few times to get a call through with no luck then suggested that I come back later in the day. On my way out I ran into Erin [a friend of hers] waiting in line and she let me use her cell phone to call the election commission. I got through to Joan Nixon at the election commission immediately. I ran the phone to the election official and she authorized me to vote over the phone. I went straight to the booth and cast my vote. I walked out still in disbelief that it actually worked out. The whole thing dependant on the actions of a series of so many people . . . it felt like a miracle!

That night I was glued to the t.v. until 2:00 A.M. watching the election coverage. I went to bed but couldn't sleep because I knew that Bush had Ohio. Kerry's concession was very emotional . . . the loss was devastating. I went from being part of one voiceless segment of the population (disenfranchised ex-felon) to another (rational American voter). I am angry that Bush will be president for 4 more years and scared of the damage that he will do. But I do *not* think that voting is futile. I'm glad that I was able to show my support. I'm very proud that I voted and very appreciative of all of the people that made it possible. I can't even begin to express the tremendous gratitude that I feel for everyone that played a part in restoring my citizenship rights. I am amazed and encouraged by the passion and dedication of the people working on this issue.

I am a different person already. I have a sense of accomplishment, redemption, and dignity now. I feel validated and empowered to overcome other obstacles in my life. Last week I talked with my son about my past, poor judgment and its consequences. We had never talked about it before. I was more anxious about this conversation with Ethan than anything else I've ever had to do. It turned out to be very positive. So I guess you could say that I celebrated by sharing my story with my son.

Following the election, disenfranchisement remained in the spotlight. Three months after George Bush was reelected, New York senator Hillary Clinton introduced legislation to amend the Help America Vote Act so as to allow felons who had completed their sentences to vote in federal elections—even if they lived in states that barred them from voting at the local and state levels. The bill was co-sponsored by California senator Barbara Boxer, by New Jersey senator Frank Lautenberg, and by John Kerry. As of the summer of 2005, however, the amendment had not been passed.

At the state level, too, an increasing number of politicians moved to address disenfranchisement, to offer the possibility of voting, as Jamaica S. had, to more ex-felons. Most of the changes and the political pressure for change occurred in states that had already abolished permanent disenfranchisement but had kept fairly broad restrictions in place. Legislators on the house judiciary committee in Rhode Island recommended allowing people on parole and probation to vote and, following this, the state senate approved a bill automatically restoring the vote to residents once they left prison. A similar proposal in Oklahoma went down to defeat. In New Jersey, the commissioner of corrections went on record stating his belief that disenfranchisement laws were weakening American democracy. In Nebraska, legislators voted to replace the state's onerous disenfranchisement provisions with a simple two-year ban on voting after felons had completed their sentences. Governor Dave Heineman vetoed the legislation in March. Not long afterward legislators overrode his veto.

The biggest success, however, was in Iowa, where, in a high-profile ceremony on July 4, 2005, Governor Tom Vilsack, surrounded by legislators from both parties, issued an executive order to restore voter eligibility to Iowa's ex-felon population. The order didn't overturn Iowa's disenfranchisement codes; instead, Vilsack used the governor's power to grant clemency to create a blanket restoration of the vote for about 50,000 people who had fully served their sentences and were no longer on either probation or parole. The executive order also directed the department of corrections to submit a list of eligible offenders each month to the governor's office for consideration for a restoration of citizenship. It was a powerful gesture, weakened only by the fact that, presumably, a future governor could choose to allow the pool of Iowa's disenfranchised to build back up, since the disenfranchisement codes are still on the statute book and the reenfranchisement relies on the willingness of the governor of the moment to issue, on a regular basis, mass clemencies regarding voting rights.

In contrast to Iowa, reformers in Tennessee suffered a punishing defeat in May 2005. For months, sympathetic legislators and voting rights activists had worked to craft reenfranchisement legislation that would be palatable to conservatives. Finally, they believed they had succeeded. House bill 1722 proposed automatic reenfranchisement after felons had fully served their sentences and had paid off all mandated court costs. To mollify opponents, its authors added language specifically excluding from these provisions those convicted of murder, rape, voter fraud, and treason. For the first time in years, proponents of reenfranchisement felt fairly certain they had the votes to enact a significant law change. But, on May 19, their hopes were dashed. The bill was defeated 55 to 39 in the house, with 12 Democrats casting *no* votes.

As in Tennessee, so it remained throughout much of the South: Alabama, Kentucky, Mississippi, Virginia, and, of course, in Florida. Despite an increasing clamor in the winter of 2005 from state legislators opposed to the laws, including the senate majority leader and the chair of the senate criminal justice committee, disenfranchisement stayed firmly on the books in the state that had played such a pivotal role in the past two presidential elections. Iowa's reforms notwithstanding, universal adult suffrage remained, therefore, a dream. A democratic dream. An American dream.

Note on Sources

In researching *Conned,* I read dozens of books, academic papers, and articles, and interviewed hundreds of people. I debated long and hard as to whether to liberally sprinkle footnotes throughout the text. In the end, for the sake of readability, I decided not to. Where I have quoted directly from books and articles, those quotes are footnoted. At some places, I have chosen to refer readers to other authors and to academic reports for more specialized commentary on statistical information or on legal aspects of this complex topic.

Where a quote comes from an interview I conducted with one of my sources, I generally chose not to footnote. These interviews were almost all conducted between the months of June and November 2004, although some were from earlier journalistic forays of mine into the field of felon disenfranchisement. The great majority of the interviews with disenfranchised individuals were carried out in person, in private homes, in coffee shops and restaurants, in law offices, hospitals, community centers, jails, prisons, and rehab clinics along the route of my cross-country journey. A few were telephone interviews.

Where possible, I have tried to double-check all of the claims and details provided me by these individuals. At times, however, not all details could be verified. Occasionally, I found that sources had massaged the truth somewhat in their descriptions of events. In those instances I incorporated the facts that I had uncovered into the narrative.

Interviews with attorneys, academics, politicians, and grassroots activist organizations were carried out mainly during 2004, although many were also interviewed during my previous intertwinement with the subject, most especially in 2000 and 2001. Again, unless the interviews were first conducted for an article I worked on for a magazine or newspaper, I have generally not footnoted each of these encounters.

Conned contains large amounts of very specific data: on state prison populations, on changes in the size of America's incarcerated population over the decades, on drug arrests, on numbers of people on parole and probation, and so on. Again, were each and every bit of information footnoted, were every legal case formally cited, the book would drown in a sea of references. At the risk of inviting a surge of "Where did you get this information?" questions, I have decided not to source all of this material.

As a journalist, I have written on this subject for many years; in my newspaper and magazine articles I do not footnote my work, and I feel that such a format works best in this book too. Where necessary, I have identified sources for the numbers that I use in the text itself. Elsewhere, I have assumed it to be fairly self-evident. Numbers on parole, for example, generally come from state departments of probation and parole; numbers currently in prison come from state departments of corrections. Federal incarceration data, and detailed national data on all fifty states, comes from the U.S. Bureau of Justice Statistics. Data on state racial demographics comes from U.S. Census files.

It is my hope that in keeping footnotes to an absolute minimum, I have allowed the narrative to flow more smoothly and have created a book that lay audiences will not be frightened away from reading.

Notes

Introduction: De Tocqueville's House of Mirrors

1. Author interview with Jamaica S., Nashville, Tennessee, September 8, 2004. All interviews with felons were carried out either in person or over the telephone by the author, the vast majority of them in person. The bulk of these interviews were conducted between June and November 2004.

2. Data on state disenfranchisement numbers, and on the impact such disenfranchisement has on different racial groups, has been generated in numerous studies by University of Minnesota professor Chris Uggen and Northwestern University professor Jeff Manza, as well as in reports released by the D.C.-based Sentencing Project and by Human Rights Watch. Of particular value here is the article "Democratic Contraction? The Political Consequences of Felon Disenfranchisement in the United States," *American Sociological Review* 67 (2002), 777–803. The bulk of these reports documenting numbers removed from the political process were published between 1998 and 2004. The book *Invisible Punishment: The Collateral Consequences of Mass Imprisonment*, edited by Marc Mauer and Meda Chesney-Lind (New York: The New Press, 2002) also contains valuable information on the numerical impact of disenfranchisement laws.

3. For a detailed discussion of the philosophical debate around felons and suffrage, see Alec Ewald's "Civil Death: The Ideological Paradox of Criminal Disenfranchisement Laws in the United States," *Wisconsin Law Review* 5 (2002), 1045–1137.

Chapter 1: Permeating the Entire Confederation

1. Details on the criteria used for the purge lists were gathered from newspaper sources, from interviews with elections supervisors and voting rights attorneys, and from copies of correspondence between state officials in various government agencies.

2. E-mail to author, October 14, 2004.

3. Rules of Executive Clemency of Florida, adopted September 10, 1975.

4. The technical details surrounding Rule 9A, and the ways in which different governors have used this, were explained to the author by attorney Randall Berg of the Florida Justice Institute during discussions in November 2004.

5. In October 2004, the *Miami Herald* ran a series of investigative articles exploring how the franchise had become increasingly restrictive under Governor Jeb Bush. The investigation found that 80 percent of those released between 2001 and 2003 had not been reenfranchised. See Debbie Cenziper and Jason Grotto's article "Clemency Proving Elusive for Florida's Ex-Cons," *Miami Herald*, October 31, 2004.

6. A couple of years after the election, Jeff Manza's and Chris Uggen's work was published as "Democratic Contraction? The Political Consequences of Felon Disenfranchisement in the United States," *American Sociological Review* 67 (2002), 777–803. See also Jamie Fellner and Marc Mauer, "Losing the Vote: The Impact of Felony Disenfranchisement Laws in the United States," Human Rights Watch and the Sentencing Project, 1998.

7. Alexis de Tocqueville, *Democracy in America and Two Essays on America* (New York: Penguin Classics, 2003), 42.

8. Michael Lind, *Made in Texas* (New York: Basic Books, 2004), 193–194.

9. Interviews conducted by author during research for "The Other Election Scandal," *Rolling Stone*, August 2001.

Chapter 2: The Legal Literacy Test

1. *Viola N. Richardson v. Abran Ramirez et al.*, No. 72-1589. The case was argued before the U.S. Supreme Court on January 15, 1974; it was decided June 24, 1974. The justices voted 6–3 that disenfranchising felons did not deny them equal protection under the Fourteenth Amendment to the U.S. Constitution. Justices Douglas, Marshall, and Brennan dissented.

2. For detailed state-by-state estimates on total numbers disenfranchised, see the Demos report "Punishing at the Polls: The Case Against Disenfranchising Citizens With Felony Convictions," authored by Alec Ewald (New York: Demos, 2003).

3. *Farrakhan v. State of Washington*, 338 F.3d 1009.

4. The ACLU requested this information in mid-2001. From late 2001 onward, Washington State provided detailed breakdowns of this data to the ACLU's Seattle office.

5. Information provided author during meeting with ACLU staff in August 2004.

6. Information provided author during meeting with members of various grassroots organizations in Seattle, August 2004.

7. Washington State Sentencing Guidelines Commission, "Representation and Equity in Washington State: An Assessment of Disproportionality and Disparity in Adult Felony Sentencing, FY 2000," Olympia, 2002, 43, 48.

8. Numbers generated by the Washington secretary of state's office. For more detailed breakdown of this data, see http://www.secstate.wa.gov/elections/voter_participation.aspx.

Chapter 3: S-Man and the One-Armed Bandits

1. Alexis de Tocqueville, *Democracy in America and Two Essays on America* (New York: Penguin Classics, 2003), 74.

2. Numbers provided by the Nevada Department of Corrections. The department estimates that 65 percent of Nevada's prison inmates come from, and return to, southern Nevada. Between 20 and 25 percent come from the urban areas in the north

of the state, and about 10–15 percent come from the sparsely populated rural and desert counties.

Chapter 4: The Great-Grandmother Brigade

1. For more details on the Mormon disenfranchisement codes, see FindLaw entry entitled "Free Exercise of Religion," in the section on the U.S. Constitution and the First Amendment: http://caselaw.lp.findlaw.com/data/constitution/amendment01/05.html. See also Maria Kokiasmenos's paper, "The Dictates of Conscience: Mormon Polygamy and Conflict with the Federal Government" (Georgetown University Law Center: 2004).

Chapter 5: Sent to Prison for Cooking Sausages

1. In New Orleans, 140 pretrial detainees held at Orleans Parish Prison were registered to vote in the months leading up to the November 2004 election by a variety of voting rights groups, led by an organization named Voice of the Ex-Offender (VOTE). See "Campaign Turns Inmates into Voters," by Lolis Eric Elie, *Times Picayune*, August 18, 2004; and Michael Perlstein's "Eligible Orleans Inmates Cast Votes," *Times Picayune*, October 26, 2004. In Washington, D.C., the Committee United for the Rehabilitation of Errants (CURE) registered several hundred jail inmates in the run-up to the election. According to CURE's executive director Charles Sullivan, on August 7 alone the organization registered 188 eligible jail inmates. On August 14, the group registered 186 inmates at the privately operated Correctional Treatment Facility.

2. The lawsuit against Ohio's secretary of state had been filed by the Prison Reform Advocacy Center (PRAC) on behalf of the Committee United for the Rehabilitation of Errants and the Racial Fairness Project. PRAC brought the lawsuit after releasing a study that showed twenty-one boards of elections in the state were wrongly telling people on probation and parole that they could not vote. On September 13, 2004, the state agreed to send letters to

all citizens on parole in Ohio, informing them of their right to vote and letting them know they had until October 4 to register to vote.

3. Notes from the phone interviews are kept in Rudd's office. Author has copies of these files.

4. Connections' full name was "Connections: Communities Helping With 'Any Positive Change.'"

5. The HAVA money, according to Connections' publicity information, was used to produce educational materials explaining ex-felons' right to register and to vote. The materials ranged from posters to brochures distributed in county elections offices.

6. Alexis de Tocqueville, *Democracy in America and Two Essays on America* (New York: Penguin Classics, 2003), 207.

Chapter 6: Snakes and Ladders

1. Mike Tolson, "A Deadly Distinction," *Houston Chronicle*, February 5, 2001. In the article, Tolson quotes Holmes and writes that the quote was first reported in a 1998 article in the same newspaper.

2. Ibid. The data in this paragraph is reported in Tolson's article.

3. Ryan S. King and Marc Mauer, "The Vanishing Black Electorate: Felony Disenfranchisement in Atlanta, Georgia" (Washington, D.C.: Sentencing Project, September 2004).

4. In interviews with the author, MASS Inc. personnel estimated they had sent letters to 10,000 ex-probationers in Dallas and another 8,000 in Fort Worth. The letters informed recipients of their right to vote and also included a voter registration card. Unfortunately, MASS Inc. did not have the resources to do follow-up work to find out how many of these people actually filled in their voter registration cards and then subsequently voted. Staff at MASS Inc. believe that most of the disenfranchised in Dallas are concentrated in six highly impoverished zip codes.

5. For more detailed information on Texas's incarceration patterns, see Dana Kaplan, Vincent Schiraldi, and Jason Ziedenberg's report, "Texas Tough?: An Analysis of Incarceration and Crime Trends in the Lone Star State," Center on Juvenile and Criminal

Justice, 2000. The report cast doubt on the success of Texas's tough-on-crime policies. "In 1980, when Texas had a prison population of 30,000," the authors wrote, "the state's crime rate was 10% above the national average. Eighteen years, and 130,000 prisoners later, the Lone Star State's crime rate was 11% above the national average."

6. Information on the mechanics of this information flow was gathered by the author during interviews with officials from the Texas secretary of state's office.

7. For more details on the history of lynching in towns such as Waco, see Michael Lind's *Made in Texas* (New York: Basic Books, 2004). For a more general exposé of the lynch culture of the late-nineteenth and early twentieth centuries, see Ida B. Wells's writings on the topic, collected in *Southern Horrors and Other Writings: The Anti-Lynching Campaign of Ida B. Wells, 1892–1900,* edited by Jacqueline Jones Royster (Boston: Bedford Books, 1997).

8. The author's article "Busted," appeared in *Blackbook* magazine's summer 2002 issue. Photographs by Andrew Lichtenstein.

9. The author's work on the private prison scandals of Texas appeared in "Small Town Blues," *American Prospect,* June 2003; and "Incarceration, Inc.," *Nation,* July 19, 2004.

10. Lind, *Made in Texas.*

11. Anne Applebaum, *Gulag* (New York: Random House, 2003). Paperback edition: (New York: Anchor Books, 2004), 103.

12. Alexis de Tocqueville, *Democracy in America and Two Essays on America* (New York: Penguin Classics, 2003), 675.

13. Marisa Demeo and Steven Ochoa, "Diminished Voting Power in the Latino Community: The Impact of Felony Disenfranchisement Laws in Ten Targeted States," report for the Mexican-American Legal Defense and Education Fund, December 2003. The states studied in the report were Arizona, California, Florida, Nebraska, Nevada, New York, North Carolina, Texas, Virginia, and Washington.

Chapter 7: Waterloo Sunset

1. Alexis de Tocqueville, *Democracy in America and Two Essays on America* (New York: Penguin Classics, 2003), 592.

2. These numbers are quoted in Gregg Hennigan's article, "Bill Would End Felony Disenfranchisement," *Cityview*, March 17, 2004.

3. "Iowa Prison Population Forecast, FY 2003–2013," Iowa Department of Human Rights, Division of Criminal and Juvenile Justice Planning report, September 2003.

Chapter 8: Bluegrass Blues

1. Kentucky Criminal Justice Council, Final Recommendations, January 2000.

2. Tom Loftus, "Felons Face Tougher Rules to Regain Right to Vote," *Courier-Journal*, September 6, 2004.

3. Ibid.

4. www.lexingtonprosecutor.com.

Chapter 9: In Graceland's Shadow

1. Alexis de Tocqueville, *Democracy in America and Two Essays on America* (New York: Penguin Classics, 2003), 425.

2. Ibid., 402.

3. For a breakdown of the varying disenfranchisement and reenfranchisement rules in Tennessee over the years, see information provided by the Tennessee Department of State on its Web site at http://www.state.tn.us/sos/election/webcon.htm.

Chapter 10: Appalachian Autumn

1. According to this data, six of the seventeen governors had restored the vote to fewer than two hundred people during their years in office. Only five governors had restored the vote to more than five hundred individuals. The low point occurred in FY 1998–1999, when only seventeen Virginians had their right to vote restored.

2. Letter from Anne P. Petera, secretary of the commonwealth, March 10, 1999.

3. For a more detailed analysis of the intersection of race and criminal justice issues in Virginia, see the report "Unequal Justice: African Americans in the Virginia Criminal Justice System," of the Virginia Advisory Committee to the United States Commission on Civil Rights, April 2000. The report found that blacks in Virginia experienced incarceration rates more than eight times those of whites in the state. Between 1985 and 2000, the report (page eight) found that only 7.5 percent of applicants for restoration of rights had had their right to vote restored.

Chapter 11: The Mississippi Hustle

1. The state's somewhat casually maintained court records were confusing, indicating that he had been given a suspended sentence and a probation term for the crime—an unusually light penalty if he had indeed been convicted of a new crime of armed robbery—yet also suggesting that he had returned to prison. Robert had appealed an order of the Circuit Court of Hinds County denying his petition for post-conviction relief. The Court of Appeals affirmed the lower court's ruling, ruling that "On July 6, 1989, [Robert] pled guilty to armed robbery. The trial court judge found [Robert]'s guilty plea to be voluntarily, intelligently and knowingly made. The trial court judge then sentenced him to serve a term of twenty years in the custody of the Mississippi Department of Corrections, with fifteen years suspended and five years of probation." Questioned in a follow-up phone interview on August 29, 2005, Robert recalled that he had served ten years for the new crime and two years for violating the terms of his parole.

2. *Cotton v. Fordice*. U.S. Fifth Circuit Court of Appeals, No. 97-60275. 157 F.3d 388. On October 15, 1998, the court ruled that because Section 241 of the 1890 constitution had been amended in 1950 to exclude "burglary" from the list of disenfranchiseable offenses, and had been further amended in 1968 to include "murder" and "rape," it was no longer racially motivated, and was free of the "discriminatory taint associated with the original version. . . . Viewed

in this light [section] 241 as it presently exists is unconstitutional only if the amendments were adopted out of a desire to discriminate against blacks. Brown [the lead plaintiff] has offered no such proof regarding the current version of [section] 241."

3. Mississippi does not collate this data. The author generated these numbers by reviewing several years worth of Judiciary Committee resolutions on reenfranchising individuals.

4. Numerous newspaper and television reports have covered Lott's links to the CCC. These include Derrock Z. Jackson, "The Racist Links Around Trent Lott," *Boston Globe*, February 10, 1999, as well as articles by Stanley Crouch in the New York *Daily News* and by Leonard Pitts in the *Miami Herald*. The specific details of the numbers of Mississippi legislators who belong to the organization can be found in John Kifner's *New York Times* reports on the topic in the late 1990s.

5. Details of this were reported by Carolyn Stephens Maxwell, in "Area Students to March Against KKK at State Fair," *Jackson Advocate*, September 30, 2004. "White supremacist and Nationalist Movement founder Richard Barrett has been granted a permit by state officials to set up a booth inside the fairgrounds during the entire 12 days" of the fair, Maxwell wrote. "Barrett plans to have Edgar Ray 'Preacher' Killen, the main person suspected as having orchestrated the 1964 Klan-led murders of the three civil rights workers, sign autographs and gather signatures on a petition to leave Killen alone."

6. Jamie Fellner and Marc Mauer, "Losing the Vote: The Impact of Felony Disenfranchisement Laws in the United States," report by Human Rights Watch and the Sentencing Project, October 1998.

7. The Maryland-based Center for Voting and Democracy reports that Musgrove received 49.6 percent of the votes, as against 48.5 percent for Mike Parker.

Chapter 12: The Governor and the Pot Smoker

1. Guy Hunt was removed from office April 22, 1993. He was succeeded by Democratic lieutenant governor James E. Folsom Jr.

2. This quote is documented in the U.S. Supreme Court decision, April 16, 1985, in the *Hunter v. Underwood* lawsuit challenging the disenfranchisement of people convicted of misdemeanors in Alabama. The decision noted that "the enumerated crimes contain within them many misdemeanors. If a specific crime does not fall within one of the enumerated offenses, the Alabama Boards of Registrars consult Alabama case law or, in absence of a court precedent, opinions of the Alabama Attorney General to determine whether it is covered by 182. . . . Various minor nonfelony offenses such as presenting a worthless check and petty larceny fall within the sweep of 182, while more serious nonfelony offenses such as second-degree manslaughter, assault on a police officer, mailing pornography, and aiding the escape of a misdemeanant do not because they are neither enumerated in 182 nor considered crimes involving moral turpitude. . . . It is alleged, and the Court of Appeals found, that the crimes selected for inclusion in 182 were believed by the delegates to be more frequently committed by blacks."

3. Riley received 672,225 votes, versus 669,105 for Siegelman.

Chapter 13: The Name of the Game Is Total Control

1. E-mail from Jeff Long to Donna Uzzell, May 4, 2004.

2. Greg Palast and Miles Rappaport both wrote on the topic of disenfranchisement laws soon after the election. Palast's book, *The Best Democracy Money Can Buy* (New York: Penguin Group, 2002), contains a section on Florida's purging of the voter rolls.

3. In the U.S. Congress, John Conyers (D–Michigan) and Corrine Brown (D–Florida) were particularly vocal in pushing for national legislation to end the practice of permanent disenfranchisement.

4. *Thomas Johnson v. Jeb Bush*. 353 F.3d 1287. No. 02-14469.

5. The formal certificate from the Office of Executive Clemency restoring Johnson's civil rights was not signed until September 3, 2004. But all the rest of the paperwork, including the issuing of Johnson's voter registration card, had been filled in two years earlier.

6. Berg made this claim during interview with the author in Miami, November 2, 2004.

7. Debbie Cenziper and Jason Grotto, "Clemency Proving Elusive for Florida's Ex-Cons," *Miami Herald*, October 31, 2004.

8. In the run-up to the election, newspapers in Florida reported that Accenture's Tallahassee lobbyists included a former chairman of the state GOP and a former top aide to Jeb Bush. See Chris Davis and Matthew Doig, "Elections Official Defends Contract," *Herald Tribune*, July 30, 2004.

9. Telephone interview with Peter Soh, October 13, 2004.

10. *Newsday's* report on Accenture's Saudi connections is mentioned in a *Herald Tribune* article by Chris Davis and Matthew Doig, "Shining Light on Company Behind Felon Voter List," July 14, 2004.

11. E-mail to author, October 20, 2004.

12. The August 13, 2004, memo was sent to all supervisors of elections, from Dawn K. Roberts, director of the Division of Elections.

Chapter 14: Heartburn

1. Alexis de Tocqueville, *Democracy in America and Two Essays on America* (New York: Penguin Classics, 2003), 880.

Index